Creole Languages and Language Acquisition

Trends in Linguistics
Studies and Monographs 86

Editor

Werner Winter

Mouton de Gruyter
Berlin · New York

Creole Languages and Language Acquisition

edited by
Herman Wekker

Mouton de Gruyter
Berlin · New York 1996

Mouton de Gruyter (formerly Mouton, The Hague)
is a Division of Walter de Gruyter & Co., Berlin.

∞ Printed on acid-free paper which falls within the guidelines
of the ANSI to ensure permanence and durability.

Library of Congress Cataloging-in-Publication-Data

Creole languages and language acquisition / edited by Herman Wekker.
        p.   cm. − (Trends in linguistics. Studies and mono-
graphs ; 86).
        Papers presented at a conference held Dec. 1990. Uni-
versity of Leiden.
        Includes bibliographical references.
        ISBN 3-11-014386-0
        1. Creole   dialects−Acquisition−Congresses.   2. Lan-
guage acquisition−Congresses.   I. Series.
        PM7831.C73   1996
        417'.22−dc20   95-43116
                                                        CIP

Die Deutsche Bibliothek − Cataloging-in-Publication-Data

Creole languages and language acquisition / ed. by Herman Wekker. − Berlin ; New York : Mouton de Gruyter, 1996
    (Trends in linguistics : Studies and monographs ; 86)
    ISBN 3-11-014386-0
    NE: Wekker, Herman [Hrsg.]; Trends in linguistics / Studies
    and monographs

Typesetting and Printing: Arthur Collignon GmbH, Berlin.
Binding: Lüderitz & Bauer, Berlin.
Printed in Germany.

Contents

Part III: Creolization as relexification

Introduction:
Creole languages and language acquisition

Herman Wekker

As John Lumsden writes at the beginning of his contribution to this volume, creole languages are natural languages, and hence

> the study of creole grammars must be a particular instance of the study of the grammar of natural languages in general. That is, creoles must be the product of the same cognitive faculties which produce any other natural language. Therefore, a synchronic study of a creole language in itself has no properties which distinguish it from studies of non-creole languages.
>
> But creoles do differ from other natural languages in their historical evolution. Where most languages evolve slowly, responding mainly to pressures which are interior to a largely unilingual population group, creoles are the result of the social confrontation of several languages and the genesis of a creole language is relatively abrupt. Creoles differ massively from any single one of the source languages which contribute to their origin and, moreover, they develop these differences in a relatively brief period and in a particular social context.

This means that comparing creole grammars with the grammars of the source languages to which they are historically related has a great deal of special interest. Creole languages offer the possibility of observing rapid linguistic change under rather unusual circumstances.

The present volume contains a selection of the papers presented at an international three-day workshop on creole languages and language acquisition, held at the University of Leiden in December 1990. The Leiden Creole Workshop (organized with the assistance of Pieter Muysken) formed part of a research project at NIAS (the Netherlands Institute for Advanced Study in the Humanities and Social Sciences) in the year 1990/1991. The NIAS project was entitled "The logical problem of language acquisition", and set out to investigate the acquisition of parts of the grammar in children and adults. The coordinators of the project were Teun Hoekstra and Harry van der Hulst (both of the Linguistics Department of the University of Leiden). The project group also included Toni Borowsky, Ger de Haan, Allan James, Peter Jordens, Charlotte Koster, David Lebeaux, Rita Manzini, Ann Mills, Tom Roeper, and myself. I thank all of them for helpful discussions, and for making our NIAS year such a memorable experience. I am also grateful to the director and staff of NIAS for providing the right atmosphere to do scholarly work.

The purpose of the Leiden Creole Workshop was to bring together linguists from three fields: 1) the theory of language acquistion, 2) pidgin and creole studies, and 3) the acquisition of creole languages. The central issue discussed during the workshop was whether the specific circumstances of the genesis of creole languages might have implications for our view of language acquisition in general. Conversely, it was argued, the theory of language acquisition could throw new light on the genesis of existing creole languages.

It turned out that there are numerous questions that creolists, historical linguists and acquisition researchers share with one another. For example, if creole grammars resemble child grammars in certain respects, due to the genetic programming of natural languages, then how does creole language development proceed? The central issue is: to what extent is acquisition input-driven, and to what extent is it programmed by innate (universal) mechanisms, given that the child's language environment is far from homogeneous? A related issue is how language development takes place in contemporary creole-speaking communities, where the ambient language is often very heterogeneous, involving complex layers of linguistic systems. Problems of this kind are addressed by Adone, Aitchison, Bickerton, Carrington, and DeGraff in section 1 of this volume.

Another question is to what extent the process of creolization is analogous to second- rather than to first-language acquisition, or whether it is a combination of the two. If creolization is a case of second-language acquisition, then the process takes place gradually and involves the systematic expansion of the jargons of adult learners. This topic is dealt with by Alleyne, Koefoed–Tarenskeen, and Wekker in section 2 of this volume.

Other researchers agree that creolization is a function of second-language acquisition but claim that relexification, while probably playing a role as a mental process in all cases of second-language acquisition, has a central role in creolization due to the particular social circumstances under which creoles are created. The topic of relexification is discussed by Lefebvre and by Lumsden in section 3 of this volume.

The three sections are entitled: 1) Creolization as first-language acquisition, 2) Creolization as second-language acquisition, and 3) Creolization as relexification. The volume contains ten papers.

Part I consists of three papers.

Aitchison's paper deals with the question whether language acquisition and creolization proceed via small steps, involving undergeneralization, or in large leaps, involving overgeneralization. The question is explored with particular reference to the treatment of the so-called "predicate marker" *i* in Tok Pisin by a group of first-generation creole speakers. Her general conclusion is that the use of *i* is declining, and that the process of atrophy is complex, showing both overgeneralization and undergeneralization. The various syntactic environments in which *i* occurs are treated differently: in one, overgeneralization is found, where a construction associated originally with *i* is being extended. In two others, undergeneralization is found, in which *i* is becoming increasingly linked to particular lexical items. In any case, the process does not seem to be instantaneous, and is still incomplete.

Bickerton, in a paper entitled "Creoles and the bankruptcy of current acquisition theory", claims that the very existence of creole languages poses a challenge to acquisition theory. He discusses the case of Hawaiian Creole, where the pidginized input that gave rise to the creole was radically ill-formed in at least three ways: a) it was structurally restricted (containing no sentences that could be unambiguously analyzed as containing embedded clauses); b) it was radically variable (containing elements from more than one language and little or no structural consistency); and c) it was morphologically impoverished (in particular, it lacked inflections as well as determiners, prepositions, complementizers and verbal auxiliaries). He notes Hawaiian Creole is a natural language which is somehow connected with, yet goes far beyond, the pidgin data he surveys; he shows how a complete (and quite complex) rule system could arise from a pidgin in which there was complete anarchy.

In his "Comment on Bickerton's paper", Roeper argues that there is very little that is different in Bickerton's approach to the assumptions made by researchers in first-language acquisition: a) Universal Grammar is innate, b) particular grammars are fixed by input, and c) children's utterances reflect both the impact of input and spontaneous, unmodelled, projections from unmarked aspects of Universal Grammar. In Roeper's view, creole languages are no different.

In his paper "Ambient language and learner output in a creole environment", Carrington stresses the importance of creating a corpus produced in the learning environment by the learner as well as the participants in his/her language socialization. There are two reasons for this: first, existing descriptions do not allow the analyst to have a clear idea of the learner's target, and second, our knowledge of variation suggests that, within the Caribbean sociolinguistic setting, it is difficult to predict the mix of features that will constitute the input to a learner. He uses Caribbean creole data from the environments of two informants to support the argument. He emphasizes the need for an integrated corpus for the study of the (moving) target language and the learner's language.

The central question for DeGraff ("Creole languages and parameter setting: A case study using Haitian Creole and the pro-drop parameter") is whether creole parameters show settings that are similar to those exhibited by the child's grammar in the initial stages of language acquisition. His paper attempts to answer this question by examining Haitian Creole with respect to pro-drop. He argues that Haitian Creole is a null-subject language, thus coinciding with the child's initial hypothesis. The evidence presented comes from two domains: (i) existential, weather, and *seem*-type verbs, which do not require phonologically realized subjects; (ii) "subject pronouns", which behave like clitics spelling out the agreement features of the inflection phrase, and identifying *pro* in subject position. DeGraff argues that certain properties of the inflection phrase in Haitian Creole regulate the appearance of clitics, nonpronominal subjects and variables in preverbal position. He shows that the creole allows long-distance extraction from subject position over lexically filled COMP, even though it does not allow subject inversion. His analysis also explains certain facts about serial verb constructions, by assuming that the second verb is part of an embedded clause. He examines the larger implications of pro-drop setting in Haitian Creole for the relationship between creole languages and language acquisition.

Part II consists of three papers. The first is by Alleyne. He casts doubt on the current innatist claims about the human capacity for language, asking whether creology really recapitulates ontogeny. He discusses some of the problems he has with Universal Grammar and its relationship with the human language faculty. He is also critical of a number of assumptions about creole languages which are still inadequately accounted for, as well as a number of creole commonplaces that have been accepted as fact in the literature, but which are merely approximations to facts. The examples he deals with here are: (i) the zero marking of the perfective, and (ii) the alleged invariable verbal theme. His conclusion is that the treatment of states and processes, as exemplified by some French-based creoles, cannot be explained in terms of a cognitive blueprint, even less in terms of a linguistic blueprint. He argues that it is a function of the worldview of the population(s) amongst whom these language developments took place. Causality seems to play an important role: states are derived from processes (they are not perceived neutrally or abstractly, independent of the processes which give rise to them). Unlike English or French, for example, creole languages like those of the Indian Ocean see nature not as a set of inert states, but as a world of dynamic forces and processes. States are caused and are potentially explicable. There is an intricate network of causality involving human nature, and the supernatural.

The paper by Koefoed and Tarenskeen ("The making of a language from a lexical point of view") is concerned with the genesis of the vocabulary of Sranan. The authors take it for granted that a vocabulary is not created by some innate language-acquisition device. They demonstrate how the creole lexicon can result from second-language acquisition or relexification. A majority of lexical items will derive from the superstratum language, together with relics from the substratum language, especially in some culturally significant domains. There are also autonomous innovations and loans from languages with which the community has been in contact. They argue that one would not normally expect many innovations in certain semantic domains. However, this is exactly what they find in the Sranan lexicon.

In my own contribution ("Creolization and the acquisition of English as a second language") I discuss creolization in terms of second-language acquisition by adults. I emphasize the role of the learners in creating the creole, their sociohistorical and linguistic background, the purposes for which they were learning the language, and the strategies they applied in the complex process of language acquisition. I see creolization as a gradual process of imperfect second-language acquisition by successive cohorts of adult slaves, extending over generations. This makes it possible to account for the process in terms of: (i) transfer from the learners' L1s (i.e., substrate influence), and (ii) innate language-learning strategies (i.e., indirect access to Universal Grammar). I discuss, in particular, the origin of Sranan, relating it to the acquisition of English as a second language.

Part III opens with a paper by Lefebvre ("The functional category "agreement" and creole genesis"). It reports on the ongoing Université du Québec à Montréal project which sets out to demonstrate that Haitian Creole was created through relexification. The general approach lies in a detailed comparison of the grammar of Haitian Creole and the grammar of its source languages, French and Fon. Her paper is divided into three parts. In part 1 she presents the theory of relexification, in part 2 a case study showing that, in the genesis of Haitian Creole, the AGR of Fon has been relexified, which explains the remarkable parallelism between the structure of the clause in Haitian and in Fon. Consequently, the structure of the clause in Haitian and in Fon differs in a similar way from the structure of the clause in French. Finally, she discusses the relevance of this study for the theory of relexification, for theories of creole genesis in general, and for acquisition.

Lumsden ("On the acquisition of nominal structures in the genesis of Haitian Creole") argues that the special contribution of creole studies to our understanding of language acquisition can be found in detailed studies which compare the grammar of the creole with the grammars of the source languages to which it is related. In his paper, he focuses on the nominal phrase in Haitian Creole, arguing that at least one aspect of this phrase must be considered a marked option in the repertoire of Universal Grammar. This constitutes a problem for the Universalist theory. He tries to show that, on the other hand, the relexification theory provides a natural explanation for the data. He examines nominal structures in Haitian Creole, comparing the creole with French and Fon. The discussion concentrates on arguments and adjectives in nominal phrases.

As editor of the present volume, it is my hope that second-language acquisition researchers, creolists, and historical linguists will intensify the kind of cooperation that we find reflected in the contributions which follow. Our common purpose is to solve the "logical problem of language acquisition" from as many perspectives as possible, and there is still a great deal that workers in different fields can learn from one another.

My thanks are due to the participants of the Leiden Creole Workshop for the stimulating discussions in a very pleasant atmosphere, and the contributors to the present volume for submitting their papers so promptly. It is not their fault that the publication of this book has taken longer than I care to admit. We received financial support for the Workshop from the Royal Dutch Academy of Sciences, the Dutch Foundation for Linguistic Research, NIAS, and the Arts Faculty of Leiden University. Their generous support is hereby gratefully acknowledged. I also thank the secretaries at NIAS and at the English Department of the University of Groningen for their assistance and the meticulous care with which they have handled the various versions of this "Babylonic" manuscript.

Part I
Creolization as first-language acquisition

Small steps or large leaps?
Undergeneralization and overgeneralization in creole acquisition

Jean Aitchison

Language acquisition is said by some to proceed via small steps, involving undergeneralization, and by others in large leaps, involving overgeneralization. This debate is also applicable to creole acquisition, and is explored in this paper with particular reference to the treatment of the so-called "predicate marker" *i* in Tok Pisin by a group of first-generation creole speakers.[1] The overall conclusion is that use of *i* is declining, and that the process of atrophy is complex, showing both overgeneralization and undergeneralization. The various syntactic environments in which *i* occurs are treated differently: in one, overgeneralization is found, where a construction associated originally with *i* is being extended. In two others, undergeneralization is found, in which *i* is becoming increasingly linked to particular lexical items. However, the neatening-up process is not instantaneous. It is still incomplete, and may continue for several generations. It is possibly being implemented by stable groups of speakers, rather than by babies.

1. Introduction

"Small steps" versus "large leaps" is an ongoing debate in first-language acquisition. Small-step supporters assume that children acquire language piecemeal, in tiny fragments, then only gradually knit the pieces together. Large-leap proponents assert that children acquire language in broad sweeps, as they add far-reaching rules to their grammars, or, (more recently), as they set parameters (Chomsky 1986). The first view typically results in undergeneralization, the second in overgeneralization.

The same debate is relevant to creole acquisition, the learning of a pidgin as a first language. When a first-generation creole speaker alters the pidgin, how does this happen? Is it done via small-scale lexical innovations, which are then generalized? Or via broad syntactic rules? Or by a mixture of the two?

These questions are examined by looking at how a group of first generation creole speakers have altered one particular construction in Tok Pisin (New Guinea Pidgin, Neo-Melanesian), a pidgin/creole spoken in Papua New Guinea. The structure is the so-called "predicate marker" *i*, which, it has been claimed, is a candidate for regularization by creole speakers: "there appears to be considerable variation in second language speakers' use of *i*, and one would expect such inconsistent input to be regularised by first-generation creole speakers" (Mühlhäusler 1985: 154). Hopefully, the processes involved will shed light on creole acquisition as a whole.

The paper is organized as follows: first, it outlines some recent important findings in child language and language change which provide a backdrop against which the facts presented in the paper can be evaluated. Second, it briefly describes the function of the putative "predicate marker" (PM) *i* in pidgin Tok Pisin (L2 speakers). Third, it analyses the use of the predicate marker in the creolized Tok Pisin of the informants discussed here (first-generation L1 speakers). Finally, it summarizes the processes of change involved, and draws out the implications for creole language acquisition.

2. Child language and language change

The following findings are gathering increasing support among workers in child language and language change. They are relevant to any discussion of creole acquisition, and in particular to the materials presented in this paper.

i. The existence of a critical period is in doubt. There is unlikely to be a "critical period" for language acquisition, in the sense proposed by Lenneberg (1967). Lenneberg proposed that age two to thirteen was a period set aside by nature for acquiring language. In his opinion, this coincided with lateralization, the specialization of language to one side of the brain. After this time, language was relatively immutable, he claimed. Research now suggests that Lenneberg's arguments for the critical period are flawed (for a summary of recent research see Aitchison 1989 a). Experiments indicate that lateralization is already present at birth: babies only a few days old process speech sounds with their left hemispheres. This finding removes the neurological underpinnings of the theory. In addition, empirical work indicates that there is no sudden cut-off-point for language at adolescence. At the most, it can be shown that younger brains have greater plasticity than older ones, so early acquisition, particularly of phonology, is an advantage.

ii. Babies do not change language. The notion of sudden change between generations is a myth, and child language alterations differ in character from those found in language change (e. g., Bybee–Slobin 1982; a summary of evidence can be found in Aitchison 1991).

iii. Peer groups matter more than parents. Language gets changed and stabilized among peer groups, and the greatest amount of change takes place when peer group influence is strongest. In our society, this occurs during adolescence, when family ties weaken, and peer-group influence increases (e. g., Cheshire 1982). A related finding is that constant usage of a language is more important for fluency than the age at which it was first learnt.

iv. Nothing happens out of nothing. In language change, and in child language, all new structures are reanalyses (or misanalyses, misperceptions) of existing material. Neither adults nor children conjure structures out of nothing (a summary of evidence for language change can be found in Aitchison 1991, for children, in Aitchison 1989 a).

v. Language tolerates useless junk. Pointless variety and irregular constructions get smoothed out very slowly, maybe over several generations. Useless junk is either eventually abandoned or re-analyzed ("exaptation", Lass 1990, cf. Bailey–Maynor 1988, for a summary of evidence, see Aitchison 1991).

vi. L1 speakers can handle more variation than L2 speakers. Native speakers of a language can sustain a greater level of irregularity, and more stylistic variation, than second-language speakers (Aitchison–Agnihotri 1985; Trudgill 1986). L2 speakers may neaten languages in order to lighten the load on memory.

From the point of view of creole acquisition, these findings suggest that pidgin-to-creole changes are unlikely to happen suddenly, at an early age. They may happen slowly, over time, and continue beyond childhood. They are most likely to develop and get consolidated among a stable peer group. Furthermore, they may take several generations to become established, and possibly involve considerable variation before they are stabilized.

Incidentally, first-generation speakers do not necessarily speak only the pidgin/creole. The child of a mixed-language marriage often grows up speaking one or both of the parental languages alongside the pidgin/

creole. The development of one of these as a subsequent "main language" depends on a variety of social factors. In addition, creole speakers inevitably interact with pidgin speakers, so the "original" input is not necessarily forgotten and left behind. Such social considerations are likely to influence the path of creolization, which in any case does not follow a single route everywhere (Mühlhäusler 1990 b).

3. Tok Pisin "predicate marker" *i*: General background

Tok Pisin (New Guinea Pidgin, Neo-Melanesian) is widely spoken in Papua New Guinea (Wurm — Mühlhäusler 1985). Its use as a pidgin dates back to the nineteenth century. It can now be regarded as a lingua franca, of particular importance in the contexts of the Christian religion and medical care. Recently, improved transport and a population shift towards towns has resulted in intermarriage between speakers of different languages. Consequently, there has been an upsurge in first-generation creole speakers, children who have acquired Tok Pisin as a first language, especially in urban areas (Mihalic 1990). Predictably, this has resulted in considerable alterations to Tok Pisin.

The structure examined in this paper is the so-called "predicate marker" (PM) *i*, which tends to be inconsistent in the pidgin. Superficially, therefore, it is a candidate for "neatening up" by L1 speakers (Mühlhäusler 1985: 154), and preliminary reports suggest that this is indeed an area where there are significant differences between L2 and L1 speakers (Sankoff 1977; Lynch 1979; Mühlhäusler 1985; for some more recent work, see note at the end of this paper). This paper therefore analyses the use of predicate markers in the speech of six first-generation speakers of creolized Tok Pisin.

3.1. Origins of i

The so-called "predicate marker" *i* in Tok Pisin is the source of considerable controversy. A widely held view is that it arose due to convergence, or "collusion" between English *he* in usages such as *My uncle, he hurt his leg* and an obligatory "subject-referencing pronoun" required preverbally in many substratum Oceanic languages (Keesing 1988), as was surmised by Hall (1966: 83):

Its use reflects a merger of the substandard English habit of recapitulating a subject by means of a pronoun − as in *John, he's an idiot* ... and the Melanesian Micronesian feature of morphologically distinct pronouns that recapitulate subjects and introduce predicates, as in Marshallese *ládrik e-ğérabal* 'the boy, he works'.

The Oceanic subject-referencing pronoun occurs not only before active verbs (as in Hall's example), but also before stative verbs which are often translatable into English adjectives, as in the following Kwaio example (Keesing 1988: 74):

(1)   *fou   lo'oo   e   gelo*
         stone DEM SRP (it) be-heavy
         'This stone is heavy.'

This account is disputed by Mühlhäusler (1987, 1990 a), who claims that the so-called predicate marker is primarily pronominal in origin, based on *he* rather than substratum influence. His arguments centre around the fact that the use of *i* was restricted and variable in early texts (end of the nineteenth century), but gradually increased, especially after 1920.

Whatever its origin, or the causes of its growth (discourse factors, according to Sankoff 1977), there is no doubt that *i* is an intrinsic part of Tok Pisin grammar, even though a problematical one, in that its function is ambiguous. It is unclear whether it should be regarded as a predicate marker, or a repeated pronoun − or even simply a mark of identity, a salient feature which identifies the speaker as talking Tok Pisin. The term "predicate marker" has been retained here, even though this may not be its true function.

As for spelling, early accounts of Melanesian pidgins represented the PM as *he*, as in the following nineteenth century example from Vanuatu, locally known as Tanna (quoted in Keesing 1988: 31, 144):

(2)   *Tanna man he   no   too   much like work.* (1859)
         Tanna man PM not very much like work
         'A man from Tanna does not like work very much.'

Currently, the predicate marker is standardly written as *i*.

3.2. Pidgin use of i

Use of *i* is extensive in mid to late twentieth-century pidgin Tok Pisin, and texts are often bespattered with predicate markers. For example: (PM = "predicate marker" TR = "transitive")

(3)   *Orait,   pren   bilong mi Don   i   kamap, mitupela i*
         Alright friend of   me Don PM came   we-two   PM
         go   long Serakum.   Mitupela i   go,   mitupela i   lukim
         go to   Serakum we-two   PM go we-two   PM see-TR
         yam long bikples,   mitupela i   godaun,   brukim
         yam to   big-village we-two   PM go-down cross-TR
         liklik hanwara, mitupela i   goap   long liklik ples,
         small creek   we-two   PM go-up to   small village
         mitupela i   lukim ol   i   bilas (Laycock, 1970: 44).
         we-two   PM see-TR them PM adorn
         'Well, my friend Don came, and we two went to Serakum. We
         two went, we looked at the yams in the main village, we two
         went downhill, crossed a small creek, we two went up to the
         hamlet, we two looked at the people putting on decorations.'

In this text, which contains 126 words, the predicate marker occurs 22
times, an approximate average of one every six words (5.7). Similarly,
Text 6 in the same collection contains 166 words, and 28 predicate markers which is one predicate marker per 5.9 words.

   Its exact conditions of use are unclear, mainly because of regional variation (Mühlhäusler 1985: 373, 1990 a). Syntactically, there are three main
(overlapping) contexts in which it is found, which could be accounted for
by a single rule of *i*-insertion before verbs. Oversimplifying somewhat,
these are as follows (pidgin examples from Laycock 1970; Dutton 1973;
Mihalic 1971; Mühlhäusler 1990):

(i) Between a main clause subject NP and the predicate:

(4)   a. *San i   lait.*
            Sun PM shine
            'The sun shines.'
         b. *Dispela haus   i   bikpela.*
            This   house PM big
            'This house is big.'
         c. *Em   i   lukim   mi.*
            he/she/it PM see-TR me
            'He (she, it) sees me.'
         d. *Ol   i   go long ples.*
            They PM go to   home-village
            'They went home.'

It is, however, often omitted after *em* in equative sentences:

(5)   a. *Em tasol.*
       it   all
       'That's all.'
    b. *Em papa bilong mi.*
       He father of   me
       'That's my father.'

There are further complications and regional variations in its use in conjoined clauses and in modals (Mühlhäusler 1990), but these are not of crucial importance for the purpose of this paper.

(ii) Between verbs, in cases where verbs are "chained". This involves several overlapping constructions, though the surface syntax is similar in all:

(6)   a. *Yu mekim i pundaun.*
       You make-TR PM fall-down
       'You knocked it down.'
    b. *Mi larim i stap.*
       I   leave-TR PM be
       'I let (it) be, left (it) alone.'
    c. *Em i kisim i kam.*
       He PM get-TR PM come
       'He brings (it).'
    d. *Mipela i wok i go.*
       We   PM work PM go
       'We keep on working.'

In cases where there is a prototypical serial-verb construction (the object of the first verb is also the subject of the second), the predicate marker occurs between the NP and the verb:

(7)   a. *Mitupela i lukim ol i bilas*
       we-two PM see-TR them PM adorn/decorate
       'We looked at them adorning themselves.'
    b. *Mipela putim mambu i gondaun long saitsait*
       we   put-TR bamboo PM go-down on every-side
       'We placed the bamboo on all sides.'

There is therefore some similarity between *i* in serial verb constructions and its use in main clauses, since in both cases it occurs between a subject NP and the predicate.

(iii) To introduce subjectless clauses:

(8)   a. *I   gat   tupela kanu.*
          PM have two   canoe
          'There are two canoes.'
       b. *I   no   ken   tru.*
          PM not will truly/really
          'It's not possible.'
       c. *I   tudak   pinis.*
          PM darkness finish
          'It's already too dark.'

The inclusion or omission of *i* in the three syntactic contexts discussed above is thought to be governed to a large extent by phonological factors (though there is some disagreement as to how much conditioning is phonological, and how much syntactic). It is mostly omitted after high vowels, sometimes omitted after other vowels (though pronouns are treated slightly differently from nouns), and retained after consonants. More specifically:

(i) It is invariably omitted after the first and second singular pronouns *mi* and *yu*, and intermittently after high vowels elsewhere:

(9)   a. *Mi lukim   wanpela pukpuk*
          I   see-TR a   crocodile
          'I saw a crododile.'
       b. *Yu laikim   wanem?*
          you want-TR what
          'What do you want?'

(10)   a. *Meri   (i)   gat   bel*
          woman (PM) have stomach
          'The woman is pregnant.'
       b. *Papa bilong mi (i)   sik*
          father of   mi (PM) ill
          'My father is ill.'

(ii) It is usually used after other vowels, though is intermittently omitted after pronouns ending in *a*, such as *mipela* (first person plural), *yupela* (second person plural):

(11)   *Banana i   mau.*
          Banana PM ripe
          'The banana is ripe.'

(12)   a. *Mipela (i)   kam   nau.*
            We   (PM) come now
            'We are coming now.'
        b. *Yupela (i)   stap we?*
            you-PL (PM) are   where
            'Where are you people?'

The question which needs to be considered, therefore, is the extent to which first-generation creole speakers have retained or altered this somewhat ungainly system, in which *i* is ambiguous between a repeated pronoun and a predicate marker, and whose occurrence is complicated by phonetic factors.

4. Creole *i*

In the creole, the most widespread observation is that the use of the predicate marker is considerably reduced. For example: "it is my impression that the use of *i* is declining, and many L1-speakers omit it very frequently indeed" (Lynch 1979: 6, cf. Sankoff 1977: 71). Its decline is to a large extent due to phonological factors: pidgin Tok Pisin is mostly spoken slowly, and it is relatively easy to distinguish predicate markers in the flow of speech. Creolized Tok Pisin is spoken fast, seemingly at the same speed as "full" languages. There are therefore numerous occasions when a predicate marker would be imperceptible, most notably when it follows a vowel. This leaves a somewhat chaotic situations. Predicate markers clearly exist in the creole, but their distribution has not yet been reliably charted (though a number of preliminary observations have been made, e. g., Woolford 1979 a; and, since this paper was written, other studies have appeared, see note at end).

Mühlhäusler (1985: 155) suggests that there may be a variety of conditioning factors: phonological (deletion after a high vowel), lexical (preferentially used with certain lexical items, such as *ron* 'run' and *go* 'go'), and syntactic (used in emphatic statements).

This paper therefore explores the interplay between these factors by examining the use of *i* in the speech of six first generation L1 speakers.

4.1. Informants and methodology

The informants discussed in this paper are six young women aged between 17 and 20, who lived in Lae, and who all knew one another. Five

of them claimed to have acquired Tok Pisin as their first language, sometimes alongside another language, and the sixth claimed to have learnt
Tok Pisin at a very young age. All of them can be regarded as first-
generation L1 speakers of Tok Pisin, since all of them had parents who
primarily spoke other languages, and all of them considered Tok Pisin to
be their "main" language, the one they preferentially spoke to one another. They all also spoke English, and were employed in jobs which
required them to use English. Four of the six informants were relatives
who originally came from the southern Highlands area around Goroka.
The other two were sisters who came from Lae. Five of the six lived in
the same hostel, and the sixth frequently visited her kinsfolk.

Each informant was interviewed separately, and asked questions about
life and life style (e. g., "What is your favourite food, and how do you
cook it?", "Have you ever been seriously ill, and can you tell me about
it?"). This gave a set of comparable texts, which were then analyzed (various aspects of their speech have been discussed in Aitchison 1984, 1989b,
1990, 1992). Since I myself was staying in the same hostel, they regarded
me as someone friendly, though somewhat ignorant and incompetent: my
efforts at cutting a coconut in half were a cause of great mirth. The texts
therefore represented a level of speech which was halfway between formal
and informal. Afterwards, they sometimes criticized each other's recordings, with comments such as (translated): "You should have spoken more
slowly, it will be difficult for Jean to hear everything".

To the casual observer, there were no obvious "rules" underlying the
use of *i* among the informants. Predicate markers gave the impression of
being random, optional elements, as in the following (all examples are
from my own data, with the initial of the informant following in paren-
theses; HAB = "habituality marker", IR = "irrealis", PL = "plural",
PM = "predicate marker", TR = "transitive"):

(13)   *na em miksim sampela kain lip ol sa kolim*
        and she mix-TR some-PL kind leaf they HAB call
        salak ia, em i kisim em, sa hatim long faia
        salak here, she PM get-TR it, HAB heat-TR on fire
        nau na i bin sa putim lo(ng) bel
        now and PM PAST HAB put-TR on stomach
        bilongen (Ja)
        of-her
        'And she pounded up some kind of leaf they call "salak", she
        took it, heated it up on the fire and put it on her stomach.'

(14)   *Na   sista   i   stap long ... em   stap   long   tambilo, wok*
        and   sister PM   stay   in   she   stay   in   town   work
        nait, em, telefon   i   ring gen   na   taim em toktok
        night she   telephone PM   ring again and   while she talk
        long mi   yet   an   telefon   ring olsem na,   em   bin
        to   me   still and   telephone ring so   and she PAST
        go   long kisim   telefon   na   em   i   isi   isi
        go   to   get-TR   telephone and she PM   casual casual
        tumas. (H)
        very
        'And the nurse staying in ... she stays in town, works in the
        night [i. e., the night nurse], she, the telephone rang again and
        while she was still talking to me, and the telephone rang, so
        she went to get the telephone, and she was very casual.'

An investigation was therefore carried out, in order to see to what extent
the occurrences of *i* were rule-governed, with particular attention to the
question of overgeneralization and undergeneralization. The following
aspects of *i* were examined:

i.   Frequency of usage
ii.   Phonological environment
iii. Syntactic environment
iv.   Lexical environment
v.   Interaction of syntax and lexicon.

4.2. *Frequency of* i

The widespread observation (noted earlier) that the number of predicate
markers is considerably reduced in the creole was confirmed in this study.
The number of sure predicate markers was 176, which occurred in a total
corpus of over 7,000 words. The most frequent user had on average one
predicate marker per 22 words, and the least frequent user one per 69,
with the overall average being one marker per 45 words. These figures
may be an underestimate of the number of intended predicate markers,
because owing to the speed of speech, after a vowel they would often
have been imperceptible, as in:

(15)   *bel   bilong mi   (i??) pen.*
        stomach of   me PM   hurt
        'My stomach hurt.'

However, even allowing for misperceptions, the frequency of predicate markers is very different from that in the pidgin texts mentioned earlier, where the figure was one marker per six words.

4.3. Phonological environment of i

The presence or absence of *i* was not totally phonologically conditioned, since it occurred after both consonants and vowels, including high vowels. Moreover, the informant with the fastest speed of speech (200 words per minute) was not the one with the smallest proportion of predicate markers.

Not surprisingly, *i* was commonest after consonants (58 percent). But a further 28 percent of occurrences were after vowels (including 11 high vowels), and the remaining 14 percent of occurrences were in clause-initial position. Examples of these different environments are given below:

(16)   *Na   ren   i   wasim   mi.* (H)
         And   rain PM   wash-TR   me
         'And the rain soaked me.'

(17)   *Faia   i   lait* (L)
         Fire   PM   is-alight
         'The fire is ablaze.'

(18)   *I   gat   kainkain   mumu* (Ja)
         PM   have   various-kinds   mumu
         'There are various kinds of mumu.' (underground oven)

These figures and examples therefore indicate that there is no absolute phonological conditioning, merely phonological preferences primarily imposed by perception. They suggest that syntactic and/or lexical conditioning were likely to be important.

4.4. Syntactic environment of i

As in the pidgin, there were three syntactic environments for the appearance of *i*. These occurred in the following quantities:

(i) Main clause, between a subject NP and a predicate: 80 occurrences. (These included a small number in which the subject was in fact omitted, but there was evidence of an understood NP, typically via conjoining. They were clearly different from subjectless clauses in which no subject was evident.) For example:

(19)   a. *Telefon   i   ring gen* (H)
           telephone PM ring again
           'The telephone rang again.'
      b. *Na em i   kam, em i   kam nau, na   em i*
           and he PM came he PM came now and he PM
           askim   mi wanem kain sik   mipela kisim (B)
           ask-TR mi what   kind illness we   catch
           'And he came, he came, and asked me what kind of illness I
           had got.'

(ii) Postverbal *i* ("chained verbs"): 53 occurrences. These involved various overlapping categories, as shown below:

(a) Directional:

(20)   a. *Mi wokabaut i   go lo(ng) wok* (H)
           I   walk   PM go to   work
           'I walk to work.'
      b. *Mipela kisim ol lip i   kam* (H)
           we   get   PL leaf PM come
           'We bring leaves.'

(b) Durative:

(21)   a. *Mipela wok i   go inap painim   foa o klok* (H)
           we   work PM go until find-TR four o'clock
           'We keep working until four o'clock.'
      b. *Liklik buk tasol i   kamap   i   go* (Ja)
           little   boil only PM come-up PM go
           'Only a little boil kept swelling up.'

(c) Prototypical "serial":

(22)   a. *Oke, wetim   ka i   kamdaum* (B)
           okay wait-TR car PM come-down
           'Okay, I wait for the car to arrive.'
      b. *Mi gat ol ska i   stap yet long han   bilong mi* (Ji)
           I   have PL scar PM stay still on   hand of   me
           'I've still got scars on my hands.'

(iii) To introduce subjectless clauses: 43 occurrences. For example:

(23)   a. *I   gat   kainkain   mumu* (Ja)
          PM have many-kinds mumu
          'There are various kinds of mumu (underground oven).
       b. *I   go Sande* (S)
          PM go Sunday
          'It gets to Sunday.'

The question which needs to be answered, therefore, is the extent to which these environments involved far-reaching syntactic rule(s) (as apparently in the pidgin), and the extent to which they were lexically governed.

4.5. Lexical environment: Preceding item

The directly preceding lexical environment turned out to be of critical importance in the main-clause examples of *i* (omitting the few examples of conjoining with no directly preceding NP). More specifically, the number of "full" NPs followed by *i* was compared with the number of pronouns followed by *i*: the pronouns considered were *em* 'he, she, it' and *ol* 'they' (since *i* was frequently indistinguishable after a vowel, and all other pronouns end in vowels).

The overall figures were: NP 48, *em* 16, *ol* seven cases − suggesting that *i* was preferentially inserted after a full NP. This supposition was confirmed when all main clauses beginning with a full NP, *em*, or *ol* were considered, as shown in Table 1.

Table 1. Main clause NP and presence/absence of *i*

	+*i*	?*i*	−*i*
"Full" NP	48	36	28
em	16	12	111
ol	7	1	52

The first column in Table 1 shows cases where *i* was clearly present, and the last column cases where it was clearly absent. The middle column shows the number of times when it would mostly have been imperceptible due to a preceding vowel, as in:

(24)   a. *Ai bilong mi (i ??) raun* (Ji)
         eye of   me PM go-round
         'I was dizzy.'
    b. *Em bai (i ??) go* (Ji)
         she IR PM go
         'She would go.'

These figures therefore indicate that *i* was preferentially included after a full NP, but was omitted after a pronoun, even though there was considerable variability. This impression is strengthened, and some of the variation was explained when the figures were examined speaker by speaker, and context by context. This showed the following:

(i) Seven (out of 16) examples of *em + i* occurred in the output of B, whose speech showed signs of decreolization (B was the girl who did not live in the hostel, and her Tok Pisin was the most anglicized. For example, she alone put an *-s* plural on the word *ston* 'stone', a word which cropped up in the speech of most informants in descriptions of a *mumu* 'underground oven', she alone used habitual *sa* inappropriately, and she was the informant with the least number of predicate markers). If she is omitted from the count, the preference for omitting *i* after *em* is stronger.

(ii) In 21 (out of 28) cases when *i* was omitted after a full NP, another pronoun was repeated:

(25)   a. *Lip bilong pamkin,   em malomalo* (S)
         leaf of   pumpkin it tender
         'Pumpkin leaf, it's tender.'
    b. *Ol man long Papua yes ating   ol   sa   kaikai*
         PL man of Papua yes I-think they HAB eat
         tapiok   tumas (Ja)
         tapioca much
         'Papuans, yes I think they eat lots of tapioca.'

This suggests that *i* is often in complementary distribution with pronouns, and that a pronominal copy is felt to be necessary after a full NP if *i* is absent. If the "pronoun copying" examples are added to the full NP + *i* examples, then 69 full NPs were followed by either *i* or a pronoun, and only seven were definitely without them. However, the phenomenon of pronoun copying was primarily a characteristic of the two Lae girls (18 examples), rather than the four Goroka girls (three examples), indicating some regional variation. (Some interesting regional variations in Tok Pisin are documented in Reesink 1990).

In short, examination of the subject NP in main clauses showed that *i* was typically omitted after the pronouns *em* and *ol.* However, *i* or a pronoun was preferentially included after a full NP. This appears to be a situation in which *i* has been analysed as a copied pronoun, and the copying has then spread to other pronouns (overgeneralization).

4.6. Lexical environment: Following item

One hundred and ten of the 176 predicate-marker occurrences (62 percent) directly preceded one of four verbs, *go* 'go', *kam* 'come', *stap* 'be, stay', *gat* 'have'. This number includes cases in which negatives, aspect or tense particles intervened between the predicate marker and the verb (e. g., *i sa gat, i no stap*) or which were compounds of the original verb (*gobek, kamdaun*). However, even if these had not been included, the number of occurrences of *i* which directly preceded these four verbs was over 50 percent.

These broke down as: *go* (60 occurrences), *kam* (22), *stap* (9), *gat* (19). Apart from these four verbs, no other lexical item had any real conditioning effect, except possibly for the negative: *i no* occurred eight times (three of these in conjunction with one of the verbs above). For example:

(26)   *Sapos yu   kaikai nating,   i   no   gutpela tumas* (S)
        if   you   eat   nothing-but PM not good   very
        'If you eat food plain, it's not very good.'

The four key verbs interacted with the syntax in interesting ways, as will be discussed in the section below.

4.7. Lexicon and syntax: Interaction

Table 2 shows the interaction of syntax and the lexicon. It indicates how the various lexical categories were distributed among the three main syntactic environments. The category "other" includes both verbs and words normally translatable as adjectives in English.

As Table 2 shows, *i* predominantly occurs between subjects and predicates in main clauses for lexical items outside the main four. The variety of predicates which can follow the initial NP confirms the impression obtained earlier, that subject NP + *i* was a syntactic rule (one of pronoun copying). Occasional examples suggested that a repeat of a noun or phrase was more likely to have a predicate marker, which indicates that

Table 2. Interaction of syntax and lexicon

	Main clause NP *i* V	Post-verb V (NP) *i* V	Subjectless clause # *i* V	*Total*
go	13	29	18	60
kam	11	11	–	22
stap	5	3	1	9
gat	1	–	18	19
Other	50	10	6	66

such markers may be a feature of careful speech, and have the role of a "marker" of good pidgin:

(27)   a. *Praktis finis, mi kambek,   praktis i   finis, mi*
          practice finish I   come-back practice PM finish I
          kambek   long haus   gen (S)
          come-back to   house   again
          'After the practice, I come back, after the practice, I come back home.'
       b. *Na   pitpit boil, pitpit i   strong liklik* (H)
          and pitpit boil pitpit PM tough little
          'and the pitpit (a vegetable) boils, pitpit is fairly tough.'

The relative rarity of lexical items apart from the main four in "chained" constructions suggests that chaining of various kinds is on the decrease. One reason may be the decline in knowledge of the substratum languages, some of which use chained verbs. Another reason is the decreasing need for such constructions, as alternative methods of expressing the functions for which they are used are developed: for example, relative clauses introduced by *we* are becoming established (Aitchison 1992, cf. Woolford 1979 b), so reducing the need for serial-verb constructions, and preverbal markers are partly taking over the functions of postverbal ones (Aitchison 1989 b).

As the postverbal constructions decrease, therefore, they are becoming increasingly tied to a small number of lexical items, mainly *go*, and to a lesser extent *kam*. The relative rarity of postverbal *stap* is interesting in view of its ubiquity in the pidgin, where it is especially common as a postverbal marker expressing continuation (e. g., *go i stap* 'to keep going'). Among the speakers discussed here, it was used only in cases where it overlaps with English *stop*, as in the following examples:

(28)   a. *Mi gat ol ska i   stap yet long han   bilong mi* (Ji)
         I   have PL scar PM stay still on   hand of   me
         'I've still got scars on on my hands.'
     b. *Mipela rausim   ol haphap paiawut i   stap long*
        we   throw-out PL pieces firewood PM stay on
        mumu (H)
        mumu
        'We chuck away the bits of firewood which remain on the
        mumu.'

These examples suggest that it is on the verge of losing its postverbal
durative function, and becoming a straightforward lexical item "stay",
"remain". The contraction of meaning of *stap* is inevitably leading to
a reduction in the number of examples of postverbal *i* and postverbal
constructions in general.

Go was the most extensively used verb with *i*. It was particularly common postverbally, occurring both in durative constructions, and directional ones:

(29)   *Mipela wok i   go inap painim   foa o klok* (H)
        we   work PM go until find-TR four o'clock
        'We keep working until four o'clock.'

(30)   .. *na   troimwe   i   go* (H)
           and throw-away PM go
        '... and throw it away.'

In addition, it was used in subjectless clauses, meaning "it has now
reached", "and so on to", "it went on", "it happens":

(31)   a. ... *na i   go lunchtaim* (Ji)
           and PM go lunchtime
        '... and it gets to lunchtime.'
     b. ... *na long dispela wik i   go olsem* (H)
           and in   this   week PM go thus
        '... and during this week it went on like this.'
        ... *na mi sa   go waswas orait i   go i   go*
           and I HAB go wash   alright PM go PM go
        wanem?
        what
        '.. and I wash, then what happens?'

In brief, this was the only verb which retained its pidgin usages, and
expanded them. In the short run, it is keeping postverbal *i* alive. In the

long run, it is a potential candidate for reanalysis as a single lexical item *igo*. This time has not yet been reached, though there were some signs of this possibility, when pronouns which preferentially do not occur with *i* are found occurring with *i go*:

(32)   *Ol   i   go long wara* (Ji)
        they PM go to   water
        'They go to the water.'

In subjectless clauses, *i gat* was as common as *i go*, as an idiomatic expression "there is", "there are", as in:

(33)   *I   gat planti kain kaikai mipela sa   kukim* (S)
        PM have many kind food   we   HAB cook-TR
        'There are numerous kinds of food we're accustomed to cook.'
        Na sapos long nait i   gat danis, mipela sa   go
        and if   in   night PM have dance we   HAB go
        danis (S)
        dance
        'And if in the evening there is a dance, we go and dance.'

I go and *i gat* in subjectless clauses are therefore idiomatic, lexically governed expressions.

The interaction of the syntax and the lexicon therefore shows that the use of *i* has become splintered into three main usages:

i. Syntactically governed *i* in main clauses containing a subject. Here it functions as a copied pronoun, and the copying rule has in the speech of some speakers been generalized to other pronouns, and so is in complementary distribution with them
ii. Lexically conditioned *i* in postverbal constructions, attached primarily to the verbs *go* and *kam*
iii. Lexically conditioned *i* in clause initial position, mainly in the idiomatic phrases *i gat* and *i go*

The creole use of *i* therefore shows overgeneralization in (i), and undergeneralization in (ii) and (iii).

5. Summary and implications

As the data and analysis have shown, the use of *i* by these six first-generation creole speakers was considerably reduced, compared with its usage by pidgin speakers. This was partly due to the speed of creolized Tok Pisin, which often caused *i* to coalesce with the preceding vowel, resulting in its virtual omission in certain environments. However, it was not simply phonologically conditioned, in that it did intermittently occur in all phonological environments.

The three syntactic environments in which *i* occurs have become separated, so that *i* is treated differently in main clauses containing a subject, postverbally, and in subjectless clauses.

In main clauses after a subject, overgeneralization occurs, via the following sequence of events:

i. After a "full" NP *i* is preferentially retained, and interpreted as a copied pronoun
ii. Its interpretation as a pronoun means that *i* does not occur after the pronouns *em* and *ol*, where it would be redundant
iii. Owing to the speed of speech, *i* tends to coalesce with the preceding vowel in some phonological environments
iv. Other pronouns are then inserted in places where *i* would be unnoticed, and so is (mostly) in complementary distribution with them. This is overgeneralization, in that it represents the extension of an *i*-copying rule to other pronouns

The general situation is one found fairly often in language change, when a syntactic feature which has been lost due to phonological attrition recurs in a different guise (such as plural marking in French, which has moved from the ends to the beginning of words, being now marked by the preceding article).

In the two other syntactic environments, undergeneralization has occurred, in that the presence of *i* is primarily lexically conditioned. Postverbally it has become restricted mainly to the verbs *go* and *kam*. This has occurred for a number of interrelated reasons:

a. decline in knowledge of the substratum languages, some of which use similar constructions;
b. increase in the use of preverbal markers, at the expense of postverbal ones, which in the long run may be one way in which a language achieves typological consistency;
c. increase in alternative methods of introducing complex sentences;
d. contraction in meaning of the verb *stap* to those senses which overlap with English *stop*.

In subjectless clauses (apart from conjoined ones), *i* is used idiomatically mainly with the verbs *go* and *gat*.

It is possible that, in the long run, *i* in the lexically conditioned environments will coalesce with the adjacent verbs and cease to have an independent existence of its own.

The overall conclusion is that *i* is gradually on the decline. A plethora of interacting factors are all slowly eroding its use. But the process of atrophy is not a straightforward one. Considerable variation occurs, which has not yet been tidied up into a fully categorical system. The situation found here suggests that young creoles are sometimes glamorized in the literature, and presented as instantaneous, neat systems. In practice, the neatening-up process might not be complete for generations (cf. Arends 1986) – in line with the finding that first-language speakers can often tolerate more variability than second-language speakers. Such changes are probably not being carried out by babies, but by stable groups of speakers, interacting among themselves.

To return to the question asked at the beginning of the paper, small steps or large leaps? The answer seems to be: "both". Speakers have split up an existing construction, and are simultaneously undergeneralizing it by restricting its use in some environments to particular lexical items, and overgeneralizing it by extending its use beyond its original bounds in other environments. Such an answer is unlikely to appeal either to the small-step, or the large-leap adherents: first-generation creole speakers are neither working entirely piecemeal, nor are they setting parameters. This conclusion shows that there are no blanket answers, merely a need to focus more closely on the interacting factors which are involved in creole development. As the playwright Oscar Wilde once said via one of his characters: "truth is rarely pure, and never simple".

Note

1. The final version of this paper was produced in February 1991. Since then, several further publications on Tok Pisin *i* and resumptive pronouns have appeared. These do not substantially alter the content, but note should be taken of (at least) Keesing (1991), Romaine (1993), Schlonksy (1993), Verhaar (1991).

References

Ahlqvist, Anders (ed.)
    1982   *Papers from the 5th International Conference on Historical Linguistics.* (Current Issues in Linguistic Theory 21.) Amsterdam: John Benjamins.
Aitchison, Jean
    1984   "Social networks and urban New Guinea Pidgin (Tok Pisin)", *York Papers in Linguistics* 11: 9–18.

1989 a   *The articulate mammal: An introduction to psycholinguistics.* (3rd edition.) London: Unwin Hyman.

1989 b   "Spaghetti junctions and recurrent routes: Some preferred pathways in language evolution", *Lingua* 77: 209−229.

1990   "The missing link: The role of the lexicon", in: Jacek Fisiak (ed.), 11−28.

1991   *Language change: Progress or decay?* (2nd edition.) Cambridge: Cambridge University Press.

1992   "Relative clauses in Tok Pisin: Is there a natural pathway?", in: Marinel Gerritsen−Dieter Stein (eds.), 295−316.

Aitchison, Jean−Rama Kant Agnihotri

1985   " 'I deny that I'm incapable of not working all night': Divergence of negative structures in British and Indian English", in: Roger Eaton−Olga Fischer−Willem Koopman−Frederike van der Leek (eds.), 3−14.

Arends, Jacques

1986   "Genesis and development of the equative copula in Sranan", in: Pieter Muysken−Norval Smith (eds.), 103−127.

Bailey, Guy−Natalie Maynor

1988   "Decreolization?", *Language in Society* 16: 449−473.

Bybee, Joan−Dan Slobin

1982   "Why small children cannot change language on their own: Suggestions from the English past tense", in: Anders Ahlqvist (ed.), 29−37.

Cheshire, Jenny

1982   *Variation in an English dialect.* Cambridge: Cambridge University Press.

Chomsky, Noam

1986   *Knowledge of language.* New York: Praeger.

Dutton, Tom E.

1973   *Conversational New Guinea Pidgin.* (Pacific Linguistics D-12.) Canberra: The Australian National University.

Eaton, Roger−Olga Fischer−Willem Koopman−Frederike van der Leek (eds.)

1985   *Papers from the 4th International Conference on English Historical Linguistics* (Current Issues in Linguistic Theory 41.) Amsterdam: John Benjamins.

Fisiak, Jacek (ed.)

1990   *Historical linguistics and philology.* Berlin−New York: Mouton de Gruyter.

Gerritsen, Marinel−Dieter Stein (eds.)

1992   *Internal and external factors in syntactic change.* (Trends in Linguistics 61.) Berlin−New York: Mouton de Gruyter.

Hall, Robert A., Jr.

1966   *Pidgin and creole languages.* Ithaca: Cornell University Press.

Hall, Kenneth C. (ed.)

1979   *The genesis of language.* Ann Arbor: Karoma.

Keesing, Roger M.

1988   *Melanesian Pidgin and the Oceanic substrate.* Stanford: Stanford University Press.

1991   The expansion of Melanesian Pidgin: Further early evidence from the Solomons. *Journal of Pidgin and Creole Languages* 6, 215−229.

Lass, Roger

1990   "How to do things with junk: Exaptation in language evolution", *Journal of Linguistics* 26: 79−102.

Laycock, Donald C.
1970   *Materials in New Guinea Pidgin (Coastal and Lowlands)*. (Pacific Linguistics D-5.) Canberra: The Australian National University.
Lynch, John
1979   Changes in Tok Pisin morphology. [Paper presented at the 13th Congress of the Linguistic Society of Papua New Guinea, Port Moresby.]
Mihalic, Francis
1971   *The Jacaranda dictionary and grammar of Melanesian pidgin*. Milton, QLD, Australia: The Jacaranda Press.
1990   "Obsolescence in the Tok Pisin vocabulary", in: Verhaar (ed.), 263−273.
Mühlhäusler, Peter
1985   "Syntax of Tok Pisin", in: Stephen A. Wurm−Peter Mühlhäusler (eds.), 344−421.
1987   "Tracing predicate markers in Pacific Pidgin English", *English Worldwide* 8: 97−121.
1990 a   "On the origins of the predicate marker in Tok Pisin", in: Verhaar (ed.), 235−249.
1990 b   "Tok Pisin: Model or special case?", in: Verhaar (ed.), 171−185.
Muysken, Pieter−Norval Smith (eds.)
1986   *Substrata versus universals in creole genesis*. Amsterdam: John Benjamins.
Reesink, Ger
1990   "Mother tongue and Tok Pisin", in: Verhaar (ed.), 289−306.
Romaine, Suzanne
1993   The decline of predicate marking in Tok Pisin. In *Atlantic meets Pacific: A global view of pidginization and creolization* edited by Francis Byrne and John Holm. Amsterdam: John Benjamins.
Sankoff, Gillian
1977   "Multilingualism in Papua New Guinea", in: *New Guinea area languages and language study*, Vol. 3. (Pacific Linguistics C-40.) Canberra: The Australian National University.
Schlonsky, Ur
1992   "Resumptive pronouns as a last resort", *Linguistic Inquiry* 23: 443−468.
Trudgill, Peter
1986   *Dialects in contact*. Oxford: Blackwell.
Verhaar, John W. M.
1990   *Melanesian pidgin and Tok Pisin: Proceedings of the First International Conference of Pidgins and Creoles in Melanesia*. Amsterdam: John Benjamins.
1991   "The function of *i* in Tok Pisin", *Journal of Pidgin and Creole Languages* 6: 231−266.
Woolford, Ellen
1979 a   "Variation and change in the *i* 'predicate marker' of New Guinea Tok Pisin", *Papers in Pidgin and Creole Linguistics* 2. (Pacific Linguistics A-57.) Canberra: Australian National University.
1979 b   "The developing complementizer system of Tok Pisin: syntactic change in progress", in: Kenneth C. Hill (ed.), 108−124.
Wurm, Stephen A.−Peter Mühlhäusler (eds.)
1985   *Handbook of Tok Pisin (New Guinea Pidgin)*. (Pacific Linguistics C-70.) Canberra: The Australian National University.

Creoles and the bankruptcy of current acquisition theory

Derek Bickerton

The central question in any discussion of creole languages and language acquisition should be the implications that these languages have for any valid theory of acquisition. The claim of this paper is simply that creole languages, by virtue of their mere existence, pose a challenge to acquisition theory that no existing theory of acquisition is capable of answering. In this paper I propose to spell out as clearly as possible just what that challenge consists of.

I have already discussed the relationship of creole languages to language acquisition in a number of works (see especially Bickerton 1981, 1984). Unfortunately, the main focus of those works was on determining the means by which creole languages originated, consequently the issues most crucially affecting language acquisition were not distinguished and expressed as clearly or as sharply as they might otherwise have been. Some of the more specific (perhaps overly specific) predictions about normal acquisition based on creole evidence have been frequently discussed (by Cziko 1986, 1988, 1989; Mapstone–Harris 1985; Youssef 1988, among others). Unfortunately, however, some more far-reaching issues have been largely ignored by acquisitionists. Central to these issues is whether the acquisition of a mature syntactic capacity requires well-formed linguistic structures as input.

The belief that well-formed syntactic input is essential to language acquisition is shared by literally every school of thought in the field of acquisition. While input plays its strongest role in approaches such as that of Snow (1977), which requires input to be not merely well-formed but actively tailored to the child's growing cognitive capacities, it is no less crucial in the work of generativists such as Berwick (1985: 95), who assumes that the acquisition device must receive "a representative sample of sentences generated by the target grammar in question", and defines "representative" as meaning that all grammatical rules of the target grammar must be represented and that grammatical sentences must appear with greater frequency than errors. In the same way, Lightfoot (1989), while requiring only "degree-0" input (simple one-clause sentences) for his acquisition model, insists that input be "robust", that is, contain a very high ratio of grammatical to ungrammatical sentences. At least one scholar (Pinker 1984) specifically admits the inadequacy of his own approach to account for creole acquisition and at the same time insightfully links this inadequacy to the input issue: "the theory is fairly data-driven, and at present cannot account in any simple way for the creation of novel grammars under conditions of radically degenerate linguistic input documented by Bickerton (1981)" (1984: 357).

In most parts of the world, we have no direct evidence of the input from which creole languages were formed (although a great deal can be inferred from the structure of the resulting languages). In Hawaii, however, creolization took place recently enough for the input to the creole to be documented and analysed. (I will deal shortly with the claim that the input discussed here is not the real input.) In Hawaii (Bickerton–Odo 1976; Bickerton 1981, 1984), the pidginized input that gave rise to a creole language was radically ill-formed in at least three ways:

a. It was structurally restricted (that is, it contained no sentences that could be unambiguously analysed as containing embedded clauses).
b. It was radically variable (that is, it contained elements from more than one language and it had little or no structural consistency).
c. It was morphologically impoverished (in particular, it lacked all grammatical and many derivational inflections as well as a high percentage of such word-classes as determiners, prepositions, complementizers and verbal auxiliaries).

All of these properties can be demonstrated from the pidgin input that gave rise to Hawaiian Creole. For instance, the sentences in (1) below demonstrate the type of structural restriction that was all but universal in pidgin input. Letters and numbers after each extract represent, respectively, the ethnicity of the speaker (F, Filipino; J, Japanese; K, Korean) and the year of arrival in Hawaii; glosses for the extracts indicate possible alternative bracketings of similar material by speakers of a natural language.

(1)   a. *bipo,   ai gat wan haus,   kip   chikin.* (F, 1914)
            before I   got one house keep chicken
            'I used to have a house [where I kept roosters].'
         b. *pau   kawl, kaukau.* (F, 1916)
            finish call   eat
            '[When I've called (on the phone) I'll eat.'

c. *daes wai −a− koria kim − kim neim wan moa taim*
that's why   korea kim   kim name one more time
mi mari. (K, 1916)
I   marry
'Because I got married again to a Korean [whose name was Kim].'

This lack of structure in pidgin inputs can be fully illustrated only if somewhat longer extracts are provided:

(2)   *samtaim   besbol-maen   − futubol-maen   − pati, no,*
        some-time baseball-man   football-man   party no
        wintaim pati, no? misez kashiwada pleis, yu no
        win-time party no Mrs. Kashiwada place you know
        da haus   get lawng taim bifo,   no? (J, 1918)
        the house get long   time before no
        'A long time ago, baseball and football players used to celebrate their victories with parties at Mrs. Kashiwada's place, you know that house she has?'

(3)   *aena tu   macha churen,   samawl churen,   haus   mani*
        and   too much children small   children house money
        pei, beri had   taim, no moa mani, pua, eskul
        pay very hard time   no more money poor school
        churen   − mai churen   go sakul teiki haus   mani
        children   mai children go school take house money
        pei, evriting   pua, tu   hawd. (K, 1916)
        pay everything poor too hard
        'I had several small children of school age and I had to find the rent money. We had a hard time because we were very poor.'

(4)   *ai go oloa, ai go dak da shuga, aen den, pau   kat*
        I   go oloa I   go cut the sugar   and then finish cut
        kein, no moa kein, no moa jab, a? ai go kalapana
        cane, no more cane no more job Q I   go Kalapana
        sai, ai go plaent taro, wan baeg oni   tri   dala,   wan
        side I   go plant taro one bag only three dollar one
        hemo   taim wan yia, wan eika hemo   wan eika meik
        harvest time one year, one acre harvest one acre make
        ova   tauzan. (F, 1916)
        over   thousand

'I went to Oloa to cut sugar-cane, but cane-cutting finished there and there was no work so I went to Kalapana to grow taro. It took a year to harvest, but though you only got three dollars a bag, you could make a thousand dollars from one acre.'

Clearly, there is no way in which a child exposed to data of this kind could acquire, from the data itself, the capacity to produce sentences containing relative clauses, embedded questions, embedded factives or adjunct clauses.

The second property, radical variability, derives in part from significant differences between the pidgins of different language groups, influenced by the speaker's mother tongue. For instance, Japanese and Filipino immigrants showed diametrically opposed tendencies with regard to word order (Bickerton−Givón 1976). Immigrants from both groups were divided into three stages, based on the degree of phonological and lexical mother-tongue interference in their speech, Stage 1 being the most heavily influenced. Stage 1 Japan-born speakers placed objects before verbs with an overall frequency of 67 percent (N = 340), while Japan-born speakers as a whole did so with a frequency of almost 50 percent (N = 954). Stage 1 Philippine-born speakers placed nonpronominal subjects after verbs with a frequency of 51 percent (N = 45; N is relatively low because the bulk of sentences in pidgin discourse have pronominal or null subjects), while Philippine-born speakers as a whole did so with a frequency of almost 33 percent (N = 122).

If the word-order deviations described above were categorical, a child might in principle conclude that two distinct varieties were being spoken, and decide to learn only one, only the other, or both. But the situation is not so easy as that. Alongside heavy mother-tongue influence, we find what Givón (1979) has called the "pragmatic mode", in which the speaker begins an utterance with whatever topic is uppermost in his/her mind, or in the context, and follows it with other material (the "comment"). This can result in Japanese speakers producing sentences in which the subject precedes the verb (5 a) or in Filipino speakers producing sentences in which the verb follows its complement (5 b):

(5)   a. *ye, dea   wok   hazban.* (J, 1925)
          yes there work husband
          'Yes my daughter's husband works there.'
       b. *waianae ebri   sandei   get.* (F, 1914)
          Waianae every Sunday get
          'Every Sunday there's (a cockfight) at Waianae.'

Thus, children exposed to pidgin input could not even determine the basic word order of the language they were supposed to be acquiring. Indeed, since the relative positions of S and O could vary in both verb-final and verb-initial sentences, a data-driven child would have had to determine that the input was drawn from a free-word-order, wholly nonconfigurational language. From such an input no believer in data-driven acquisition could have predicted the strictly configurational SVO form that the nascent creole would in fact take.

Radical variability is, however, by no means limited to word order. One characteristic of well-formed input is that it contains overt representations of all the subcategorized arguments of verbs, except where some regular process of the language (e. g., control, NP-movement, *wh*-movement) makes it possible to determine quite unambiguously the intended referent of the phonologically-null argument. This is by no means the case in pidgin input, where any argument may be omitted and where no regular processes exist to identify phonologically-null arguments (this can be done only pragmatically, if at all). Sentences that omit external arguments are very frequent:

(6) a. *bambai,   kam   hia,   ei?* (J, 1917)
        by-and-by come here eh
        'Later on we came here, didn't we?'

     b. *no kaen du nating.* (F, 1919)
        no can   do nothing
        'You can't do anything.'

     c. *nata   pleis no go.* (K, 1916)
        another place no go
        'I didn't go anywhere else.'

Internal arguments too may be freely omitted:

(7) a. *ai sel wan sainis   gai.* (F, 1914)
        I   sell one Chinese guy
        'I sold it to a Chinese guy.'

     b. *sambadi klin,   wan wahine podgi.* (F, 1916)
        someone clean one woman Portuguese
        'Somebody cleaned it, a Portuguese woman.'

     c. *awl fren   giv, no?* (J, 1918)
        all friend give no
        'They gave them all to their friends, didn't they?'

Children exposed to large numbers of such sentences could not hope to derive from them any systematic means of linking null elements with overt expressions. Indeed, one may doubt whether they could have learned the subcategorization frames of even the commonest verbs.

Similar variability could be found in the expression of grammatical elements, the occurrence of which, in any given context, simply could not be predicted. To take only a single example out of many possible ones, definite articles might be omitted where English would require them (8 a) or, more rarely, inserted where English would not require them (8 b):

(8)   a. *kawpe prais tu   mach hai,   ei?* (J, 1907)
coffee price too much high eh
'The price of coffee was very high, wasn't it?'

   b. *yu   no   da bambu,   hi kaen,   yae,   da bambu.* (F, 1910)
you know the bamboo he can   yes   the bamboo
'You know one can do that with bamboo, yeah, with bamboo.'

Thus, there was no way in which any child could have derived the correct distribution of such items.

As for the third property of pidgin input, the degree of morphological impoverishment can be documented from the examples already given. The following items were missing virtually without exception: verbal morphology (past and third person singular marking, participial *-ing* and *-ed*), auxiliary *do*, *have* and *be* whether as auxiliaries or main verbs (with the exception of *been*), modals other than *can* and *must*, a number of prepositions (*to*, *by*, *at*), complementizer *that*, *who/whom/which* as relative pronouns (except for *who* with indefinite referent), genitive *'s*, indefinite articles, and adverbs in *-ly*. The following items were retained but with greatly lowered frequencies and/or unpredictable distribution: the form *been*, definite articles, complementizer *for*, the remainder of prepositions, pronouns, anaphors, and subordinating conjunctions.

Yet despite structural restriction, radical variability and morphological impoverishment, children exposed to input of which examples (1) to (8) are typical succeeded in producing a language which is fairly represented by sentences such as the following:

(9)   a. *dei   gon   get naif pok   yu.*
they going get knife poke you
'They will stab you with a knife.'

   b. *dei   wawk fit   go skul.*
they walk   feet   go school
'They went to school on foot.'

c. *da gai gon   lei da vainil bin   kwot mi prais.*
the guy going lay the vinyl been quote me price
'The guy who was going to lay the vinyl had quoted me a price.'

d. *da gai stap da intasekshan da oni   wan gon   no.*
the guy stop the intersection the only one going know
'The guy who stops at the intersection is the only one who will know.'

e. *a tel am wai no   meik am go aut go it   raet.*
I tell her why not make it   go out go eat rat
'I asked her why she didn't make it go out and eat rats.'

f. *a no kea hu   stei hant insai dea.*
I no care who stay hunt inside there
'I don't care who's hunting in there.'

g. *a bin   laik go pei am.*
I been like go pay him
'I would have liked to pay for it.'

All of the sentences in (9) contain embedded clauses (even where, as in (9 a) and (9 b) their English equivalents do not). Examples (9 a) and (9 b) show ways in which arguments can be incorporated in sentences even in the absence of governing and Case-assigning prepositions such as *with* or *to*. (9 c, 9 d), and (9 f) show relativization, employing a zero operator where the relative has a head noun in (9 c) and (9 e), even though English requires overt relativizers in such sentences, but using a reflex of English *who* exclusively in headless relatives, as in (9 f). Example (9 e) shows a complex sentence with two infinitival clauses embedded in a causative embedded in an embedded question. Sentences (9 c), (9 d), (9 f), and (9 g) show how the massive losses in verbal inflexions and auxiliaries were made up by using a reflex of *been* as a past-before-past tense marker, a reflex of *stay* as a partial replacement for auxiliary *be*, and reflexes of *go/going* indicate future or conditional states and actions.

Clearly, we are here in the presence of a natural language, somehow connected with, yet going far beyond, the pidgin data surveyed in (1) to (8); we find a complete (and quite complex) rule system where in the pidgin there was complete anarchy. Equally clearly, although the words in these sentences are all drawn from English, their grammar is not English grammar. But neither is it the grammar of Hawaiian, Chinese, Portuguese, Japanese or any of the other languages that were spoken in late nineteenth − or early twentieth-century Hawaii. Yet it is homogeneous;

the speakers of (9) will not (save with the relatively trivial exceptions we find among speakers of any natural language) disagree with one another about the grammaticality of sentences like these. There can be no doubt that, although the speakers of (9) have not acquired any pre-existing language, they have acquired language.

I should say a word here about some alternative explanations of the data which have been attempted. Goodman (1984, 1985), Holm (1986), and Carden—Stewart (1988) have objected to the account set forth above on two grounds. They claim, first, that data such as those of (1) to (8) do not represent the actual pidgin that gave rise to the creole but only some type of degenerate speech that followed, rather than preceded, the emergence of the creole. Second, they claim that there existed, prior to 1900, a systematic and fully-developed pidgin, linked historically to pidgins in the Pacific and elsewhere, that was the true ancestor of the creole.

Unfortunately, as shown by Roberts (to appear), the evidence on which these claims are based is seriously flawed. All the cited works rely exclusively on three citations by Goodman (1985). The first of these purports to show that the speech of Hawaiian seamen in the 1830s was simply a variety of Pacific Pidgin English, with negligible admixture from other languages (Goodman professes to believe that only later Japanese immigrants had the habit of inserting numerous expressions from their own language into the pidgin). The extract comes originally from Richard Dana's *Two years before the mast*, but its immediate source is Clark (1979). As Clark shows, Dana's seamen used a high proportion of Hawaiian in their pidgin (not just individual words but also whole sentences) and some at least of those sentences consisted of the pidginized Hawaiian described by Bickerton—Wilson (1987). Goodman carefully omits all of these, and his "citation" is made possible only by splicing together two extracts from different speakers on quite different occasions (a fact of which Goodman fails to apprise the reader).

Similar treatment is afforded to the other two citations, which purport to show that a local variety of English was well established by the 1880s. Goodman, following Reineke et al. (1975), cites the following extract:

> The colloquial English of Hawaii is even now sufficiently *sui generis* to be noticeable to strangers. It is not a dialect, but a new language with English as its basic element, wrought upon by the subtle forces of other languages, not as much in the matter of a changed vocabulary as a changed diction.

However, he fails to cite the passage following this in the original article (*The Friend*, April 1886, p. 4):

They have been at the great feast of language and have stolen the scraps
... The native boy is a rarity who has not several phrases in Chinese and
Portuguese and when it comes to single words the stock in trade of most
native boys is not at all small. It is true also of the Chinese and Portuguese
and Japanese, for some of the latter, who have been in the country a very
brief time, have picked up some Portuguese words and a few native expressions, and a stray English word of uncertain lineage ... The worst of it is,
they think this olla podrida is English undefiled!

Similar treatment is afforded a further citation from the same source (*The
Friend*, August 1887, p. 63). The passage Goodman cites states: "English
is already settled in its place as the controlling language of the country."
Goodman fails to cite the two sentences that immediately follow this: "It
is the governing language of the laws and the courts. It is supreme in
business and in journalism."

Amazingly, the three citations detailed above constitute the only evidence for Goodman's claim that by 1888 "the pidgin had already become
fairly fixed in form". As against these, Bickerton—Wilson (1987) contains
abundant data, drawn from contemporary documents as well as from
the memories of living speakers, that both pidginized Hawaiian and a
macaronic pidgin of mixed English and Hawaiian were widely used right
through the early decades of the present century, and Roberts (to appear),
in the course of an exhaustive survey of late nineteenth-century books,
magazines, and court records, has amassed many more contemporary
citations of pidgin Hawaiian, macaronic pidgin, and the use of the immigrants' native languages as a means of communication in Hawaii. No-
where in all of this literature have we found a single citation of the systematic English-based pidgin whose existence Goodman treated as incon-
trovertible fact. The only possible conclusion is that no such pidgin existed.

If this is so, and if immigrants at all stages communicated via a language that was structurally restricted, radically variable and morphologically impoverished, then, contra Goodman and others, either the speakers recorded in the early 1970s and discussed in Bickerton—Odo (1976)
actually provided the input to the first creole speakers, or the input provided at an earlier period was equally or even more structurally restricted,
equally or even more radically variable, and equally or even more morphologically impoverished.

But if syntax can be acquired from input of this level of impoverishment, then no theory that requires well-formed data as input can be an
adequate theory of language acquisition. Since all extant theories of
acquisition contain this requirement, it follows that, as yet, there do not
exist any that could be called adequate theories.

References

Berwick, Robert C.
1985   *The acquisition of syntactic knowledge.* Cambridge, MA: MIT Press.
Bickerton, Derek
1981   *Roots of language.* Ann Arbor: Karoma.
1984   "The language bioprogram hypothesis", *The Behavioral and Brain Sciences* 7:
           173–221.
Bickerton, Derek–Talmy Givón
1976   "Pidginization and language change: From SXV and VSX to SVX", in: San-
           ford E. Steever–Carol A. Walker–Salikoko A. Mufwene (eds.), 9–39.
Bickerton, Derek–Carol Odo
1976   *General phonology and pidgin syntax.* (Vol. 1 of final report on NSF Grant #
           GS-39748.) [Mimeo.] Honolulu: University of Hawaii.
Bickerton, Derek–William H. Wilson
1987   "Pidgin Hawaiian", in: Glenn G. Gilbert (ed.), 61–76.
Clark, Ross
1979   "In search of Beach-la-Mar: Towards a history of Pacific Pidgin English", *Te
           Reo* 22: 3–64.
Cziko, Gary
1986   "Testing the LBH: A review of children's acquisition of articles", *Language*
           62: 878–898.
1988   "The LBH: A reply to Youssef", *Journal of Child Language* 15: 669–671.
1989   "A review of the state-process and punctual-nonpunctual distinction in chil-
           dren's acquisition of verbs", *First Language* 9: 1–31.
Gilbert, Glenn G. (ed.)
1987   *Pidgin and creole languages: Essays in memory of John E. Reinecke.* Honolulu:
           University of Hawaii Press.
Givón, Talmy
1979   *On understanding syntax.* New York: Academic Press.
Goodman, Morris
1984   "Are creole structures innate?", *The Behavioral and Brain Sciences* 7:
           193–194.
1985   "Review of Bickerton (1981)", *International Journal of American Linguistics*
           51: 109–137.
Holm, John
1986   "Substrate diffusion", in: Pieter Muysken–Norval Smith (eds.), 259–278.
Lightfoot, David
1989   "The child's trigger experience: degree-0 learnability", *The Behavioral and
           Brain Sciences* 15.
Mapstone, E. R.–Paul L. Harris
1985   "Is the English present progressive unique?", *Journal of Child Language* 12:
           433–441.
Muysken, Pieter–Norval Smith (eds.)
1986   *Substrata versus universals in creole genesis.* Amsterdam: Benjamins.
Pinker, Stephen
1984   *Language learnability and language development.* Cambridge, MA: Harvard
           University Press.

Reinecke, John−David De Camp−Ian F. Hancock−Stanley M. Tsuzaki−R. E. Wood
  1975   *A bibliography of pidgin and creole languages.* Honolulu: University of Hawaii
            Press.
Roberts, Julian M.
  to appear *The origins of pidgin in Hawaii.*
Snow, Catherine E.
  1977   "Mother's speech research: From input to interaction", in: Catherine E.
            Snow−Charles A. Ferguson (eds.), 31−49.
Snow, Catherine E.−Charles A. Ferguson (eds.)
  1977   *Talking to children: Language input and acquisition.* Cambridge: Cambridge
            University Press.
Steever, Sanford E.−Carol A. Walker−Salikoko A. Mufwene (eds.)
  1976   *Papers from the parasession on diachronic syntax.* Chicago: Chicago Linguistic
            Society.
Youssef, Valerie C.
  1988   "The language bioprogram hypothesis revisited", *Journal of Child Language*
            15: 451−458.

Comment on Bickerton's paper

Thomas Roeper

The claim that creole languages provide us with a radically new view of acquisition theory is, perhaps, entertainingly flamboyant, but it is little more than that. There is no departure whatsoever in Bickerton's approach from the assumptions made by researchers in first-language acquisition: a) Universal Grammar is innate, b) particular grammars are fixed by input, and c) children's utterances reflect both the impact of input and spontaneous, unmodeled, projections from unmarked aspects of Universal Grammar. Creole languages reflect precisely the same thing as far as I know.[1]

Bickerton states that "the belief that well-formed syntactic input is essential to language acquisition is shared by literally every school of thought in the field of acquisition". He then argues that the spontaneous emergence of new structures, not based upon input of the same form, shows that this assumption is wrong.

This view is a simplification which leads to a distortion. The central belief of acquisition theorists is the following logical one: in order for a child to acquire knowledge of a particular language, the child must have representative input from that language. For instance, a child will not acquire Object-verb structure correctly if no instances of Object-verb sentences are presented to her. The notion that input must be "well-formed" is an idealization which we know not to be true in general for either creole or non-creole languages. The notion "well-formed" means not obscured by nongrammatical performance phenomena. If every instance of an Object-verb sequence were interrupted by hesitation and uncertainty, then the input would be not well-formed. How does the child learn the rule of compound formation which puts the Object before the verb, e. g.: *soda-drinking*? If the child heard:

(1)   *soda ah I mean coke-drinking, or even non-soda is bad.*

then, unaware of the structure of the language, the child would have heard a sequence with:

(2)   Object Object verb Object [*soda, coke, drink, non-soda*]

From utterances of this kind, language, any language, is unlearnable. Even a creole language would not be learnable from input of this sort. The information is in a sense "contradictory" and the child will know it by application of Universal Grammar: the Object cannot be in three different places. The child needs clear, simple instances like *soda-drinking.* Universal Grammar must be powerful and specific enough, so that the child does not think that the repetitions of the Object in (2) are possibly grammatical, as they are in cases like *John I like him* (Object Subject verb Object).

The second claim Bickerton makes is: spontaneous productions in creole which are not found in any input provide a challenge to acquisition theory. But such productions are precisely what one finds in normal acquisition. It is not the case that children exhibit properties only of the target language in acquisition. The very fact that English children exhibit small-clause-like structures, unacceptable in isolation for adults, is an example:

(3)   *it big.*

Other unmodeled utterances from children are interesting:

(4)   a. *You don't be quiet.*
         b. *Allison didn't be mad.*
         c. *This didn't be colored.*
         d. *did there be some.*
         e. *did it be ...?*
         f. *does it be on every day ...?*
         g. *does the fire be on every day?*
         h. *do clowns be a boy or a girl?*
         i. *I didn't been there* (aspectual *been*).[2]

These sentences, like others with *do*-insertion (*he did left*), exhibit *do*-insertion with verbs that normally do not take an Object (no theta-assignment) and therefore should "raise" to the Tense position. The fact that insertion occurs with *be* means that linguistic theory cannot explain these facts simply in terms of theta-assignment. There may be an explanation in terms of some theory of "aspect" which is also relevant to creole languages, but once again, first-language acquisition reveals facts of precisely the same kind we find in creoles.

In addition we find copying structures, acceptable in German but not in English, in the language of children:

(5)   *What did you say what you wanted?*

Recently Hoekstra—Jordens (1991) have pointed out that in Dutch children will dissociate possessors from their Objects, prior to learning /'s/, in a way that resembles Hungarian:

(6)   a. *Cynthia niet pajama.* (= not Cynthia's pajama)
        b. **Cynthia's not pajama.* (ungrammatical in Dutch and English)

These are all examples of a child making spontaneous projections from Universal Grammar which do not correspond to the properties of the target language.

More interesting errors at more sophisticated levels occur. In German one can have *wh*-words in either order (7 a), (7 b), but not English (7 c), (7 d):

(7)   a. *Wer kauft was?*
        b. *Was hat wer gekauft?*
        c. *Who bought what?*
        d. **What did who buy?*

However, I recently noted that a child said, twice, a sentence in English which resembles German for which no model is possible:

(8)   *Do you know what I wonder who is?*

The child exhibits a freedom with the movement of *wh*-words that is allowed by Universal Grammar but disallowed in English. The child must then, somehow, learn something which excludes such sentences from her grammar. Specifying what the child learns which moves the child to what seems to be a narrower grammar (from German to English) is then the challenge of acquisition theory. The next step is based on some input from the target grammar which in turn has the elimination of these so-called "superiority violations". Conceivably, differences in the case-properties of German and English are involved, but the issue remains open.

The instances which Bickerton provides of spontaneous utterances in creole are very interesting and serve to suggest which forms are "unmarked" in Universal Grammar. The fact that they occur spontaneously provides simply more evidence of the generative power of grammar to produce novel structures, just like the evidence we find in the acquisition of non-creole languages. The true challenge faced by linguistic theory and acquisition theory lies elsewhere. It is equally a challenge for the acquisition of creole languages: how are certain interpretations excluded? How does a child know that a bound-variable reading is possible for (9 a) but not (9 b):

(9)   a. *Who is lifting his hat?*
       b. *Whose hat is he lifting?*

That is, (9 a) can refer to a set of people each of whom lifts their hat, while (9 b) can allow at most one person to lift his own hat. Evidence (Roeper–Mallis–Akiyama 1985) suggests that children know this by the age of three. Relevant input is impossible, since the fact that one interpretation of (9 a, b) is not bound (*he*= someone else) does not indicate that it cannot be bound in (9 b) alone.

The putative answer to this question is that Universal Grammar says something like: a bound reading does not exist if the *wh*-word has been moved (as it is in *whose hat$_i$ is he lifting trace$_i$*). However, particular language variation may also occur. We find that a bound variable reading is excluded when an indirect question is involved in English (10 a) but not when the *wh*-word is in situ (10 b):

(10)   a. *How did he say what to lift?*
       b. *How did he say to lift what?* (both *wh*s answered)

But this does not hold for Spanish, where children and adults will give a bound-variable reading for both cases.[3] These questions are being pursued by Ana Perez at the University of Massachusetts. English-speaking children will at first function as the Spanish children, allowing the bound-variable interpretation and then shifting. In our work (de Villiers–Roeper–Vainikka 1990) they are forced to shift by Universal Grammar when they learn, in English, that certain verbs subcategorize for indirect questions. How then do they learn that? That is the next question.

The role of "well-formed" input in language acquisition pertains only to choices that children make about particular languages. Universal features of grammar can emerge spontaneously – and they do. The challenge for acquisition theory is the same as the challenge for linguistic theory: how do we specify the properties of Universal Grammar so that we can state and explain exactly what the child knows without input?

Notes

1. This comment is written from the perspective of one who is acquainted with first-language acquisition and not creole. Therefore, I evaluate only the claims about first-language acquisition.
2. See Roeper (1991) for discussion.
3. The term bound-variable is much-disputed. We use it here as a descriptive term to refer to paired readings.

References

de Villiers, Jill—Thomas Roeper—Anna Vainikka
    1990   "The acquisition of long-distance rules", in: Lynn Frazier—Jill de Villiers (eds.), 257—297.
Frazier, Lynn—Jill de Villiers
    1990   *Language processing and language acquisition.* Dordrecht: Kluwer.
Hoekstra, Teun—Peter Jordens
    1991   "From adjunct to head". [Paper presented at the GLOW workshop on acquisition, University of Leiden.]
Perez, Ana
            Empty categories in language acquisition. [Unpublished dissertation, University of Massachusetts.]
Roeper, Thomas—M. Rooth Mallis—Satoshi Akiyama
    1985   "The problem of empty categories and bound variables in language acquisition". [Unpublished MS, University of Massachusetts.]

Ambient language and learner output in a creole environment

Lawrence D. Carrington

1. Introduction

Carrington (1989) argued that in studying language acquisition in a Caribbean sociolinguistic complex, both the description of the language to be acquired and the account of the process of acquisition should be based on the same corpus produced in the learning environment by the learner and the participants in his/her language socialization. The principle was presented as necessary for two reasons; firstly, because existing descriptions of the systems of communication do not allow the analyst to have a predetermined reference point for the learner's target, and secondly, because our knowledge of variation suggests that, even within a tightly defined sociolinguistic setting, it is difficult to predict the mix of features that will constitute the input to a learner. The 1989 paper exemplified the problem by reference to the environment of one informant. This paper uses data from the environments of two informants to amplify the argument and to highlight the necessity for an integrated corpus for the study of the target language and learner's language.

2. The established environments for acquisition studies

Most documented knowledge of language acquisition has been established by observation of children exposed to a specific language for which an ample referential description is already available. The language being acquired has been usually modeled by formally educated mainstream users. Despite the shift that the study of linguistic variation has occasioned in sociolinguistics and in general linguistics, it is fair to say that acquisition studies tend to treat variation as a footnote rather than as a determinant of descriptive methodology and field procedure. Such studies may confirm the reality of variation and may even occasionally explore it, but generally speaking, variation would not have been deliberately included as a conditioning factor of their design and methods.

3. The creole environment

By contrast, the nature of creole environments obliges analysts to consider the phenomenon of variation in the design of acquisition studies. Creole studies have given a high profile to variation and, while there has been very little study of language acquisition in such environments, it is a reasonable extrapolation that a learner faces a moving target. That target is ill-defined both because of the paucity of grammatical studies that cover the range of sociolinguistic environments in which a child might learn to speak and because we are still unable to predict the mix of linguistic features that might correlate with a tightly defined environment.[1]

The delimitation of the true target is important not only because of the established needs of acquisition studies but also because of ideas associated with the language bioprogram hypothesis. We need to know with some certainty what is genuinely part of the input so that we can tease it apart from what is developmental and what may be innate.

4. An appropriate corpus

Working in Trinidad, I have begun to experiment with the creation of a corpus intended to allow both the description of the target communication system (i. e., the community repertoire) and the description of the acquisition process to come from the same data. Before discussing the corpus and methodology, however, I hasten to neutralize the charge of reinventing the wheel by ignoring the available descriptions of the language of the environment in which I am working. It must be understood that the descriptions of language in Trinidad are only very partial.[2]

Even if there were what might be described as full descriptions, I would still argue that the descriptions available and our knowledge of creole grammar are not primary resources for the delimitation of the target language; they are ultimate resources.

5. A target of the acquisition process

In Trinidad, the official language is English; the vernacular language in the environment of the informants is of English-lexicon creole type. The experimental corpus is being created out of the tape-recorded conversations of the informants and the participants in their learning environments. The audio recordings of conversations with the child and within earshot of the child allow a partial description of the grammar of the speech of the environment. This is assumed to represent the core of the target of the learner. Those data are supplemented by the analysis of instances within the recordings when the informant is specifically (or obliquely) corrected or instructed to perform specific linguistic tasks (including repetition).[3] The Appendix provides a listing and examples of the occurrence of various forms associated with the predicate system of the speech of the households of two primary informants, P and S. The symbol # marks examples taken from the speech of the primary informants in cases where they display the same marking characteristics as the rest of their households. A continuation of the Appendix shows some characteristics of the speech of informant P which are not recorded in the speech of the rest of her household.

6. Profiles of the informants

Informant P was recorded between the ages of two years and eight months and three years exactly (2;8 and 3;0). She is the second youngest of seven children in a rural household. Her mother (a teenager), her grandmother (almost 40) and her grandmother's husband (late forties) show very different varieties of the spectrum of possible outputs in rural Trinidad. Their home is on the north coast of Trinidad about 60 miles by road from the capital. The informant's grandmother had secondary-level education up to the fifth form (approximate student age 16) in a semi-urban setting; her grandmother's husband had limited elementary schooling in a rural setting; her mother left secondary school in their village setting at form two (approximate age 13); four of the other children in the household are at school. The family's income comes from peasant agriculture. Informant S was recorded between the ages of one year and eleven months and two years four months (1;11 and 2;4). She is the youngest of four children in an out-of-town household in an area of mixed socioeconomic type about eight miles east of the capital city. Her mother (late twenties) was educated at secondary level for five years but earned no certificates. Her father (also late twenties) is a draughtsman with a firm of engineering consultants. His education is technical-institute level. Three brothers aged nine, seven and five complete the household. They attend a neighboring primary school.

7. Trinidadian and the speech of the learners' environments

According to the relevant literature, informant S can be expected to be exposed in greater proportion than informant P to varieties of language that are closer to the acrolectal end of a post-creole continuum. The data support that expectation but that knowledge by itself is too gross to be of major value for the purpose of studying acquisition. It does not allow prediction of form-function units or of the distribution of such units. Available sociolinguistic descriptions of the relevant settings do not allow us to assign a specific coherent grammar to a given sociolinguistic profile with more than gross probability.

8. A look at the actual data

It would be an error to assume that a child in the setting of Trinidad necessarily functions with a target (i. e., available model) that includes the features described by the literature as established features of Trinidadian. In the case of reference to established pattern (e. g., habitual), the descriptions of Trinidadian vernacular would lead one to expect *does* and its variants. However, such forms are singularly absent from the recording of the environment of informant P. Instead, P's environment offers zero as in example (1 a). The informant produces zero at (1 b), as well as suffix /-ɪn/ (2 a, b), although this latter is not recorded in the speech of her environment.

(1)   a. wɔt jʊ ø se? (P 6)
          'What do you say?'
   #   b. dɑ ø mek kɪedẑ
          'That makes Koolaid.'

(2) # a. m a watʃɪn muːvi (P 15)
          'm ... I watch movies.'
   #   b. a watʃɪn dajnasti
          'I watch Dynasty.'

   The data from the environment of informant S over the same grammatical area of the predicate show a larger number of forms and features than from the environment of P. There are several instances of forms of English *be* and, unlike the environment of P, hers features the use of *does* as one of the means of expressing established pattern.

(3)   a. ðat ɪz waɪ aɪ dʌz bi hɛrɪn bɔwt sara, sara! (S 7)
       'That is why I keep hearing about this Sarah!'
    b. an sʌmtaɪmz aɪ it plɛnti an aiz kʌm leta
       'And sometimes I eat a lot and I come later.'
    c. ɪz risɛs aʌz bi hɔŋgri, nʌt lʌntʃ taim
       'Recess time is when I am hungry, not lunch time.'

By comparison with the case of "established pattern", data from the environments of both informants show the use of a copula in equation type sentences as predicted by the literature. See examples (4), (5 a, b), and (6) from the environment of informant P and (19 a, b) from the environment of informant S.

(4)   da ɪ nɔt ʃuga (P 12)
    'That is not sugar.'

(5)   a. dajz kuled (P 13)
       'That's Koolaid.'
    b. se da glas ɪz tu drɪŋk wɔta
       'Say "that glass is to drink water".'

(6)   daɪz wɔtʔ (P 14)
    'What's that?'

(7)   a. an dɪːz di neks wʌn (S 19)
       'And this is the other one.'
    b. dɪːz di jʌŋgʌ wʌn
       'This is the younger one.'

In contrast to the examples recorded in the environment of informant P, she herself produced a zero form in a comparable utterance (8).

(8) #   da ø maj ki! (P 17 b)
       'That's my key!'

Informant S though, matched the model recorded in her environment.

(9) #   daz i wʌkmaːn (S 19 c)
       'That's the Rockman.'

9. Suspicious elements

Structures which occur in the recorded speech of an informant but which are not evidenced in the speech of the other participants in his or her environment have to be carefully interpreted. They may fall into one of the following categories:

a. they may be acceptable community structures which, by chance, have escaped being recorded; or
b. they may be representative of a developmental stage of the child's acquisition.

There is the interesting possibility that a feature that constitutes a developmental stage for one informant may be part of the target for another child. Compare examples (10 a) and (10 b) from informant P with example (11) under informant S.

(10) # a. m a watʃɪn muːvi (P 15)
              'm ... I watch movies.'
       # b. a watʃɪn dajnasti
              'I watch Dynasty.'

(11)   ai sɪtɪn dɔŋ nɛks tʌ natʌli (S 3 a)
            'I sit next to Natalie.'

P uses suffix /-ɪn/ in an utterance compatible with reference to an established pattern although the usage is not mirrored in the recordings of her environments. Did she create the usage? Is it developmental? A common-sense view would suggest that the absence of the usage among the other members of the household is simply an accident of the recording and that at some point the usage will be recorded. Suffix /-ɪn/ used in this way is documented in Trinidad and it is in evidence in the usage of members of the household of informant S. It would be easy then to simply decide that this is part of P's input. However, such a decision would be dangerous because, if followed logically, it would result in an obviously unacceptable proposition that children produce only those structures that they have heard. We are therefore obliged to mark the feature as suspicious and seek to verify it within the same environment.

10. Specific linguistic tasks requested of informant

The specific linguistic tasks requested of the informant by members of her environment can provide data to amplify the target. In respect of the informant P, several interactions involved her being asked to convey specific information to another person in the household (messages), to repeat particular words or phrases, or to reply to questions in specified ways. One of these instances is instructive here. Some of the children of the household of P returned home to find her wearing a shirt I put on her with a wireless microphone used for the recordings. Her grandmother instructs her to tell the others how she comes to be dressed in that fashion. The sequence goes as follows:

(Sequence 1)
Grandmother: tɛl dɛm dat a man gɪv jʊ a tʃɜt
              'Tell them a man gave you a shirt.'
Child: man gɪ mi a tʃɜ.t.
              'Man gave me a shirt.'

The exchange is innocuous enough until it is compared with an earlier sequence of exchanges between the same pair in the same recording session. The grandmother goes through a ritual question and answer interaction with the child.

(Sequence 2)
Grandmother: hu gev jʊ dat pɪtʃa?
              'Who gave you that picture?'
Child: m?
              'mhm?'
Grandmother: hu gɪv jʊ?
              'Who gave you?'
Child: *Joy*
Grandmother: hu gɪv jʊ di tʃe?
              'Who gave you the chair?'
Child: *Joy*

The informant's grandmother disposes of both *gave* and *give* in reference to past action and it is clear that she considers both forms acceptable for use with and by the informant. It is not possible within the present data to determine whether she attributes a consciously different status to *gave* but examination of her use of such forms over a wider data set should allow clarification. A similar kind of information comes out of a play situation in which one child models a preferred form for the informant. In a brief exchange between S and her seven-year-old brother, he pretends to be father of the family.

(Sequence 3)
Child: dadi dwɪŋᵏ ɔːl! dadi dwɪnk ɔːl!
              'Daddy drank all! Daddy drank all!'

Brother: jɛs, a draŋk ɔ:l
               'Yes, I drank all.'

The modeling of the English strong form of the past morpheme suggests that the identification of a specific speaker with a preference for that type of form is part of the family experience. Considerations of identity such as have been treated in Le Page and Tabouret-Keller (1985) are clearly pertinent to the acquisition process.

11. The usefulness of the approach

As in all research of this type, informants are not monitored 24 hours a day each day of their lives. Consequently, a majority of their utterances and those of their interlocutors goes unrecorded. It would be folly therefore to adopt a closed attitude towards any corpus. However, the differences between the details that can be extracted from the environments of P and of S are sufficient to exemplify the notion that in a Caribbean sociolinguistic complex, learners may have quite different targets even though they may be growing up in an environment for which available descriptions may suggest greater uniformity.[4] The available descriptions are insufficiently discriminating and need to be refined by more careful study of individual Caribbean varieties. Nevertheless, even if there were a reasonable proliferation of descriptions, it would not be acceptable to assign speakers to specific predescribed varieties on the basis of either their place of residence, apparent class membership, education or any of the social considerations that correlate to specific features. Only knowledge of the mix of features in the input to a particular child can really allow proper assessment of how early, how effortless and how errorless is the acquisition of competence in a community variety in a Caribbean sociolinguistic complex. Some procedure of target delimitation is essential. The approach I have outlined seems promising and will form the basis of continuing study of my informants. The concerns here are primarily methodological but they address an important theoretical issue that cannot be side-stepped if our discussions of the processes of language acquisition in creole environments are to be productive. Acquisition studies have to make flexible use of the data of the immediate environment as well as the available knowledge of the general language variety within which the learner is being nurtured.

Appendix

Informant P

Recorded between 2;8 and 3;0, P is the second youngest of seven children in a rural household. Her mother [J], a teenager, her grandmother [M] almost 40, and her grandmother's husband [R], late 40s, show very different varieties of the spectrum of possible outputs in rural Trinidad. The grandmother had secondary level education up to the fifth form (approximate age 16) in a semi-urban setting; the grandmother's husband has had limited elementary schooling in a rural setting; her mother left secondary school in their village setting at Form 2 (approximate age 13); four of the other children in the household are at school. Examples marked by # were produced by the informant.

Informant S

Recorded between 1;11 and 2;4, S is the youngest of four children in an out-of-town household in an area of mixed socioeconomic type. Her mother, late 20s, was educated at secondary level for five years but earned no certificates; her father, also late 20s, is a technical worker with a firm of engineering consultants; his education is technical institute level. Three brothers aged nine, seven, and five complete the household. They attend a neighboring primary school.
Examples marked by # were produced by the informant.

The occurrence of suffix *-in*

Activity that is observable as in progress concurrently with the speech event

1. a. tɛl ɪm mɪstʌ sɛntɪl kʌmɪn ʌp di hɪl
'Tell him Mr. St. Hill is coming up the hill.'
b. tʌmbɔdi kʌmin ʌp
'Somebody is coming up.'
2. Activity hypothesized to take place after the speech event

a. an wɪtʃ pat jʊ kipɪn jʊ krɛɔn?
'And where would you keep your crayon(s)?'

1. a. ʌ mekɪn ɪt, ʌ hɔtɪn ɪt!
'I'm making it, I'm heating it up.'
2. Activity having duration at a time concurrent with the discourse grammar

a. de sem lʊk di kɔkrotʃ dansɪn bikʌz ɪt dʒʌmpɪn ɔl ʌbɔt
'They were saying "look at how the cockroach is dancing" because it was jumping all over.'
3. Reference to an established pattern

a. ai sɪtɪn dɔŋ neks tʌ natʌli
'I sit next to Natalie.'
4. Activity to take place after the speech event
a. ai kɔmin wɪt mɔmi
'I'm coming with Mummy.'

The occurrence of is/are + V + *ın*

5. Activity having duration concurrently with the speech event

a. no wɔnda hiz filın so hɔt
'No wonder he feels so hot.'

The occurrence of was/were + V + *ın*

6. Activity having duration at time prior to speech event

a. ıt wʌs maı dʒus dat wʌz likın
'It was my juice that was leaking.'

The occurrence of *dʌz* and variants

7. Reference to an established pattern

a. ðat ız waı ai dʌz bi hɛrın bɔwt Sara, Sara!
'That is why I keep hearing about this Sarah!'

b. an sʌmtaımz aı it plɛntı an aiz kʌm leta
'And sometimes I eat a lot and I come later.'

c. ız rises aʌz bi hɔŋgri, nʌt lʌntʃ taim
'Recess time is when I am hungry, not lunch time.'

The occurrence of zero (± English concord marking)

8. Reference to an established pattern

a. wat ʃi sɛz tru di maikrafon goz tru dat redjo wıtʃ .. wıtʃ sɛnz wevz tʌ di rejdio an ıt k.. an ıt goz dɔŋ tʊ di antɛna ...
'What she says through the microphone goes through the radio which ... which sends waves to the radio and it c ... and it goes down to the antenna ...'

b. de fɔlo wɔt jʊ dʊ, jʊ no
'They follow what you do, you know.'

The occurrence of zero

Desires current at the time of utterance

3. a. wɛ jʊ wɔ̃ mı baı fʌ jʊ?
'What do you want me buy for you?'

#9. a. mami ʌ wʌn ti
'Mummy, I want tea.'

\# b. hi wɔnt a ɛk
    'He wants an egg.'

4. Recently completed events closely contiguous to the speech event
  a. hɔwɪtes?
    'How does it taste?'
\# b. di ɛk bʌn mi!
    'The egg has burnt me!'

    b. a tiŋk i min ʃi wʌnt a kʌp o sʌmtɪŋ
      ...
      'I think she means she wants a cup or something ...'

Events completed before the speech event

5. a. we jʊ gɛ fa di krɪsmʌs?
    'What did you get for Christmas?'
\# b. ʃi tɛl mɪ da
    'She told me so.'

10. a. mʌmi, a mek a bʊk wɪt ɪt
    'Mummy, I made a book with it.'
  b. an de haf kɪl ɪt
    'And they half killed it.'
  c. hu gɪv jʊ dat
    'Who gave you that?'
  d. wi si di staɪːl di staɪl, di ovʌri
    'We saw the style, the style, the ovary.'
\# e. aw! m .. bʌ mɪ ʌw! m ..
    '(It) burnt me.'

6. Reference to an established pattern

  a. wɔt jʊ seʔ
    'What do you say?'
\# b. da mek kiedʒ
    'That makes Koolaid.'

11. Perception possible at the time of the speech event
\# a. ai si wʌkmaːn
    'I can see Rockman.'

The expression of a state or the nature of a subject, at a time concurrent with the speech event or discourse grammar

7. a. ʃi tɛl jʊ jʊ najsʔ
    'She told you you're nice?'
\# b. ʃi tɛl mɪ a najt
    'She told me I'm nice'
  c. lɪzi vɛks
    'Lizzie is vexed (angry).'

12. a. dɪs said kol, dɪs said hɔt
    'This side is cold, this side is hot.'
  b. ɪt tɪk so
    'It is about this thick.'

8. The expression of location of a subject at a time concurrent with the speech event
  a. wɔ ɪn de?
    'What's in there?'

13. The expression of location of a subject at a time concurrent with the discourse
  a. natʌli ɪn di mɪdl, sera at wʌn ɛn an ai at di ʌdʌ
    'Natalie is in the middle, Sarah at one end and I at the other.'

9.   In a clause expressing a consequence
       of an immediately preceding clause
  a. kʌ ʌ tɛ jʊ sʌmtıŋ
      'Come let me tell you something.'

The occurrence of English past marked forms

An event completed before the speech event

14.   Forms with suffix -*d*, -*t*, -*id*
   a. aı had ɔl di ıngridiʌnts
      'I had all the ingredients.'

10. a. hu gev jʊ dat pıtʃa
       'Who gave you that picture?'

internal vocalic change ± D
   b. mıs tʊk ɔt ʌ kan ʌv ɛmti ʃɛltɔks
      'Miss took out a can of empty Shell-
      tox.'
   c. ʃi sɛd ı wʌz ɛmti
      'She said it was empty.'

other strong forms
   d. sera tɔt ʃi min spre ıt
      'Sarah thought she meant to spray
      it.'

The occurrence of had + verb ±
English past marking feature

15.   An event anterior to a discourse
       grammar that is already prior to the
       speech event
   a. mıs had waʃt ıt ɔt bıfɔ
      'Miss had washed it out before.'

The occurrence of *go* and variants

An event to take place after the speech event

11. a. a go bit jʊ
       'I'll beat you.'
 # b. go ʌŋ mek dʒus wıt ıt
       'Going to make juice with it.'
 # c. dʒɛni gɔn fʊl dɔŋ
       'Jenny's going to fall down.'
    d. a gʌ tek ıt ɔt frʌm ʃi bikɔ ʃi tu ba.d
       'I'll take it away from her because
       she is too bad (naughty).'

16. a. ʌ go gɛ ıt ovʌ mʌ bɛd bat ...
       'I'll get it over my bed but ...'
 # b. goın an ple
       'Going to play.'

The occurrence of [will], [l] and variants

17. An event to take place immediately after the speech event
   a. al gɛt wʌn fʌ jʌ
      'I'll get one for you.'
18. An event to take place after the speech event
   a. wɛn it go, pʊp' wi wɪl kɔl jʌ bak, oke
      'When it goes 'pup' we will call you back, O.K.?'

The occurrence of COP *is* and variants

12. In a negative utterance, a statement of identity that is stated as false at the time of the speech event
   a. da ɪ nɔt ʃuga
      'That is not sugar.'

13. Statements of identity true at the time of the speech event
   a. dajz kuled
      'That's Koolaid.'
   b. se da glas ɪz tu drɪŋk wɔta
      'Say "that glass is to drink water".'
14. Questions of identity true at the time of the speech event

   a. daɪz wɔt?
      'What's that?'

19. Statements of identity true at the time of the speech event

   a. an dɪːz di neks wʌn
      'And this is the other one.'
   b. dɪz di jʌŋgʌ waʌ
      'This is the younger one.'
 # c. daz i wʌkmaːn
      'That's the Rockman.'
20. Questions of identity true at the time of the speech event
   a. huz at?
      'Who's that?'

21. Expression of a state true concurrently with the speech event/discourse grammar
   a. di dʒus is gʊd fʊ hɪm
      'The juice is good for him.'

The occurrence of COP *was*
22. State true prior to the speech event
   a. bʌ wʌz onli rɛli haf dɛd
      'But (it) was only really half dead.'

Some characteristics of the speech of informant P

The features listed here appear in the speech of the informant P although they do not appear in the recorded speech of the remainder of the household.

Suffix -*ın*
15.   Reference to an established pattern
a. m a watʃɪn muːvi
      'm ... I watch movies.'
b. a watʃɪn dajnasti
      'I watch Dynasty.'
      The occurrence of zero
16.   The expression of possession at the
      time of the speech event
a. tʃav ʌ kjatʃ
      'She has a glass.'
17.   Statements of identity true at the
      time of the speech event
a. daː a dɔji
      'That's a dolly.'
b. da maj ki!
      'That's my key!'

Notes

1. See Carrington (1989) for a brief description of some of the types of environments.
2. Most of the specific documentation of the structure of Trinidadian speech is from work by Winford and Solomon. See Winford 1972, 1980; Solomon 1966.
3. See Carrington (1989) for some examples.
4. Youssef (1990) is relevant here.

References

Carrington, Lawrence D.
   1989   "Acquiring language in a creole setting: theoretical and methodological issues", *Papers and Reports on Child Language Development* 28: 65–71.
Day, Richard R. (ed.)
   1980   *Issues in English creoles: Papers from the 1975 Hawaii Conference.* (Varieties of English Around the World 2.) Heidelberg: Groos.
Le Page, Robert B.–Tabouret-Keller, Andrée
   1985   *Acts of identity: Creole-based approaches to language and ethnicity.* New York: Cambridge University Press.
Solomon, Denis V.
   1966   *The system of predication in the speech of Trinidad: A quantitative study in decreolisation.* [Unpublished MA thesis, Columbia University.]
Winford, Donald
   1972   *A sociolinguistic description of two communities in Trinidad.* [Unpublished Ph. D. dissertation, University of York.]
   1980   "The creole situation in the context of sociolinguistic studies", in: Richard R. Day (ed.), 51–76.
Youssef, Valerie C.
   1990   *The development of linguistic skills in some Trinidadian children: An integrative approach to verb phrase development.* [Unpublished Ph. D. dissertation, University of the West Indies.]

Creole languages and parameter setting: A case study using Haitian Creole and the pro-drop parameter

Michel F. DeGraff[1]

Are creole languages "unmarked", i. e., do their parameters show settings significantly similar to those exhibited by the child's grammar in the initial stages of language acquisition? This paper is an effort to partially answer this question by examining Haitian Creole with respect to one parameter with an "established" initial setting. It has been shown that the child's initial grammar, G_0, is pro-drop (or null-subject). I argue that Haitian Creole is also a null-subject language. Thus, along the corresponding parameter, Haitian Creole coincides with the child's initial hypothesis. Two kinds of evidence are presented to support this claim: (i) existential, weather, and *seem*-type verbs do not require phonologically realized subjects; (ii) "subject pronouns" behave like clitics spelling out the agreement features of the inflection phrase, and identifying *pro* in subject position. I will argue that certain properties of the inflection phrase in Haitian Creole regulate the appearance of clitics, nonpronominal subjects and variables in preverbal position. My account makes at least one nontrivial prediction, which concerns [COMP-trace] effects. Haitian Creole allows long-distance extraction from subject position over lexically filled COMP, even though it does not allow subject inversion. This is a problem for Rizzi (1982), which explains apparent lack of *[COMP-trace] in Italian through extraction from postverbal position. My analysis also contributes to explaining certain facts about serial verb constructions. Assuming that the second verb is part of an embedded clause, my analysis is used in explaining the mechanisms by which the embedded arguments, when phonologically empty, obligatorily corefer with arguments of the matrix clause.

We conclude by examining the larger implications of Haitian Creole's pro-drop setting for the relationship between creole languages and language acquisition.

1. Motivation

It has often been argued that creolization occurs through children's attempts to natively learn a pidgin and that, as a result, creole languages should be closer to Universal Grammar than languages formed under more stable environments. This argument is now familiar and goes as follows. Creole languages are the result of acquisition under unusual circumstances: heavy multilingualism, restricted access to the socially dominant language, lingua franca restricted to a pidgin that is syntactically impoverished, etc. Under these circumstances, children, because of the paucity and variability of the available linguistic model, would rely almost exclusively on their genetically wired "bioprogram" in acquiring language, and contribute much more to the final product of acquisition than, say, a contemporary child learning English. In other words, the linguistic environment had a minimal triggering effect on the emerging grammar. In a nutshell, this is (a version of) the language bioprogram hypothesis (Bickerton 1984). If the language bioprogram hypothesis holds, G_0, the child's initial grammar, must substantially overlap with G_C, the intersection of the core grammars of radical creoles. In the principles-and-parameters approach, this means that the child must start the acquisition process with most parameters initially set as in G_C (under some idealization).

One rigorous method to test this hypothesis is to look at parameters with "clear" initial settings (as per the literature on child language) and compare their settings with those of their counterparts in creole languages. This is what I propose to do in this paper with respect to the pro-drop parameter. This parameter was chosen because of the amount of scrutiny it has received in the literature on language acquisition, and because it has been examined in acquisition studies of various languages. Haitian Creole was chosen as a "representative" creole language because of comprehensive available documentation, and because it is a language that I speak natively.[2]

Bloom (1970), Hyams (1986, 1987), and Clahsen (to appear), among others, have shown that the child's first approximation of the model language (be it English, Italian, or German) is "subject-optional".[3] In Hyams's and Clahsen's accounts, G_0, the initial grammar, is pro-drop: it admits phonologically-null referential subjects in contexts where overt subjects may appear (irrespectively of whether the target language admits such null subjects).[4] Ultimately, the corresponding parameter either is reset when the target language is non-pro-drop (e. g., English, French),[5] or retains its initial setting for pro-drop languages (e. g., Spanish, Italian). According to Hyams (1986, 1987), two kinds of triggers activate the resetting from pro-drop to non-pro-drop: obligatory lexical expletive subjects and the use of "infelicitous" subject pronouns. In this paper, I first determine that there are no such triggers for the child learning Haitian Creole, and that this language is in fact pro-drop. This is done by showing that: 1) obligatory expletive subjects are mostly absent from Haitian Creole: existential, weather, and *seem*-type verbs do not require phonologically realized subjects; 2) "subject pronouns" are clitics spelling out the agreement features of the inflection phrase, and identifying *pro* in subject position. My analysis of Haitian Creole as a null-subject language yields one nontrivial result, which in turn supports the analysis: [COMP-trace] effects (or lack thereof) in Haitian Creole are explicated. Also, an account for the obligatory coreference between matrix arguments and nonrealized embedded arguments in so-called serial verb constructions (and other properties of such constructions) is provided, using the structures posited for the analysis of INFL.

2. Empty expletive subjects

According to Hyams, one crucial trigger for resetting the pro-drop parameter from its default positive value to a negative value is the obligatory use of lexical expletive subjects in the target language (e. g., English *it* and *there*, French *il*). If the pro-drop parameter is set negatively for a particular language, then the language has obligatory overt subjects, and expletives in subject position must be lexical. Verbs thematically equivalent to English *seem*, which subcategorize exclusively for a sentential argument in object position, will obligatorily have an overt subject in matrix subject position if null subjects are forbidden. In English, this obligatory subject is either an overt expletive, as in *It seems that Jack is sick*, or a subject raised from embedded subject position, as in *Jack seems to be sick.*

Haitian Creole *genlè*, the equivalent of English *seem*, does not require a phonologically realized subject:

(1)   *genlè Jak damou*
         seem Jak in-love
         'It seems that Jak is in love.'

Lexical expletives are generally optional in Haitian Creole. Following are some other instances of constructions lacking a phonologically realized subject:[6]

(2)   *te   fè   frèt*
ANT make cold
'It was cold.'

(3)   *gen jwèt sou tab   la*
have toys on   table the
'There are toys on the table.'

(4)   *te   manke Bazen yon   voum vòt   pou li   monte*
ANT lack   Bazin DET   lot   vote for 3sg rise
prezidan
president
'Bazin lacked many votes needed to become president.'

(5)   *ap   rete   manje sou tab   la*
FUT remain food   on   table the
'There will remain food on the table.'

Examples (1) to (5) indicate quite clearly that expletive subjects can be null in Haitian Creole.[7] These sentences are also examples of null elements occurring in subject position of tensed sentences. Examples (6) to (10) show that this position can be occupied by a lexical NP. Assuming this NP to be assigned Case under government, PRO must be excluded from this position.[8]

(6)   *Jak genlè damou*
Jak seem in-love
'Jak seems in love.'

(7)   *Jan te   fè   yon bèl   bagay*
Jan ANT make DET nice thing
'Jan did something nice.'

(8)   *tab   la   gen   jwèt sou li*
table the have toys on   it
'The table has toys on it.'

(9)   *Bazen te   manke yon   voum vòt   pou li   monte*
Bazin ANT lack   DET   lot   vote for 3sg rise
prezidan
president
'Bazin lacked many votes needed to become president.'

(10) *manje ap   rete   sou tab   la*
      food FUT remain on table the
      'Food will remain on the table.'

A quick inspection of the other possibilities for the empty category in [NP, S] of (1) to (5) reveals that it can neither be a variable (it is not operator-bound), nor an NP-trace (it is not A-bound). Thus this empty category must be *pro*. In the principles-and-parameters treatment of the pro-drop parameter proposed by Rizzi (1986 b), this means that Haitian Creole is pro-drop and that INFL is in the set of heads licensing *pro* through government.[9] The rest of this paper will flesh out this possibility and its consequences for the grammar of Haitian Creole.

3. "Subject pronouns" as clitics

Another characteristic of non-drop languages, and a trigger helping the language learner in setting the pro-drop parameter, is what Hyams calls "the use of referential pronouns ... in 'pragmatically infelicitous' circumstances" (Hyams 1987: 17). This trigger operates through the "avoid pronoun" principle. This principle states that the use of overt pronouns must be avoided wherever a null pronominal is possible. Thus, unstressed, noncontrastive, nonemphatic subject pronouns, the reference of which can be determined from context, are phonetically realized only when the language requires their presence for grammatical reasons, i. e., when the language is non-pro-drop.[10]

Superficially, it seems that Haitian Creole uses "infelicitous referential pronouns". Contrary to "pure" pro-drop languages like Spanish or Italian, Haitian Creole apparently requires that referential subjects be phonologically realized. Indeed, referential subjects in Haitian Creole seem to behave like those in non-pro-drop languages. Compare (11) with (12):

(11) **(mwen) achte yon   chemiz*
      1sg   buy DET shirt
      'I bought a shirt.'

The asterisk in this example is intended to indicate that omission of *mwen* produces ungrammaticality. It does not mean that sentence (11) is ungrammatical whether or not *mwen* is present.

(12) *(yo) compré   una camisa* (Spanish)
      1sg buy-PAST-1sg DET shirt
      'I bought a shirt' (with emphasis on 'I' when *yo* is realized in subject position).

However, in what follows I will argue that "subject pronouns" in Haitian Creole do not appear in subject position, and that they are clitics phonologically spelling person and number agreement features of INFL.[11]

One clue to cliticization of "subject pronouns" in Haitian Creole is the obligatory adjacency of such pronouns to the verb phrase:

(13) a. *Yaya, bèl   ti   abitan   an,   ap   viv nan vil*
         Yaya beautiful little peasant DET PROG live in   town
         Sen-Mak
         Sen-Mak
         'Yaya, the beautiful little peasant, lives in Sen-Mak.'
      b. **li, bèl   ti   abitan   an,   ap   viv nan vil*
         3sg beautiful little peasant DET PROG live in   town
         Sen-Mak
         Sen-Mak

In (13), the appositive *bèl ti abitan an* is allowed to occur between the lexical subject *Yaya* and VP, but not between *li* and VP.[12]

Interestingly, adjacency to the verbal phrase is not required either when *li* is followed by the emphatic marker *menm, li-menm* being a tonic pronoun:

(14)   *Li-menm,   bèl   ti   abitan   an,   ap   viv nan*
          3sg-EMPH beautiful little peasant DET PROG live in
          vil   Sen-Mak
          town Sen-Mak
          'The beautiful little peasant herself lives in Sen-Mak.'

Example (15) shows that an appositive can follow *li* in object position. Thus the ungrammaticality of (13 b) is not due to the cooccurrence of a pronoun and an appositive.

(15)   *mwen te   wè li, bèl   ti   abitan   an*
          1sg   ANT see 3sg beautiful little peasant DET
          'I saw her, the beautiful little peasant.'

More generally, the morphemes *mwen* (first person singular), *ou* (second person singular), *li* (third person singular), *nou* (first and second person plural), *yo* (third person plural), when in preverbal position, behave more like clitics than tonic pronouns, according to the tests listed in Zwicky (1985).

Phonologically, a subject clitic in Haitian Creole may form a single unit with the first morpheme of the verbal phrase, be it with *ale* 'go' in (16), *ap* (future) in (17) or *pa* (negative)[13] in (18):[14]

(16)   *mwen   ale   >   m ale*
        ou   ale   >   w ale
        li   ale   >   l ale
        nou   ale   >   n ale
        yo   ale   >   y ale

(17)   *mwen   ap   ale > m ap   ale*
        etc.

(18)   *mwen   pa   te   ale > m pa   te   ale*
        etc.

Preverbal clitics are accentually dependent and cannot bear phrasal stress:[15]

(19)   a. Bouki *ale*
     b. *li *ale*

Nonoccurrence of subject clitics in isolation is further evidence that they are bound morphemes which need an adjacent stem on which to attach. Possible answers to the question *Kimoun ki genyen?* 'Who won?' include *Bouki* and *li-menm*, but not **li*.

Distributionally, subject clitics are distinguishable from lexical subjects in not being able to combine with other phrases to form complex NPs. A subject clitic cannot head a complex NP in subject position:

(20)   a. *Bouki   avèk li,   de   abitan   Sen-Mak, pral Leogàn*
      Bouki with 3sg two peasant Sen-Mak go Leogàn
      'Bouki and he, two peasants from Sen-Mak, are going to Leogàn.'
     b. {*mwen/ou/nou/yo*} *(*-menm*) *avèk li pral Leogàn*

This is fully expected under the hypothesis that "subject pronouns" are clitics in INFL. Note that *li*, in (20a), allows for an appositive to separate it from the verbal phrase, unlike clitic *li* in (13b). This is because *li* in (20a) is an object pronoun appearing as the complement of the comitative preposition *avèk*. The subject NPs in (20) have the structure

$$[_{np} \text{ NP } [_{pp} \text{ avèk } li]].^{[16]}$$

Examples (15) to (20) strongly suggest that "subject pronouns" are indeed clitics phonologically bound to the first morpheme in VP. Thus, I assume that, at syntax, they occur in a position adjacent to VP, i. e., in INFL.[17] The phonological facts illustrated in (16) to (18) can also be viewed as part of the primary data used by the language learner for deciding that *mwen, ou, li, nou, yo* are the AGR element of INFL and that they are not in [NP, S]. If the language learner does use indirect negative evidence, then the distribution suggested in (13) to (15), (19), and (20) confirms this hypothesis.

4. Structure of INFL in Haitian Creole

I assume the following basic sentential and inflectional structures:[18]

(21) $[_S$ NP INFL $[_{VP}$ (NEG) V $[...]]$

(22)   INFL → (AGR) [± Tense] (AUX)

(23)   AGR = [α person, β number, (γ gender)]

4.1. AUX in Haitian Creole

I also assume that the realization of AUX in (22) is subject to parametric variation.[19] I will show that, in Haitian Creole, auxiliary verbs are realized not under INFL, but under VP.

The set of syntactic diagnostics proposed by Hyams (1987: 5) to determine the existence of a non-empty AUX node under INFL includes "tag-formation, negative placement, VP deletion and Subject-AUX inversion". All these diagnostics fail for Haitian Creole. There is no tag-formation:

(24)   a. *Roro pa   te   manje, te   li?*
           Roro NEG ANT eat   ANT 3sg
        b. *Roro pa   te   manje, pa   vre?*
           Roro NEG ANT eat   NEG true
           'Roro hadn't eaten, had he?'

The negation operator *pa* always precedes the sequence of tense-mood-aspect markers and main verb. It never breaks the sequence:[20, 21]

(25) a. *Jan pa t   ava   ale nan mache*
      Jan NEG ANT IRREAL go in market
      'Jan would not have gone to the market.'
      b. **Jan te   pa   ava   al nan mache*
      Jan ANT NEG IRREAL go in market
      c. **Jan t   ava   pa   ale nan mache*
      Jan ANT IRREAL NEG go in market

"VP deletion" is ungrammatical:

(26) *Mari p   ap   vini jodi a, men Jak ap   *(vini)*
      Mari NEG PROG come today but Jak PROG come
      'Mari is not coming today, but Jak is.'

Finally, Question AUX-Inversion is ungrammatical, cf. example (27). In (27 b), interrogative mood is indicated by rising intonation or the sentence-initial marker *èske*.

(27) a. **te   ou   wè mwen?*
      ANT 2sg see 1sg
      b. *(èske) ou te   wè mwen?*
      Q-mark 2sg ANT see 1sg
      'Did you see me?'

Examples (24) to (27) indicate that Haitian Creole auxiliaries do not move from their canonical positions. Thus, tense-mood-aspect markers in this language need not occupy an independent AUX node and can be generated under VP. The Haitian child can easily analyze tense-mood-aspect markers and modals in Haitian Creole as syntactically normal verbs since most of them also occur in their full forms as main verbs in the adult language, providing the necessary triggering evidence. *Pral*, marking future, also means 'to go'; *dwe*, marking obligation or possibility, also means 'to owe'; *fini*, marking completion, also means 'to finish'; *konnen*, marking habituality, also means 'to know'; *sòti*, marking recent past, also means 'to leave', etc.[22, 23]

To summarize, auxiliaries in Haitian Creole do not undergo movement and need not form an independent AUX node under INFL. They are generated under VP. As a result, (22) rewrites in Haitian Creole as:[24, 25]

(28)   INFL → (AGR) [± Tense]

I assume that both INFL and VP have temporal specifications. To ensure compatibility between [δ Tense] in INFL and temporal features of auxiliary verbs in VP, both features must percolate up to, and unify at, the sentential level.[26] For example, [− Tense] inherited by S from infinitival INFL would not unify with tense features percolated up from a VP containing *te* (anterior) or *ap* (future, progressive). Such a clash would result in ungrammaticality.

4.2. AGR in Haitian Creole

I assume the following properties to hold for AGR in Haitian Creole:

(29)   AGR is present under INFL only if INFL is [+ Tense].

(30)   [+ Tense] in INFL is a case-assigner.

(31)   In infinitival sentences, INFL is [− Tense] and is neither a governor nor a case-assigner.[27]

(32)   INFL is not an argument position (A-position).

In addition to (29) to (32), which are fairly uncontroversial, I rely on the following additional properties of INFL in Haitian Creole:

(33)   AGR is specified for the φ-features of the subject of its clause, either directly or indirectly, provided the subject bears a θ-role.[28]

(34)   AGR, when phonological, bears φ-features and is [+ pronominal, −anaphor].

(35)   AGR, when devoid of a phonetic matrix, lacks intrinsic φ-features and is anaphoric [− pronominal, + anaphor].

(36)   φ-features, when phonologically realized in AGR, absorb Case.

Properties (33) to (36) are the essence of my analysis of Haitian Creole as a null-subject language. As in all creoles, verbs in Haitian Creole never realize AGR through morphological inflections. Instead, AGR is "realized" either as a clitic pronoun or as a null anaphor bound by an overt NP in subject position.

4.2.1. AGR as clitic

When phonological, AGR draws its possible realizations from the set of subject clitics shown in Table 1.

Table 1. Subject clitics

Person	Singular	Plural
1st	*mwen*	*nou*
2rd	*ou*	*nou*
3rd	*li*	*yo*

Each clitic in Table 1 is specified for person and number. Thus, AGR, when realized (hereafter, cl-AGR), is clearly pronominal [+ pronominal, − anaphor][29] and sufficiently rich in φ-features to identify *pro* in subject position, on a par with rich AGR in Italian and Spanish.[30] Haitian Creole differs from "pure pro-drop languages" such as Italian and Spanish as follows: in Haitian Creole, AGR may be phonologically realized only through clitics, whereas Italian and Spanish realize AGR through affixes (in tensed clauses).[31]

Given the above remarks, the surface structure for *li ale* 'he left' is:

(37)   [s [NP pro$_i$] [INFL *li$_i$*] [VP *ale*]]

One crucial property of cl-AGR is that it absorbs Case from the Case-assigning element in INFL, [+ Tense], cf. assumption (36).[32] This directly accounts for the complementary distribution of clitic pronouns and lexical NPs in preverbal position. Contrary to some of the Northern Italian dialects (Brandi−Cordin 1989), Haitian Creole does not allow for overt NPs in subject position to cooccur with cl-AGR in INFL:[33]

(38)   *(*Jan) li ale*
        Jan 3sg leave

In (38), *li* having absorbed Case assigned by [+ Tense] under INFL, *Jan* would remain Caseless and violate the Case filter.[34, 35]

As per (32), I take the position under INFL not to be an argument position. Yet, as a contentive pronominal element, cl-AGR needs to be associated with a θ-role so as not to run afoul of the θ-criterion.[36] cl-AGR gets its θ-role through coindexation with *pro* in [NP, S], an argument position, and the θ-criterion is satisfied. Being a noncontentive element, *pro* may transmit its θ-role to a coindexed phonological element (cf. Rizzi 1982: 136), in this case cl-AGR.

How about the binding principles?[37] Being [+ pronominal], cl-AGR must be free in its clause. But pro$_i$ in argument-position [NP, S] seems to bind cl-AGR, violating binding principle B. This apparent contradiction is resolved by adopting the following assumption from Rizzi (1982: 136).[38]

(39)   α binds β iff α c-commands and is coindexed with β and β is not θ-dependent on α.

cl-AGR depends on pro_i for its θ-role. Thus, given (39), pro_i does not bind cl-AGR. In the other direction, cl-AGR does not bind pro_i since cl-AGR is not in A-position.[39] As a result, the binding conditions are fulfilled.

Could the empty category in [NP, S] in (37) not be *pro* ([+ pronominal, − anaphor])? No, all the other choices are ruled out. It cannot be PRO ([+ pronominal, + anaphor]) since [NP, S] is governed by either AGR or [+ Tense] in INFL.[40] It cannot be a variable ([− pronominal, − anaphor]) since it is Caseless, cl-AGR having absorbed Case, and it is not operator-bound.[41] It cannot be an anaphor ([− pronominal, + anaphor]) since the only potential binder is not in A-position. These constraints are confirmed by the data; cf. examples (38), (40) and (41).

(40)   [PRO *(*li)* *(*ap)* *bwè* *alkòl*]   *bay* *moun* *tèt-fè-mal*
              3sg   PROG drink alcohol give people headache
              'Alcohol drinking gives headaches to people.'

Given (31), infinitival INFL is not a governor and lacks AGR. Thus, PRO is allowed to appear in ungoverned [NP, S] of the sentential subject of (40). But *li*, when it occurs, either goes under AGR, and provides a governor for [NP, S], excluding PRO, or goes in [NP, S] as a subject pronoun but remains Caseless, violating the Case filter, whence the obligatory absence of *li* in (40).

(41)   *kimoun_i* *ki* e_i *(*li)* *ale*
              who   COMP e_i 3sg   leave
              'Who left?'

When present in (41), *li* absorbs Case and e_i is left Caseless, violating the visibility condition, cf. note 41.[42, 43]

4.2.2. Empty AGR

In a finite clause without a preverbal clitic, AGR, being null, is [− pronominal, + anaphoric] (hereafter, e-AGR), and must be bound in its governing category, cf. (35).[44] Only if an external role $θ_x$ is assigned, must the binder of e-AGR bear φ-features (and the role $θ_x$). Otherwise, the binder may be the empty expletive EXE. EXE is nothing but a *pro* which may remain unidentified given its nonreferential and nonthematic nature.[45]

Two crucial properties of e-AGR concern the θ-criterion and the Case filter. Being noncontentive (phonologically empty), e-AGR need not be associated with a θ-role and need not absorb Case from [+ Tense], allowing an overt NP to occur in [NP, S].[46]

As illustrated in (42), [NS, S] can be lexical when e-AGR is in INFL:

(42)   *Jan ale.*
          Jan leave
          [$_S$ [$_{NP}$ *Jan$_i$*] [$_{INFL}$ e-AGR$_i$] [$_{VP}$ *ale*]]
          'Jan left.'

Jan is allowed in [NP, S] in (42), since Case is assigned to that position. E-AGR is coindexed with *Jan* and, not being θ-dependent on *Jan*, is bound. In turn, the R-expression *Jan* is free since its only potential binder, e-AGR, is not in A-position.

[NP, S] in (42) cannot be empty:

(43)   *-*ale*

The empty category in [NP, S] of (43) cannot be PRO since it is governed (by [+ Tense] in INFL).[47] It cannot be a variable since it is not operator-bound. It cannot be argumental *pro* since it is not licensed (identified) by a governing φ-feature-bearing element. It cannot be expletive *pro*, EXE, since *ale*'s θ-role would remain unassigned, violating the θ-criterion. It cannot be an anaphor since it would remain unbound. Thus [NP, S] in (43) must be filled by a lexical NP.

Given the analysis I have proposed so far, sentences (1) to (5) might appear problematic: they are tensed, but exhibit neither cl-AGR under INFL, nor a lexical NP in subject position that would bind e-AGR. To account for these sentences, I argue, first, that e-AGR in (1) to (5) is bound by EXE, and, second, that such binding is allowed exactly when the subject position is not assigned a θ-role.

I can take it as a natural consequence of the θ-criterion that the binder of e-AGR bears a θ-role if and only if there is an external θ-role to be assigned. Moreover, if the external role is θ_x, the binder of e-AGR must be assigned θ_x. The verbs in (1) to (5) do not assign an external θ-role.[48] We can therefore expect e-AGR to be bound by EXE.

To recapitulate, both *pro* and EXE are [+ pronominal, − anaphor]. Yet, while the former has definite reference and, besides being licensed by INFL, must also be identified by an element bearing φ-features (cl-AGR), the latter does not bear a θ-role, is not referential, and does not need an identifier. As Rizzi (1986 b: 527) remarks, an expletive is a "pronominal without content". As such, EXE should not be expected to need an identifier, i. e., it only needs to be licensed.[49] The "distribution [of EXE] is regulated by the θ-criterion and the Emex Condition" (Safir 1986: 348).[50]

4.3. Summary

In my analysis of Haitian Creole as a pro-drop language, it is the nature of INFL that regulates the appearance of *pro* in [NP, S]. This is done by assigning to AGR the features [± pronominal, ±anaphor]. The assignment of these features to AGR is quite reasonable given that it correlates with whether AGR is phonological or not. Thus, cl-AGR in INFL may license *pro* in [NP, S], and subject *pro*, when argumental, is identified by pronominal cl-AGR which bears φ-features. In absence of a preverbal clitic, INFL contains anaphoric e-AGR which requires a binder in [NP, S]. This binder may be null only when the subject position is nonthematic.

The behavior of INFL is predicted through its values ± pronominal and ± anaphor. This syntactic explanation dovetails very nicely with the identification properties of agreement. As noted by Rizzi (1986 a: 392), "pure" null-subject languages "have a rich morphological specification of agreement in the verbal inflection, ... the rich agreement "recovers" the minimal grammatical specification "[the φ-features] of the missing subject". Haitian Creole verbal inflectional morphology is nonexistent. Thus, the φ-features of the subject need to be "added" to INFL either phonologically through cl-AGR or indirectly through binding of e-AGR.

Lexical subjects in Haitian Creole are not fully optional (cf. [33] and [43]), as they are with tensed INFL in "pure" pro-drop languages. AGR in "pure" pro-drop languages always bears φ-features and is pronominal, and *pro* is always licensed, whereas AGR in Haitian Creole is pronominal (and licenses *pro*) only when it contains clitics. Pragmatic rules decide whether phonological or *pro* subjects appear preverbally, and this choice, in turn, regulates whether e-AGR or cl-AGR appears in INFL. Such a pragmatic choice obeys rules similar to those governing the use of nonpronominal vs. pronominal subjects in English and those governing the use of nonpronominal subjects or null or overt pronominal subjects in Italian and Spanish. The Case and θ-properties of cl-AGR and e-AGR account for the differences in their respective syntactic behaviors.

Lexical NPs and preverbal clitics being in complementary distribution, one could be led to explain that complementarity by saying that they both belong to subject position, which can contain at most one element.[51] However, as evidenced in section 3, the elements I posit to be clitics do behave like clitics: they phonologically attach to the first morpheme of VP and, thus, must be adjacent to VP, i. e., must be in INFL. This explains the distributional differences between preverbal clitics and lexical subjects illustrated in section 3. The complementary distribution of lexical NPs and preverbal clitics is accounted for by their Case- and θ-properties.

I will now go on to show the predictions made by the above analysis. These predictions revolve around two main features of my analysis of INFL in Haitian Creole:

i. INFL is nonbranching since auxiliary verbs occur under VP. AGR in Haitian Creole is coindexed with, and c-commands, [NP, S], thus properly governs [NP, S];

ii. INFL in infinitival sentences is [− Tense], does not govern, nor assign Case, to [NP, S], and is AGR-less.

5. [COMP-trace] effects in Haitian Creole

Rizzi (1982) claims, contrary to previous analyses, that Italian does not violate the *[COMP-trace] filter. In English, the *[COMP-trace] filter accounts for the contrast *Who do you think (*that) loves Mary?* vs. *Who do you think (that) Mary loves?* Traditional accounts have derived the filter from the empty category principle, which requires all traces to be properly governed.[52] Thus, the empty category in embedded [NP, S] needs to be properly governed. English INFL is not a proper governor, and the intermediate trace in COMP antecedent-governs [NP, S] only when COMP is empty. A lexical element in COMP forces COMP to branch, and breaks the c-commanding relation between the intermediate trace and embedded [NP, S], whence the effect.[53]

According to Rizzi (1982: 145 ff), *[COMP-trace] violations in Italian are only apparent and should be accounted for by subject inversion. Italian subjects can appear after the verb:

(44)   *Credo   che   verrà   qualcuno.*
        I-believe that will-come somebody
        'I believe that somebody will come.'

Rizzi argues that *wh*-subjects are extracted not from [NP, S] as in (45), but from postverbal position as in (46):[54]

(45)   *[$_{COMP}$ *chi*$_i$] *credi* [$_S$ *che* e$_i$ INFL *verrà*]

(46)   [$_{COMP}$ *chi*$_i$] *credi* [$_{S'}$ *che* e$_i$ INFL$_i$ *verrà* e$_i$']
           'Who do you believe that will come?'

Derivation (45) is rejected because either INFL is pronominal and binds the variable e_i, violating binding principle C,[55] or INFL is not pronominal and e_i is left without a proper governor, violating the empty category principle. In (46), *chi*$_i$ first moves from [NP, S] to VP-final position and from there moves to matrix COMP. The empty category principle is obeyed since the variable e_i' is properly governed by *verrà* and preverbal e_i by pronominal INFL$_i$.

   Thus, according to Rizzi's analysis, languages which allow long subject extraction over filled COMP must also allow for subjects to freely move to postverbal position. This prediction runs into trouble in the face of Haitian Creole data. In Haitian Creole, *wh*-subjects can be extracted over lexically filled COMP, cf. (47) and (49), yet the language does not allow subject inversion, cf. (48).

(47)   *kimoun ou kwè   (ki)   pral vini*
           who   2sg believe COMP will come
           'Who do you think will come?'

(48)   **ou kwè   pral vini   kèk   moun*
           2sg believe will come some body
           'You believe somebody will come.'

Contrary to Portuguese and French (Safir 1986: 341), Haitian Creole exhibits *[COMP-trace] violations with both factive and nonfactive verbs:

(49)   *kimoun ou regrèt (ki)   craze vaz   la?*
           who   2sg regret COMP break vase DET
           'Who do you regret has broken the vase?'

Like Rizzi (1982), Safir assumes that apparent *[COMP-trace] violations are the result of subject inversion followed by postverbal extraction, which analysis is untenable for Haitian Creole given (48).[56]

   Within my analysis, (47) and (49) readily receive an explanation. (47) has the following structure:

(50)   *kimoun*$_i$ *ou kwè* [$_S$, [$_{COMP}$ e$_i$' *(ki)*] e$_i$ [$_{INFL}$ e-AGR$_i$][$_{VP}$ *pral vini*]]

When *ki* is absent, all is well: the intermediate trace e_i' in COMP may antecedent-govern e_i. When *ki* is present, e_i' does not c-command, thus does not govern e_i. The empty category principle is not violated though, since e-AGR_i in INFL antecedent-governs e_i: it c-commands e_i and is co-indexed with it.[57] Note that the variable e_i is still free since e-AGR_i, a potential binder, is not in an A-position. Thus, in view of the Haitian Creole data, there is reason to believe that, in some languages, *[COMP-trace] violations are related to the possibility that AGR in INFL properly governs [NP, S].[58]

This analysis might also explain the following observation.[59] Consider (51):

(51)　a. *ou   te   fè*   [*Tijan (*te) vini*]
　　　　　2sg ANT make Tijan ANT come
　　　　　'You made Tijan come.'

　　　 b. *kimoun_i ou   te   fè*   (**ki*) [e_i *vini*]
　　　　　who   2sg ANT make COMP   come
　　　　　'Who did you make come?'

The embedded clauses in both (51 a) and (51 b) are infinitival as the obligatory absence of *te* in (51 a) indicates. Being infinitival, embedded INFL does not contain AGR, and does not antecedent-govern the embedded subject position, which is lexically governed and exceptionally Case-marked by the matrix verb *fè*. In (51 b), *ki* would block government and Case-marking by *fè* and produce ungrammaticality. Crucial to this prediction is that 1) infinitival INFL does not contain AGR and is, thus, not a proper governor of [NP, S], cf. (31); and 2) *ki* is not a proper governor.[60, 61]

Interpretation of negative quantifiers in Haitian Creole also provides evidence that [NP, S] can be properly governed from INFL. Haitian Creole differs from Italian in that it permits long extraction of subjects over lexical COMP at logical form (LF):

(52)　*mwen pa te mande pou pèsòn (te) vini*
　　　1sg NEG ANT ask COMP nobody ANT come
　　　LF: *pa + pèsòn_i* [*mwen te mande* [*pou* e_i *(te) vini*]]
　　　'There isn't any X such that I asked X to come.'

(53)　*mwen pa te mande pou lapolis (te) arete pèsòn*
　　　1sg NEG ANT ask COMP police ANT arrest nobody
　　　LF: *pa + pèsòn_i* [*mwen te mande* [*pou la-polis (te) arete* e_i]]
　　　'There isn't any X such that I asked the police to arrest X.'

In both (52) and (53), *pèsòn* receives wide-scope interpretation. Thus, at LF, *pèsòn* must adjoin to the matrix clause. Such movement is allowed only if the trace left in the embedded clause is properly governed. In (53) the proper governor is *arete*. In (52), there are two potential proper governors for e_i at LF: *pou* in COMP (as a lexical governor) and e-AGR_i in INFL (as an antecedent-governor). The status of *pou* as proper governor is suspicious, given (54) where the embedded clause is clearly infinitival and has PRO as subject.[62]

(54)   *mwen*$_i$ *te*   *mande Tijan*$_j$ *[pou* $PRO_{i,j}$ *(*te) bale*
        1sg   ANT ask   Tijan for   ANT broom
        lakou   a]
        courtyard DET
        'I asked Tijan to sweep the courtyard.'

The word *pou* in (54) does not properly govern embedded [NP, S], otherwise PRO would violate the PRO-theorem, cf. note 8. Therefore, the proper governor for e_i in the logical form representation of (52) can only be e-AGR_i in INFL.

This analysis predicts that, if in a language [NP, S] cannot be properly governed from INFL, then a quantifier in embedded subject position cannot receive wide scope when COMP is lexical and does not properly govern embedded [NP, S]. This is exactly the situation in French. In French, there is a subject-object asymmetry regarding long-distance movement of negative quantifiers over overt COMP: they can be moved from object position but not from subject position (Rizzi 1982: 119−121):

(55)   a. *?Je n'   ai   exigé   qu' ils   arrêtent personne*
           I   NEG have required that they arrest   nobody
        b. **Je n'   ai   exigé   que personne soit arrêté*
           I   NEG have required that nobody   be   arrested

This variation is readily explained by the differences in the structures of INFL in French and Haitian Creole. There is reason to believe that auxiliary verbs in French occur under INFL (cf. note 20 and the grammaticality of AUX-Inversion as in *As-tu mangé?* 'Have you eaten?').[63] Here, the crucial observation is that INFL is branching in French, whereas it is nonbranching in Haitian Creole. Thus in (55 b) the embedded subject, although possibly coindexed with AGR,[64] is not c-commanded (and thus not properly governed) by it, whereas in (52) the embedded subject is c-commanded (and thus properly governed) by e-AGR.[65] AGR in French is not a proper governor of [NP, S], AGR in Haitian Creole is.[66]

What is the situation in English? The English counterparts of (24) to (27) are all grammatical. English modals, even though they do not bear agreement morphemes, occur under INFL: they undergo inversion, tag-formation, precede *not* in negative sentences and take *n't*. It is thus expected that English, like French, has a branching INFL node containing both AGR and AUX, and does not allow AGR to properly govern [NP, S]. As a result, *[COMP-trace] holds.[67]

To summarize, my analysis of INFL in Haitian Creole, as containing AGR which is coindexed with and c-commands [NP, S], reconciles the possibility of subjects' long-distance extraction over lexical COMP in the absence of postverbal subjects, and accounts for some cross-linguistic variations regarding [COMP-trace] effects.[68]

6. INFL and serial verb constructions

In this section, I will examine how my analysis of INFL lends itself to explaining some interesting facts about serial-verb-phrase constructions in Haitian Creole without postulating any new apparatus. I assume that the second verb of the series, V_2, is part of an embedded clause, S'_2. The structure posited for INFL in section 4 is used in describing the syntactic mechanisms by which the unrealized arguments of V_2 corefer with arguments of the verb V_1 of the matrix clause S'_1.

6.1. Serial-verb-phrase constructions in Haitian Creole

There are two main types of serial-verb-phrase constructions in Haitian Creole: those involving verbs of motion, as in (56), and those involving verbs of transfer, as in (57).[69]

(56)   *Bouki voye timoun yo   ale (lekòl)*
        Bouki send kids   DET-PL go school
        'Bouki sent the kids away (to school).'

(57)   *Malis te   pran yon flè   bay Boukinèt*
        Malis ANT take DET flower give Boukinèt
        'Malis gave a flower to Boukinèt.'

In both types of serial-verb-phrase constructions, the possible realizations of V_2 are much more restricted than those of V_1. In motion-type constructions, V_2 is taken from {*vini* 'come'/, *ale* 'go'/, *rive* 'arrive'/, *sòti* 'leave', ...}, and in transfer-type constructions, V_2 is taken from {*bay* 'give'/, *pote* 'bring'/, *mete* 'put', ...}. But, in spite of its lexical restriction, V_2 can always appear alone in a nonserial matrix clause:

(58)   *timoun yo   ale (lekòl)*
         kids   DET-PL go   school
         'The kids have gone away (to school).'

(59)   *Malis bay Boukinèt yon   flè*
         Malis give Boukinèt DET flower
         'Malis gave a flower to Boukinèt.'

Note that *bay* in (59) occurs in a double-object constructions. This indicates that, at least in contemporary Haitian Creole, serial-verb-phrase constructions are not a substitute for missing tertiary predicates.

Serial-verb-phrase constructions differ from other constructions containing verb series. I will briefly survey the differences between serial-verb-phrase constructions and coordinate structures. The latter are distinguished by the obligatory use of the conjunction morpheme *epi*.

Serial-verb-phrase constructions differ from sentential coordination in allowing extraction of the object of either V_1 or V_2, potentially violating Ross's Coordinate Structure Constraint:[70]

(60)   a. *Kisa$_i$ Malis te   pran e$_i$ bay Boukinèt*
          what Malis ANT take   give Boukinèt?
          'What did Malis give to Boukinèt?'
       b. *Kimoun$_i$ Malis te   pran yon   flè   bay e$_i$?*
          who   Malis ANT take DET flower give
          'Who did Malis give a flower to?'

Serial verb phrase constructions also differ from coordinate structures in having neither a lexical subject nor a clitic pronoun in the position preceding V_2. This is impossible in sentential coordination.[71] Also, in serial-verb-phrase constructions, the theme argument of V_2 may be unrealized. But in coordinate structures, the θ-roles of each verb must all be phonologically realized. These constraints are illustrated in (61):

$$(61) \quad Malis_i \text{ } te \text{ } pran \text{ } yon \text{ } flè_j \text{ } epi* \left(\left\{ \begin{array}{c} pro_{i,\ k}[_{AGR}li_{i,\ k}] \\ [_{NP}Bouki] \end{array} \right\} \right) te \text{ } bay$$

$$Boukinet* \left(\left\{ \begin{array}{c} li_j \\ yon \text{ } mango \end{array} \right\} \right)$$

Malis ANT take DET flower and {3sg/Bouki} ANT give
Boukinèt {3sg/a mango}
'Malis$_i$ took [a flower]$_j$ and {he$_{i, k}$/Bouki} gave {it$_j$/a mango}
to Boukinèt.'

An important characteristic of serial-verb-phrase constructions is the absence of tense-marking verbs before V_2, cf. (62),[72] whereas such verbs are permitted in coordinate constructions, cf. (61):

(62)   *Bouki te*   *voye timoun yo* $\left(*\left\{ \begin{array}{c} te \\ ap \\ pral \end{array} \right\} \right)$

Bouki ANT send kid   DET-PL {ANT/PROG/FUT}
ale (*lekòl*)
go school
'Bouki sent the kids away (to school)'.

Finally, V_2 cannot be considered a preposition since it allows extraction of its object (as in [60 b]). Preposition stranding is not allowed in Haitian Creole:

(63)   a. **kimoun$_i$ ou pote bonbon pou e$_i$?*
       who   2sg bring candy for
   b. *pou kimoun$_i$ ou pote bonbon e$_i$?*
       for who   2sg bring candy
       'Whom did you bring candies for?'

6.2. *Previous analyses of serial-verb-phrase constructions*

Since "serial verbs" were introduced in the literature by Stewart (1963) and Stahlke (1970), several analyses have been proposed to account for their properties.[73] Williams (1971) proposes to generate them through embedded or conjoined clauses, followed by deletion of COMP, [NP, S] and INFL of the second clause. Schachter (1974) suggests that serial-verb-phrase constructions are generated by the rule

(64)   S → NP INFL VP$^+$

Both Williams's and Schachter's proposals are untenable in view of the framework adopted for my analysis: deletion rules are not allowed, and the extended projection principle forbids (64).[74] Déchaine (1988) shows

inadequacies in other analyses which are based on movement of NP or
V_2, such movement being derived from Case- or θ-constraints.

In Déchaine's own account, serial-verb-phrase constructions are considered complex predicates derived in the lexicon through operations on
V_1 and V_2's θ-grids.[75] V_1 and V_2 form a complex predicate by coalescing
their argument structures under certain thematic restrictions specified in
the lexicon. Déchaine's analysis shifts most of the burden of explaining
serial-verb-phrase constructions to the lexicon and operations defined
there. To her, the D-structure of (57) contains the substructure:

(65) $[_{V'}$ V $[_{VP}$ NP$_{\langle theme \rangle}$ $[_{V'}$ *pran-bay* NP$_{\langle goal \rangle}]]]$

representing a complex predicate. At syntax, *pran* must move to assign
Case to the theme NP, resulting in the structure:

(66) $[_{V'}$ *pran* $[_{VP}$ NP$_{\langle theme \rangle}$ $[_{V'}$ *bay* NP$_{\langle goal \rangle}]]]$

More recently, Baker (1989) analyses serial-verb-phrase constructions as
double-headed VPs, proposing a parameter whose setting allows VPs in
certain languages to "count as the projection of more than one distinct
head" (1989: 519). His analysis assigns the structure in (68) to the Sranan
sentence in (67).

(67)   *Kofi naki Amba kiri.* (Sranan)
        Kofi hit   Amba kill
        'Kofi struck Amba dead.'

(68) $[_S$ *Kofi* $[_{VP}[_{V'}[_V$ *naki*] $[_{NP}$ *Amba*]$[_{V'}[_V$ *kiri*]]]]]$

In such a structure, the shared object *Amba* is θ-marked directly by *naki*
under sisterhood and indirectly by *kiri* through predication.

One problem with (68) is that it extends X-bar theory in a way that
seems to violate its very motivations. One basic assumption of X-bar
theory is that a head subcategorizes exclusively for maximal projections.
But Baker allows V', a nonmaximal projection, as a complement (or adjunct) of V.

Another problem with Baker's analysis is that it forces *kiri* in (68) to
assign its theme-role by predication to the NP sister of its first projection
V', whereas in matrix sentences (such as *Kofi kiri Amba*) the same theme-
role is assigned directly to the NP sister of V.

Finally, some Haitian Creole data cannot be analyzed under Baker's
analysis. See (76) and note 84 for a counterexample to Baker's analysis.
This counterexample is a clear instance of a serial-verb-phrase construction where the intervening NP is not θ-marked by V_2.[76]

6.3. *My analysis of serial-verb-phrase constructions in Haitian Creole*

The analysis of serial-verb-phrase constructions I now propose derives directly from general principles of grammar and the structure of INFL in Haitian Creole as explicated in section 4, plus some minimal assumptions about the lexicon. I will argue that the structure of serial-verb-phrase constructions is parallel to that of English purposive clauses. Compare (69) and (70):[77]

(69)   *Malis te   pran yon flè* [− *bay Boukinèt−*]
        Malis ANT take DET flower give Boukinèt
        'Malis gave a flower to Boukinèt.'

(70)   *I bought a book* [− *to give* − *to Bill*]

The absence of auxiliary verbs in VP of S'$_2$ (cf. [62]) clearly indicates that S'$_2$ is an infinitival clause. *Te* (anterior), *ap* (progressive, future), or *pral* (future) cannot occur in S'$_2$ because [− Tense] in infinitival INFL would conflict with temporal features of such auxiliary verbs, cf. (28) and remarks following it.[78] The embedded subject position in (69), a θ-position, is ungoverned and Caseless ([− Tense] is neither a governor nor a Case-assigner, cf. [31]): thus only PRO can appear there. Moreover, PRO is controlled since there is a possible binder in the upstairs clause.[79]

The embedded clause can also be introduced by the prepositional complementizer *pou*. In this case, S'$_2$ is finite and has a lexical NP which is assigned Case by [+ Tense]:

(71)   *Malis te   achte yon flè*   [*pou* [*Bouki te   bay*
        Malis ANT buy   DET flower for   Bouki ANT give
        Boukinèt −]]]
        Boukinèt
        'Malis bought a flower for Bouki to give to Boukinèt.'

Thus, in (56) and in (57), what prevents [NP, S] from being lexically realized is the Case filter, given that S'$_2$, in those cases, is infinitival and [− Tense] does not assign Case.

As for the null object of *bay* in (69), being an empty category in Case-marked θ-position (cf. [59]), it must be a variable. This variable is bound by an empty operator in COMP of S'$_2$.

[NP, VP$_2$] does not have to be empty though; witness (72):

(72)   *Malis te   achte yon   flè* [− *bay Boukinèt espwa*]
         Malis ANT buy   DET flower give Boukinèt hope
         'Malis bought a flower to give hope to Boukinèt'
         or 'Malis bought a flower and (by doing so) gave hope to
         Boukinèt.'

These observations about the two empty categories in subject and object positions of S'$_2$ in (69) are sufficient to account for the following two properties of serial verb phrase constructions:
i. whether or not the embedded subject is empty correlates with whether S'$_2$ is infinitival or not. [− Tense] in infinitival clauses not being a Case-assigner, a lexical subject cannot occur in preverbal position of S'$_2$. Infinitival INFL lacking AGR, clitics are also prohibited from appearing in preverbal position of S'$_2$:

(73)   *Malis te pran yon flè* [(**{pro$_{i,k}$[$_{AGR}$li$_{i,k}$]/[$_{NP}$Boukí]}) bay Boukinèt −*]

ii. The operator in COMP of S'$_2$, being empty, lacks referential properties and does not strongly bind the variable in object position of V$_2$, i. e., it does not denote a range of possible referents for the variable.[80] Thus, the variable and its operator must be bound by a referring element in the higher clause.
    Thus far I have accounted for the following structure for (69):[81]

(74)   *Malis$_k$ te pran* [*yon flè*]$_l$ [$_{S'}$ O$_j$ [$_S$ PRO$_i$ *bay Boukinèt* e$_j$]]

Now, what principles account for the correct bindings of PRO$_i$ by *Malis* and of e$_j$ by *yon flè*, i. e., for $i = k$ and $j = l$? The correct bindings are determined by lexical knowledge and by pragmatics through what I call a "binding heuristic". Step 1: the empty operator in COMP of S'$_2$ (if any) and the empty category it binds are always coindexed with the internal argument of V$_1$, which is adjacent to S'$_2$. Step 2: PRO subject of V$_2$ is bound by the subject or object of the matrix clause in a manner compatible with binding principles and pragmatic and contextual well-formedness.[82]
    This heuristic predicts the following binding:

(75)   *Malis$_i$ te pran* [*yon flè*]$_j$ [$_{S'}$ O$_j$ [$_S$ PRO$_i$ *bay Boukinèt* e$_j$]]

Yon flè becomes the binder of O$_j$ and e$_j$ in step 1. In step 2, PRO$_i$ can be bound by either *yon flè* or *Malis*. Binding principles suffice to determine that *yon flè* cannot bind both e$_j$ and PRO$_i$. If, after step 2, *yon flè* did bind PRO$_i$, then $i = j$ and binding principle C is violated since e$_j$, an R-expression, is not free in the domain of its operator O_j. Therefore, *Malis*, not *yon flè*, must bind PRO_i.[83]

Examples (76) and (77) illustrate the possibilities in serial-verb-phrase constructions for both subject and object control. Presumably, because of pragmatic knowledge associated with the relevant lexical items, the controller of PRO is V_1's external argument in (76) and its internal argument in (77). This is quite similar to the choice between subject and object control in pairs such as *promise* and *persuade*.[84]

(76) *Bouki*$_i$ *achte* [*yon   tikè-avion*]$_j$ [PRO_i *ale Nouyòk*]
      Bouki buy   DET plane-ticket   go New York
      'Bouki bought a plane ticket to go to New York (and went to New York).'

(77) *Bouki*$_i$ *voye* [[*timoun yo*]$_j$ [PRO_j *ale (lekòl)*]
      Bouki$_i$ send kids$_j$ DET-PL PRO_j go   school
      'Bouki sent the kids to school.'

I summarize this section by noting that, without adding substantial assumptions, my analysis accounts for the main characteristics of Haitian Creole serial verbs: (non)occurrence of lexical subjects and subject clitics in S'_2 of embedded clauses, coreference between unrealized arguments of V_2 and arguments of V_1. In fact, serial-verbs-phrase constructions are shown to differ from "ordinary" subordinate constructions in ways which are readily accounted for by existing grammar modules, namely the Case filter and binding theory. In its parsimony, my analysis is superior to those (too) quickly surveyed in section 6.2.

7. Summary and conclusion

In section 2 of this paper, I show that Haitian Creole allows subject-less tensed sentences. These sentences indicate that Haitian Creole is a pro-drop language with INFL licensing *pro*. In section 3, I provide data supporting the hypothesis that Haitian Creole subject clitics are agreement markers appearing under INFL. Section 4 presents an analysis of INFL as the repository of abstract tense features and subject-agreement features. INFL contains agreement features either directly when AGR is phonological and pronominal, or indirectly when AGR is unrealized and anaphoric. When realized as a subject clitic, AGR is sufficiently rich in φ-features to identify *pro* in thematic subject position. Expletive *pro*, EXE, is licensed by INFL, but need not be identified by φ-feature-bearing INFL. This analysis characterizes AGR in terms of ± anaphoric and ± pronominal features in a manner consistent with its phonological (non-)realization. Such characterization of AGR allows a parsimonious account of the data at hand without the introduction of ad hoc machinery.

Sections 5 and 6 explicate diverse syntactic properties of Haitian Creole that such an hypothesis accounts for. In section 5, I look at the possibility of proper government of [NP, S] from INFL and its import with respect to [COMP-trace] effects. Across languages, AGR, whether phonological or not, is possibly coindexed with [NP, S] (at least, when it shows subject agreement and/or serves as an identifier for *pro* in subject position). Thus, when INFL is nonbranching, i. e., when auxiliary verbs are syntactically indistinguishable from main verbs and occur under VP, AGR would properly govern [NP, S]. In Haitian Creole, auxiliary verbs occur under VP and INFL is nonbranching. Consequently, AGR properly governs [NP, S] and allows subjects' long distance extraction over lexical COMP in absence of subject inversion.

In the course of my exposition, I also hint at ways that my analysis could be extended to account for cross-linguistic variations with respect to [COMP-trace] effects. Those variations seem related to the position of auxiliary verbs and the branching structure of INFL.[85]

Section 6 shows how the structure of INFL in Haitian Creole predicts some syntactic properties of serial verb constructions. The embedded clause S'$_2$ in Haitian Creole serial-verb-phrase constructions is infinitival. Thus subject clitics cannot appear in S'$_2$ since AGR is missing, and PRO is licensed to appear as subject of V$_2$, controlled by an overt argument of the matrix verb. The empty category which sometimes occurs in [NP, VP$_2$] is a variable bound by an empty operator in COMP, which in turn is bound by a matrix argument. (Non)occurrence of lexical NPs as subject of V$_2$ and coreference between arguments of V$_1$ and V$_2$ are thus explained.

The data and analysis presented in these sections make a case for analyzing subject clitics in Haitian Creole as elements of AGR in INFL, and for classifying Haitian Creole as a null-subject language.[86]

8. Postscript: Implications for the creole languages— language acquisition relationship

Regarding the status of subject pronouns in the creole and child grammars, there is an intriguing parallel. As shown above, subject pronouns in Haitian Creole tensed clauses are clitics in INFL. Read and Schreiber (1982) present evidence that children have enormous difficulty in parsing English pronominal subjects as independent constituents. They tend to lump such subjects with the following VP. Read and Schreiber (1982: 89) attribute the problem of parsing pronominal subjects to both a "relative lack of semantic specificity ... and a lack of phraselike prosody". The parallel becomes even more noteworthy when one realizes that subject pronouns in Haitian Creole are derived from the strong forms of French subject pronouns, e. g., *mwen* from *moi* and *li* from *lui*, and that the French weak pronouns *il* and *je/j'* are lost in Haitian Creole. One possible scenario, suggested by Anthony Kroch (personal communication), has to do with the frequency of double-subject constructions in colloquial French (assuming, of course, that modern colloquial French is not too different from seventeenth- and eighteenth-century colloquial French). In such constructions, a strong pronoun is followed by a much less salient subject clitic: *lui, i'vient* 'him, he's coming'; *moi, j'pars* 'me, I'm leaving'. It is thus tempting to trace the historical source of Haitian Creole preverbal "pronouns" as French strong pronouns which have become subject clitics, maybe due to pressures from the child's innate acquisition strategies.

A link can also be drawn regarding the syntactic status of INFL in the child grammar, G_0, and the grammar of Haitian Creole. TMA markers in Haitian Creole syntactically behave as constituents of VP, as noted in subsection 4.1. Shepherd (1983: 188) makes similar observations with respect to modals in Antiguan Creole and child English: "[S]tandard English makes a syntactic distinction (between modals and quasi-modals) which is absent in the creole and in the speech of children". Hyams (1986) indirectly supports Shepherd's findings by presenting evidence that children learning English are quicker to learn the semi-auxiliaries *have to* and *going to*, which appear in VP, than the true modals *must, will*, etc., which belong to INFL. If children's grammars are pro-drop and all their auxiliary verbs occur under VP, then one should expect, given the above analysis, that children allow *[COMP-trace] violations (like Haitian Creole speakers). Interestingly enough, Thornton (1990) provides examples where children do indeed produce *wh*-questions exhibiting such violations: e. g. *Which one do you think that has a tail?*. Within my analysis, such examples do not violate the empty category principle, AGR being a proper governor for the embedded subject trace.[87]

It would be interesting to determine the status of other creole languages, specially the most "radical" ones, with respect to the pro-drop parameter (and other parameters whose initial settings are most uncontroversial). Saramaccan is also a null-subject language:

(78)   *(a) (bi-) kendi/koto* (Byrne 1987: 76)
        it   TNS hot/cold
        'It was hot/cold.'

(79)   *tuú   tåa di wómi gó diså déé   fåmii   feen*
        true say the man go leave the-PL family of-him
        'It's true that the man left his family.'   (Byrne 1987: 77)

Kouwenberg (1990: 46) gives Papiamento examples where expletive subjects of tensed sentences with *seem*-type, existential and weather verbs
are phonologically empty:[88]

(80)   *pro (tawata) parse ku   Maria ta (wata) malo*
              PAST   seem COMP Mary be PAST   ill
        'It seems/seemed that Mary is/was ill.'

(81)   *pro tin/   tawatin   hopi   hende*
              have PAST-have many people
        'There are/were many people.'

(82)   *pro tawata jobe*
              PAST rain
        'It was raining.'

Given these observations and assuming the accuracy of Bloom (1970)
(or some reinterpretation of it, cf. note 3), Clahsen (to appear), and specially Hyams (1986, 1987), Haitian Creole (and, maybe, Saramaccan and
Papiamento) would, under the above analysis, correspond to the child's
initial grammar, G_0, at least along the pro-drop parameter. All those
grammars seem to allow nonreferential and referential *pro* instead of lexical expletives and phonological subjects, respectively.

A related and important question concerns the status of null expletives
in *seem*-type, existential, and weather constructions in French and the
West African languages involved in the genesis of Haitian Creole. French,
the lexifier language of Haitian Creole, requires lexical expletive subjects
in constructions with nonthematic subjects. Koopman (1986: 248) remarks that null pleonastic pronouns do not seem to exist in West African
languages. In particular, "the equivalent of [the *gen*] construction [cf. (3)]
does not appear to exist in West African languages. The interesting aspect
of this zero-pleonastic pronoun then is that it overtly marks a distinction
neither marked in French nor present in West African languages".[89]
Thus, the pro-drop setting of Haitian Creole (and, possibly, other creole
languages) might be due exclusively to creolization qua language acquisition.

(An abridged version of this paper's pro-drop analysis of Haitian Creole has appeared in DeGraff (1993 a). As a late postscriptum, I must also note that after the present paper was first circulated at the Leiden Workshop on Creole Languages and Language Acquisition (in December 1990), a lively and enlightening debate has taken place regarding the status of Haitian Creole as a pro-drop language, and related issues; see e. g. DeGraff (1992), DeGraff (1993 b) and Déprez (1992) and their references. Due to publication vagaries and constraints, insights from these later works (which were written after DeGraff (1993 a) and the present paper) are unfortunately not incorporated here.)

Notes

1. I thank Richard Campbell, Anthony Kroch, Mitch Marcus, and Gillian Sankoff for very helpful discussions. I have benefited from ideas of participants in various meetings: the Fall 1990 University of Pennsylvania seminars on language acquisition, on serial verbs and on pidgins and creoles, the December 1990 Leiden Workshop on Creole Languages and Language Acquisition, and the January 1991 Meeting of the Society of Pidgin and Creole Linguistics. Yet, all shortcomings are my own. This research was partially supported by an AT&T Corporate Research Fellowship and DARPA-ONR grant N00014-90-J-1863.

2. Here, one caveat is in order. The setting of one parameter in one (set of) creole language(s) does not suffice to prove anything about creole genesis, but I hope this to be one example of research to be carried out using the principles-and-parameters approach to grammar and cross-linguistic findings from language acquisition studies.

3. Contrary to Hyams and Clahsen, Bloom argues that in the child's subjectless sentences the lexical subject is underlyingly present, and that it superficially deletes because of processing limitations.

4. The terms "null-subject" and "pro-drop" will be used interchangeably.

5. But see Jaeggli (1982) and Roberge–Vinet (1989) for views that French might be null-subject.

6. The following abbreviations will be used: ANT = anterior, CONJ = conjunction, DET = determiner, EMPH = emphatic marker, FM = focus marker, FUT = future, IRREAL = irrealis, PROG = progressive, 1sg = first person singular, 3pl = third person plural, etc.

7. There exists a small class of adjectives predicating over propositions (such as *difisil* 'hard', *impòtan* 'important', *nesesè* 'necessary', *imposib* 'impossible', *fasil* 'easy') which seem to require lexical expletive subjects:

   (i)   *(li) difisil pou nou jwenn travay*
            3sg   hard   for 1pl find   job
            'It's hard for us to find a job.'

   In note 50 (see section 4.2.2), I will sketch an account for the obligatoriness of *li*.

8. Because of principles A and B of binding theory, PRO, which is both an anaphor and a pronominal, only appears in ungoverned position (cf. note 37 for a definition of the binding principles).

9. My treatment of the pro-drop parameter differs slightly from that proposed in Rizzi (1986 b: 524) where "pro is Case-marked by X^0_y," and where X^0_y is a "designated head". Here, I assume that *pro* only needs to be governed (not necessarily Case-marked) by X^0_y (as in [40] of Rizzi 1986 b).

10. As pointed out by Hyams, the "avoid pronoun" principle also accounts for the absence of obligatory lexical expletives in null-subject languages, given that lexical expletives cannot be stressed, contrasted, or emphasized, and are, pragmatically and semantically, void of content.

11. An analysis of pronominal subjects as agreement markers in INFL has been proposed before for French in Jaeggli (1982). See also Rizzi (1986 a), Brandi−Cordin (1989) where subject clitics in some Northern Italian dialects are analysed as "spelling-out of AGR under INFL". Bickerton (1990) entertains a similar possibility for a number of creole languages.

12. Given appropriate context, the English counterpart of (13 b) is acceptable:

(i)   *The beautiful little peasant had left her mother at a very young age.*
      She, the beautiful little peasant, was now living in Sen-Mak.

In no such context does (13 b) seem acceptable in Haitian Creole. Shown as (ii) is another such example where material (in roman type) is allowed to intervene between subject pronoun and VP in English, indicating the nonclitic status of English subject pronouns.

(ii)   *Linguists should be wary of their grammatical judgements. I,* for one, *do not trust my intuitions.*

Kayne (1983: 129, note 26) mentions that some French speakers allow parentheticals after subject pronouns. This, inter alia, is used to argue that French subject clitics are only phonological clitics, not syntactic clitics. Given the categorial status of (13 b), such an argument does not carry over to Haitian Creole.

13. I will argue in section 4.1 that Haitian Creole tense-mood-aspect markers, such as *ap*, are in VP, not in INFL. Also, I assume *pa* (negative) to be adjoined to VP. But see De Graff (1993b) for a more recent analysis.)

14. For clarity, only the full forms of the clitics will be used in the subsequent examples.

15. Here, I use roman type to indicate stress.

16. This is reminiscent of Akan, where the second NP of two conjoined NPs is morphologically marked with accusative Case (Richard Campbell, personal communication).

17. In Klavans's (1985) terminology, they are proclitics subcategorizing for VP and in phonological liaison with the initial constituent of VP.

18. I take the split-INFL hypothesis of Pollock (1989) to be irrelevant to this paper.

19. What I call "auxiliaries" are verbal (or quasi-verbal) elements which do not assign θ-roles, and whose only function is to contribute to the temporal, modal, and/or aspectual interpretation of their clause. The syntactic properties of such elements vary across languages, cf. Steele et al. (1981).

20. Compare with French *pas* 'not', which occurs between AUX and V:

(i)   *Jean (ne)   serait pas   allé au   marché.*
      Jean (NEG) AUX NEG go to-the market
      'Jean will not have gone to the market.'

21. Apparent counter-examples to this generalization are constructions like the following, where *pa* occurs between the epistemic modal *ka* 'might' and the tense marker *te*:

(i)   *Jan ka   pa te   vini*
           Jan might not ANT come
           'John might not have come.'

But, Magloire-Holly (1982) analyses such modals as raising verbs subcategorizing for a sentence ("EQUI verbs" in Magloire-Holly's terminology). Such an analysis defuses the counterexample.

22. Magloire-Holly (1982) extensively argues that modals in Haitian Creole behave syntactically as constituents of VP and not of INFL. But my analysis differs from hers in that she considers tense and aspect markers as constituents of INFL.

23. The conflation of modals and verbs into a single syntactic class tends to exist in other creoles as well as in some instances of child language, cf. Byrne (1987) for Saramaccan, Shepherd (1983) for Antiguan Creole and child language, and Hyams (1986) for child language. Also, in Middle and Early Modern English, modals were main verbs (Francis Byrne, personal communication).

24. [± Tense] are features under INFL which do not cause INFL to branch.

25. I do not believe that predicate-clefting can be used as a test to distinguish between constituents of INFL and those of VP. The fact that most tense-mood-aspect markers cannot be cleft seems due to their semantic properties: they are verbs lacking "event-like" characteristics. But given appropriate contexts, some modals can be cleft:

(i)   *se   pa   kapab mwen pa te   kapab vini, se vle   mwen*
           FM NEG MOD 1sg   NEG ANT MOD come FM want 1sg
           pa   te   vle   vini
           NEG ANT want come
           'It's not that I wasn't *able* to come, it's that I didn't *want* to come.' (Literally: 'It's not could I could not come, it's want I didn't want to come.')

(ii)   *se   pa   vle   mwen te   vle   vini, se dwe   mwen te*
           FM NEG want 1sg   ANT want come FM MOD 1sg   ANT
           dwe   vini
           MOD come
           'It's not that I *want* to come, it's that I *must* come.' (Literally: 'It's not want that I want to come, it's must that I must come.')

There is at least one main verb which, because of its "non-event" nature, cannot be cleft:

(iii)   a. *Jan genlè damou*
           Jan seem in-love
           'John seems in love.'
     b. **se genlè Jan genlè damou*
           FM seem Jan seem in-love
           'John only seems to be in love (he's not really in love)' (Literally: 'It's seem that John seems in love.')

Larson–Lefebvre (1990) propose a semantic account of clefts in Haitian Creole.

26. Chomsky (1986 b: 24) also assumes that "any category α agrees with itself and with its head" and that (1986 b: 77) "there is head-head agreement (index-sharing) between INFL and the aspectual verbs" of VP. I assume this notion of agreement to extend to tense, modal, and aspectual features.

27. I take a clause to be finite in Haitian Creole if and only if tense-marking verbs are allowed to precede the "semantically"-main verb, but see Mufwene—Dijkhoff (1989) for some controversy about (non)finiteness in creoles.

28. Presumably, in finite sentences, INFL serves as a bridge through which VP is predicated of [NP, S] via coindexing.

29. See Rizzi (1982).

30. See Chomsky (1982), Borer (1986 b), Rizzi (1986 b) for more details on licensing and identifying *pro*.

31. As indicated in Rizzi (1986 a: 393), the Northern Italian dialects illustrate yet another possibility which intersects with both the "pure pro-drop" case and the Haitian Creole case: in these languages, "strong AGR is realized in Phonetic Form not only in the concrete verbal morphology, but also in its abstract syntactic position".

32. As suggested in Jaeggli (1986), the Case-absorbing properties of clitics might be subject to parametrization. Preverbal clitics in languages with subject doubling (some Northern Italian dialects) need not absorb Case. As per Bickerton (1990), Hawaiian Creole also allows the cooccurrence of nonpronominal subject and clitic in preverbal position. Sentences with both lexical NP and clitic in preverbal position (without an intervening pause after the lexical NP) inform the learner that subject clitics in the target language need not absorb Case.

33. Note that *Jan, li ale* is possible with a pause after *Jan*. In this case, *Jan* is in topic position, escaping the Case filter.

34. Case filter: ... *NP ... where NP is lexical and not assigned Case.

35. Jaeggli (1982: 97) offers a similar proposal for French.

36. θ-criterion: Each θ-role is assigned to exactly one chain and each chain receives exactly one θ-role.

37. Binding principles:
   A) An *anaphor* is bound in its governing category;
   B) A *pronominal* is free in its governing category;
   C) An *R-expression* is free in the domain of the head of its chain.
   α is *bound* by β if β is in A-position, and β c-commands and is co-indexed with α. α is *free* if it is not bound.
   β is a *governing category* for α if and only if β "is the least CFC [complete functional complex] containing a governor of α in which α could satisfy the binding theory with some indexing (perhaps not the actual indexing of [α])" (Chomsky 1986 a: 171).
   α *c-commands* β if and only if α does not dominate β and the first branching node dominating α also dominates β.

38. Even though I borrow assumption (39) from Rizzi, there is one substantial difference between my account and his. According to Rizzi, the pronominal element in INFL is a potential binder with regard to the binding principles. In my account, INFL is not an A-position and does not count as a potential binder.

39. Chomsky (1986 a: 176) also argues that AGR does not count as a binder.

40. In fact, I will argue in section 5 that [NP, S] is properly governed.

41. The visibility hypothesis requires variables to have case (Chomsky 1981: 334).

42. *Li* in (41) might also be ruled out along the lines proposed by Rizzi (1986 a): *li*, as cl-AGR, licenses *pro* in subject position and *pro* "cannot be locally bound by a ... quantifier" (1986 a: 395).

43. Resumptive pronouns introduce certain puzzles which I will not address in this paper.

44. For independent reasons, Borer (1989) also proposes that AGR may be anaphoric. Also, see Byrne (1991) for an alternative to Borer's proposal.

45. See Safir (1986) for a detailed study of EXE. In the remainder of the text, I will use EXE as an abbreviation for "unidentified *pro* in nonthematic position".

46. In fact, it is tempting to claim that NOM Case is assigned by [+ Tense] in INFL to [NP, S] via binding of AGR. When e-AGR is in INFL, its binder receives NOM Case. When cl-AGR is in INFL, it must absorb Case and prevents a lexical NP from occurring in [NP, S].

47. And antecedent-governed by e-AGR in INFL. (This antecedent-government relation between [NP, S] and e-AGR will become very important in section 5.)

48. Lumsden (1990) proposes a detailed analysis of the argument structures of *rete* and *manke* in which he argues that the theme and locative arguments of each verb are generated under VP.

49. As pointed out by Borer (1989: 97) for Hebrew, expletive *pro* is freer in occurrence than referential *pro*: "the restrictions on the occurrence of *pro* in past and future third person and in present tense only hold for referential *pro*. Nonreferential, expletive *pro* may occur freely without an antecedent both in past and future and in present tense as well" (in Hebrew, past and future third person and present tense are deprived of φ-features). Borer's observation is based on Rizzi's (1982) assumption that "identification requirements on non-referential elements are less stringent".

50. In the light of this account, the obligatoriness of *li* in note 7 remains mysterious. I propose the following, admittedly tentative, explanation, which rests on two assumptions: 1) The direction of predication for Haitian Creole adjectives subcategorizing for S is uniformly to the left; 2) Haitian Creole does not allow sentential subjects. As a consequence of 1) and 2), adjectives in Haitian Creole predicate over propositions by being coindexed with *pro* in subject position which is licensed by *li* in INFL. This *pro* is, in turn, coindexed with and transmits its θ-role to S in postverbal position. Presumably, only a third person singular clitic can be coindexed with a sentential argument, which would explain why only *li* in note 7 is grammatical in preverbal position:

    (i)   *{*mwen/ou/nou/yo*} *difisil pou nou jwenn travay*

    (I am indebted to Richard Campbell for suggesting this approach.)
    Vinet (to appear) makes further observations on the behavior of expletives in Haitian Creole which in some contexts are either obligatorily present or obligatorily absent.

51. This line of argument is used by Rizzi (1986 a: 400 – 401), in arguing that subject clitics in French occur in [NP, S]. But note that Haitian Creole crucially differs from French in allowing "gap[s] in the clitic paradigm": contrary to French, Haitian Creole exhibits constructions in which both nonarguments, as in (1), and quasi-arguments, as in (2), are not realized at all, not even as clitics. See also note 12.

52. Proper government is fulfilled either lexically through government by a lexical head (lexical government), or through coindexation with a c-commanding element (antecedent-government).

53. For an alternative account of *[COMP-trace] in the barriers framework, see Chomsky (1986 b: 47 – 48). According to this account, the intermediate trace is in the specifier of

CP and cannot antecedent-govern the trace in subject position when *that* is in COMP, *that* in COMP being a closer governor (minimality condition).

54. The evidence that *wh*-extraction of subjects takes place from VP-final position comes from facts about quantification, negation and *ne*-cliticization.

55. Recall that Rizzi (1982) assumes that INFL is an A-position (it can bind an anaphor in [NP, S].

56. My native-speaker judgements about (47) and (49), as well as those of my informants, differ from those reported in Koopman (1986) according to which *ki* is obligatory whenever the subject of a finite clause is *wh*-extracted. To me and my informants, (47) sounds equally good with or without *ki*. In fast speech, the preference is to omit *ki*. There are also cases where *ki* is reduced to *k*, which is cliticized onto the preceding or following morpheme.

57. In order for e-AGR$_i$ to c-command e_i in (50), it is crucial that INFL be nonbranching, i. e., the future marker *pral* must be under VP.

58. Koopman (1982, 1986) argues that *ki*, in (47), properly governs e$_i$, and that it is the only possible proper governor for e$_i$, whence its obligatory presence. This proposal begs the following question. What would account for the obligatoriness of *ki* since the intermediate e$_i$' in COMP could also antecedent-govern e$_i$ in the absence of *ki* (as in English *Who do you think came*?)? Note that (even according to Koopman's data) Haitian Creole, unlike French, allows subordinate COMP to be empty (when the object of the embedded verb is extracted):

    (i)   *[ki sa]$_i$ Jan kwè   Mariz te   fè e$_i$ a*   (Koopman 1982: 216)
                what Jan believe Mariz ANT do DET
                'What does Jan believe Mary had done?'

59. This fact was observed, but not explained, in Koopman (1986).

60. Koopman's (1982) proposal that *ki* is a potential proper governor would not explain the obligatory absence of *ki* in (51 b). If it is a proper governor, *ki* in (51 b) should not cause ungrammaticality. Also note that Koopman's proposal for *ki* in Haitian Creole is inspired by Kayne's *que/qui* rule for French. But whereas the *que/qui* rule in French constructions such as *Qui crois-tu qui tombera?* 'Who do you think will fall?' is slightly marked ("recherché") according to Kayne (1984: 97), the use of *ki* in (47) and (49) is perfectly natural, which suggests that a different rule might be needed to account for proper government of a subject trace adjacent to *ki* in Haitian Creole.

61. An alternative explanation for (51 b) might be that *fè* subcategorizes for S and not for S', excluding a lexical COMP between *fè* and the embedded subject. But, the example below is grammatical, raising doubt as to whether *fè* subcategorizes exclusively for S: the embedded clause is S'.

    (i)   *ou te   fè [$_{S'}$ pou Tijan (*te) vini]*
                2sg ANT make for Tijan ANT come
                'You made it possible for Tijan to come.'

62. Example (54) also shows that [± Tense] is related to the appearance of PRO: when *te* is present in embedded clause, [+ Tense] governs PRO and the sentence is ruled out.

63. This example and note 20 are evidence that the tensed element has moved from VP to INFL, if not directly generated under INFL. The position to which it moves forces INFL to branch. I assume that this position is different from and adjacent to AGR/

TENSE (maybe adjoined to AGR). Morphological rules are responsible for amalgamating AGR and the raised verb. But see Pollock (1989).

64. An intriguing question arises as to whether being a potential identifier for *pro* is a prerequisite to being an antecedent-governor.

65. AGR is also a potential *pro*-identifier in Haitian Creole, cf. note 64 and section 4.2.1.

66. Italian counterparts to (52) and (53) can be found in Rizzi (1982: 125). Contrary to Haitian Creole and similarly to French, there is a subject-object asymmetry in Italian with regard to extraction of quantifiers over filled COMP (even though auxiliaries in Italian might also be under VP, cf. Hyams [1986: 48−55]). The difference between Haitian Creole and Italian might be that in Haitian Creole, AGR in INFL is always coindexed with and a proper governor of [NP, S] (whether or not it is assigned Case), whereas in Italian INFL is a proper governor only when marked for NOM Case and pronominal. Rizzi (1982) elaborates on the conditions under which INFL is pronominal in Italian.

67. Spanish is a null-subject language with *[COMP-trace] violations. It differs from both French and English by not having a rule of finite verb raising into INFL (cf. Emonds 1978). Neither does Spanish have verbal elements that, like English modals, must be generated under INFL. Spanish, like Italian and Haitian Creole, does not exhibit VP deletion, VP preposing and tag-formation.

68. One (perhaps, too) strong prediction of my analysis is that languages with rich verbal agreement and/or subject clitics, that do not distinguish syntactically between auxiliary and main verbs should show no [COMP-trace] effects. The validity of this prediction should be tested empirically.

69. For a survey and an alternative analysis of serial-verb-phrase constructions in Haitian Creole, see Déchaine (1988). For a critique of analyses of empty arguments in serial-verb-phrase constructions, see Byrne (1991).

70. Déchaine (1988) further delineates characteristics of serial-verb-phrase constructions in Haitian Creole.

71. VP coordination is very restricted in Haitian Creole.

72. In that respect, Haitian Creole serial-verb-phrase constructions differ from such constructions in both Saramaccan and Seselwa, in which V_2 can be tensed, cf. Byrne (1987) for Saramaccan and Bickerton−Iatridou (1988) for Seselwa.

73. Déchaine (1988), Byrne (1991) and Bickerton−Iatridou (1988) thoroughly criticize a number of these analyses.

74. Among other things, the extended projection principle requires VPs to have external arguments as subjects.

75. Lefebvre's (1989) account of instrumental *take*-serials in Haitian Creole is along similar lines.

76. See Byrne (1991) and Bickerton−Iatridou (1988) for additional arguments against and counterexamples to Baker's analysis.

77. My analysis of serial-verb-phrase constructions in Haitian Creole is straightforwardly derived from Chomsky's (1986 a: 109−114) analysis of English purposive clauses. Byrne (1987) and Bickerton−Iatridou (1988) have similarly argued that V_2 in serial-verb-phrase constructions is contained in an embedded clause with an empty subject.

78. Byrne (1987 and 1991) stresses that V_2 in Saramaccan serial-verb-phrase constructions may be preceded by the tense marker *bi* and is thus finite. Bickerton and Iatridou (1988) make the same remarks about Seselwa and Morisyien. The tense of S_2' must be interpreted as being the same as that of V_1 in both Haitian Creole and Saramaccan. In

Haitian Creole, this constraint can be straightforwardly accounted for by assuming that [− Tense] in infinitivals is anaphoric and must be bound from matrix INFL (cf. Borer 1989, Kroch−Santorini−Heycock 1987). But see Byrne (to appear) for an alternative account.

79. For those languages mentioned in note 78, which allow V_2 to be tensed, it must be assumed that [NP, S_2] is *pro*, licensed by INFL of S_1' and identified by its e-AGR, which is itself bound by an overt argument in the matrix clause (cf. Borer 1989).

80. See Chomsky (1981: 329), and Chomsky (1986 a: 85) for the concept of "strong binding".

81. Here, my analysis parts with that of Bickerton and Iatridou. They propose that the embedded clause in serial verb phrase constructions is IP, not CP. But I must assume it is CP (= S') in order to make room in COMP for an empty operator, as in (74), or an overt complementizer, as in (71).

82. This binding heuristic predicts that, when subject and object of V_1 do not corefer, it cannot be the case that PRO subject of V_2 is object-controlled while an empty object of V_2 and its empty operator are coindexed with the matrix subject. See note 83 for the case when subject and object of V_1 are coindexed.

83. The following sentence is a problem for this analysis.

(i)   *Malis$_i$ te   pote   [tèt-lí]$_i$ [$_{S'}$ O_i [$_S$ PRO$_i$ bay   la-polis e_i]]*
        Malis ANT bring himself   give the police
        'Malis surrendered to the police.'

In this example PRO$_i$ binds the variable e_i within its domain, violating binding principle C.

As noted by Bickerton and Iatridou concerning similar problems in Djuka serial-verb-phrase constructions and English purposive clauses, the problem is that all the potential bindees in the matrix clause are coindexed and that both the embedded PRO subject and the empty operator must be bound. Thus, as Bickerton and Iatridou (1988: 36) write, "the need to interpret null elements may simply override the normal feature specifications for *ec*'s".

84. Example (76) is a counterexample to Déchaine's (1988) double claim that in serial-verb-phrase constructions the theme argument of V_1 and V_2 must be shared and that shared arguments must bear identical θ-role. In (76), both claims are refuted: the shared argument is *Bouki* which is the agent of V_1 *achte* and the theme of V_2 *ale*.
Example (76) is also a problem for Baker (1989). In Baker's analysis, V_1 and V_2 must share their internal argument by virtue that this argument is an immediate constituent of a V' projection of both V_1 and V_2 and, as such, must be θ-marked by both verbs. In (76), I cannot see in which way *tikè-avion* could possibly be θ-marked by *ale*, unless one is willing to loosen the notion θ-role to an undesirable extreme. Baker might answer that (76) is a V'-conjunction structure. But such conjunctions are ungrammatical in Haitian Creole:

(i)   *Bouki$_i$ [$_{VP}$ achte yon   tikè-avion]   epi   *(li$_i$) [$_{VP}$ ale Nouyòk]*
        Bouki   buy   DET plane-ticket CONJ 3sg   go New-York
        'Bouki bought a plane ticket and he went to New-York.'

Moreover, (76) can undergo *wh*-movement of the object of V_2, which movement would violate the coordinate structure constraint:

(ii)   *kote*$_i$ *Bouki*$_j$ *achte* [*yon*   *tikè-avion* [$_{S'}$ [COMP e_i' [$_S$ PRO$_j$ *ale* e_i]
         where Bouki buy   DET plane-ticket   go

85. It is also possible that those variations are also linked to the referential richness of AGR. In order to be coindexed with [NP, S] in a manner relevant for antecedent-government, AGR might need to be nominal and potentially filled with φ-features (i. e., only when AGR is a potential *pro* identifier can it be coindexed with [NP, S]).

86. Safir (1986) contains perhaps the most restrictive definition of null-subject languages as those which may "avoid phonetically realizing NOM Case". Haitian Creole is a null-subject even under this definition because of its weather and *seem* constructions, where both [NP, S] and AGR are empty.

87. Thornton (1990) provides an alternative account of such examples within the theory proposed in Rizzi (1990).

88. As for (82), Kouwenberg (1990) notes the following dialectical variation: "A[ruban] informants prefer the overt version [with the subject lexically realized as *awa* 'water'], the Curaçoans the covert one."

89. Koopman argues that other such cases, where Haitian Creole is different from both French and West African languages, are "extremely difficult to find". Before (dis)agreeing with Koopman, I believe additional work is needed, where parameters with established initial settings are compared with their counterparts in creoles.

References

Baker, Mark C.
  1989   "Object sharing and projection in serial verb constructions", *Linguistic Inquiry* 20: 513–553.
Bickerton, Derek
  1984   "The language bioprogram hypothesis", *The Behavioral and Brain Sciences* 7: 173–221.
  1990   Focused subjects and pronouns. [Paper presented at the Conference on Focus and Grammatical Relations in Creole Languages, University of Chicago.]
Bickerton, Derek – Sabine Iatridou
  1988   Serial verb constructions and empty categories. [Unpublished MS., University of Hawaii.]
Bloom, Lois
  1970   *Language development: Form and function in emerging grammars.* Cambridge, MA: MIT Press.
Borer, Hagit
  1986   "I-Subjects", *Linguistic Inquiry* 17: 375–416.
  1989   "Anaphoric AGR", in: Osvaldo Jaeggli – Kenneth Safir (eds.), 69–109.
Borer, Hagit (ed.)
  1986   *Syntax and semantics.* Vol. 19. New York: Academic Press.
Brandi, Lucian – Patrizia Cordin
  1989   "Two Italian dialects and the null subject parameter", in: Osvaldo Jaeggli – Kenneth Safir (eds.), 111–142.
Byrne, Francis
  1987   *Grammatical relations in a radical creole.* Amsterdam: John Benjamins.

1991   "Approaches to 'missing' internal (and external) arguments in serial structure: Some presumed difficulties", in: Francis Byrne—Thom Huebner (eds.), 207—222.

1992   "Tense scope and spreading in Saramaccan", *Journal of Pidgin and Creole Languages* 7(2): 195—221.

Byrne, Francis—Thom Huebner (eds.)
1991   *Development and structures of creole languages: Essays in honor of Derek Bickerton.* Amsterdam: John Benjamins.

Carrington, Lawrence D. (ed.)
1983   *Studies in Caribbean Language.* St. Augustine, Trinidad: Society for Caribbean Linguistics.

Chomsky, Noam
1981   *Lectures on government and binding.* Dordrecht: Foris.
1982   *Some concepts and consequences of the theory of government and binding.* Cambridge, MA: MIT Press.
1986 a *Knowledge of language.* New York: Praeger.
1986 b *Barriers Cambridge, MA: MIT Press.*

Clahsen, Harald
(to appear) "Constraints on parameter setting: A grammatical analysis of some acquisition stages in German child language". To appear in *Language Acquisition.*

Déchaine, Rose-Marie
1988   *Opérations sur les structures argumentales: Le cas des constructions sérielles en créole haïtien.* [Unpublished MS., Université du Quebec à Montréal, Département de Linguistique.]

DeGraff, Michel
1992   "Haitian null subjects revisited", in: Claire Lefebvre (ed.), *Travaux de Recherche sur le Créole Haïtien* 11. Université du Québec à Montréal: 58—74.
1993 a "Is Haitian Creole a *pro-drop* language?", in Francis Byrne and John Holm (eds.), *Atlantic Meets Pacific: A Global View of Pidginization and Creolization.* Amsterdam. Benjamins: 71—90.
1993 b "A riddle on negation in Haitian," *Probus* 5.1/2: 63—93.

Déprez, Viviane
1992   "Is Haitian Creole really a *pro-drop* language?", in: Claire Lefebvre (ed.), *Travaux de Recherche sur le Créole Haïtien* 11. Université du Québec à Montréal: 23—40.

Givón, Talmy (ed.)
1971   *Papers from the second conference on African linguistics.* (Studies in African Linguistics supplement 2.) Department of Linguistics and the African Studies Center. University of California, Los Angeles.

Emonds, Joseph
1978   "The verbal complex V'—V in French", *Linguistic Inquiry* 9: 151—175.

Givón, Talmy (ed.)
1971   *Papers from the second conference on African linguistics.* (Studies in African Linguistics, supplement 2.) Department of Linguistics and the African Studies Center. University of California, Los Angeles.

Hyams, Nina M.
1986   *Language acquisition and the theory of parameters.* Dordrecht: Reidel.

1987 "The theory of parameters and syntactic development", in: Thomas Roeper–Edwin Williams (eds.), 1–22.

Jaeggli, Osvaldo A.
1982 *Topics in Romance syntax.* Dordrecht: Foris.
1986 "Three issues in the theory of clitics: Case, doubled NPs, and extraction", in: Hagit Borer (ed.), 15–42.

Jaeggli, Osvaldo A.–Kenneth J. Safir
1989 *The null subject parameter.* Dordrecht: Kluwer.

Jaeggli, Osvaldo A.–Carmen Silva-Corvalán (eds.)
1986 *Studies in Romance Linguistics.* Dordrecht: Foris.

Kayne, Richard S.
1983 "Chains, categories external to S and French complex inversion", *Natural Language and Linguistic Theory* 1: 107–139.
1984 *Connectedness and binary branching.* Dordrecht: Foris.

Klavans, Judith L.
1985 "The independence of syntax and phonology in cliticization", *Language* 61: 95–120.

Koopman, Hilda
1982 "Les questions", in: Claire Lefebvre–Hélène Magloire-Holly–Nanie Piou (eds.), 204–241.
1986 "The genesis of Haitian: Implications of a comparison of some features of the syntax of Haitian", in: Pieter Muysken–Norval Smith (eds.), 231–258.

Kouwenberg, Silvia
1990 "Complementizer *pa*, the finiteness of its complements, and some remarks on empty categories in Papiamento", *Journal of Pidgin and Creole Languages* 5: 39–51.

Kroch, Anthony–Beatrice Santorini–Caroline Heycock
1987 "Bare infinitives and external arguments", *Proceedings of the 18th Annual Meeting of the North Eastern Linguistics Society*, 271–285. J. Blevins–J. Carter (eds.). Department of Linguistics, University of Massachusetts, Amherst.

Larson, Richard K.–Claire Lefebvre
1990 Predicate clefting in Haitian Creole. [Paper presented at Annual Meeting of the North Eastern Linguistics Society, Montreal.]

Lebeaux, David
1987 "Comments on Hyams", in: Thomas Roeper–Edwin Williams (eds.), 23–39.

Lefebvre, Claire
1989 "Instrumental *take*-serial constructions in Haitian and in Fon", *The Canadian Journal of Linguistics* 34: 319–337.

Lefebvre, Claire–Hélène Magloire-Holly–Nanie Piou (eds.)
1982 *Syntaxe de l'Haïtien.* Ann Harbor: Karoma.

Lumsden, John S.
1990 Locative arguments and expletives in Haitian Creole. [Paper presented at the Conference on Focus and Grammatical Relations in Creole Languages, University of Chicago.]

Magloire-Holly, Hélène
1982 "Les Modaux: Auxiliaires ou verbes?", in: Claire Lefebvre–Hélène Magloire-Holly–Nanie Piou (eds.), 92–121.

Mufwene, Salikoko S. – Marta B. Dijkhoff
   1989   "On the so-called 'infinitive' in Atlantic Creoles", *Lingua* 77: 297–330.
Muysken, Pieter – Norval Smith (eds.)
   1986   *Universals versus substrata in creole genesis.* Amsterdam: John Benjamins.
Pollock, Jean-Yves
   1989   "Verb movement, universal grammar, and the structure of IP", *Linguistic Inquiry* 20: 365–424.
Read, Charles – Peter Schreiber
   1982   "Why short subjects are harder to find than long ones", in: Eric Wanner – Lila Gleitman (eds.), 78–101.
Rizzi, Luigi
   1982   *Issues in Italian syntax.* Dordrecht: Foris.
   1986 a   "On the status of subject clitics in Romance", in: Osvaldo Jaeggli – Carmen Silva-Corvalán (eds.), 391–419.
   1986 b   "Null objects in Italian and the theory of *pro*", *Linguistic Inquiry* 17: 501–557.
   1990   *Relativized minimality.* Cambridge, Mass: MIT Press.
Roberge, Yves – Marie Thérèse Vinet
   1989   *La variation dialectale en grammaire universelle.* Montréal: Les Presses de l'Université de Montréal et les Editions de l'Université de Sherbrooke.
Roeper, Thomas – Edwin Williams (eds.)
   1987   *Parameter setting.* Dordrecht: Reidel.
Safir, Kenneth J.
   1986   "Subject clitics and the Nom-drop parameter", in: Hagit Borer 1986 (ed.), 333–365.
Schachter, Paul
   1974   "A non-transformation account of serial verbs." *Studies in African Linguistics, Supplement* 5: 253–270.
Shepherd, Susan C.
   1983   "Creoles and language acquisition: Parallels in the expression of modality", in: Lawrence Carrington (ed.), 178–189.
Stahlke, Herbert
   1970   "Serial verbs", *Studies in African Linguistics* 1: 60–99.
Steele, Susan – Adrian Akmajian – Richard Demers – Eloise Jelinek – Chisato Kitagawa – Richard Oehrle – Thomas Wasow
   1981   *An encyclopedia of AUX: A study of cross-linguistic equivalence.* (Linguistic Inquiry Monograph 5.) Cambridge, MA: MIT Press.
Stewart, John M.
   1963   "Some restrictions on objects in Twi", *Studies in African Linguistics* 2: 145–149.
Thornton, Rosalind
   1990   A principle-based explanation of some exceptional *Wh*-questions. [Paper presented at the Boston University Conference on Language Development.]
Vinet, Marie-Thérèse
   (to appear) "Observations théoriques sur les explétifs: Le cas du Créole Haïtien". To appear in *Revue Québécoise de Linguistique.*

Wanner, Eric – Lila Gleitman (eds.)
    1982   *Language acquisition: The state of the art.* Cambridge: Cambridge University
              Press.
Williams, Wayne R.
    1971   "Serial verb constructions in Krio", in Talmy Givón (ed.), 47 – 65.
Zwicky, Arnold M.
    1985   "Clitics and particles", *Language* 61: 283 – 305.

Part II
Creolization as second-language acquisition

Does creologeny really recapitulate ontogeny?

Mervyn C. Alleyne

Creole linguistics and creole languages have entered fully into the current debate about what is innate and what is environmentally determined in human language. One innatist claim is that creole languages represent more directly than other languages what is biologically determined in human language. The innate capacity for language is deemed to be also manifested in child language acquisition. Hence the logical link between child language and creole genesis. In an attempt to specify what is the form and substance of this human faculty, there is the concept of Universal Grammar, for which there are a few versions or at least a few modifications of the original concept. The version referred to as the Language Bioprogram has been identified first and chiefly with creole languages and proposes a quite specific blueprint for the construction of the grammar of human language as a product of the human mind. It may seem at first sight that only one of these versions and reformulations can be right, especially where these versions present innate capacity or Universal Grammar as a set of fixed structures. But although the authors of these versions seem to leave themselves open to such criticism, it is really the case that all of them are possible, no one of them is "right", since they are all abstract representations of a human faculty for language, the existence of which is now undeniable. They are all possible, but extremely unlikely, ways in which this faculty works and is structured, but we shall have to await much more work from neurobiologists and (psycho)linguists to be more convinced as to the precise nature of this faculty (particularly whether it is a specific device for language or whether it is a general device for learning).

My present problem with Universal Grammar and its relationship with the human language faculty derives from what is my own nonspecialist commonsensical view of the neurobiological development of *homo sapiens*. Language must have unfolded in phylogeny through a process of progressive specialization and maturation of the human mind and the vocal apparatus. The progressive specialization of the physiological apparatus to produce the sounds of human language is rather well established. But semantic and syntactic aspects of language and their underlying cognitive structures seem to be dealt with differently. One could of course say that Universal Grammar is really the point where man's development reached its final maturation at some period and there is no further modification of this fundamental blueprint. The notion of Universal Grammar as a once-and-for-all phylogenetic blueprint seems more consistent with the creationist view of humankind than the evolutionary view. And ontogenetically, even if we assume that the innate language device is present as a genetic factor in the ovarian cell, it clearly cannot really be there until developmentally the vocal tract and the cognitive capacity or linguistic knowledge have reached a certain level of maturation. I therefore agree with Lamendella that "the current cognitive nature of man may be viewed as the result of continued neurobiological specialization in the direction of more abstract and complex processing and away from adaptation to a narrow ecological niche"; and, I would add, parallel with the development of more complex cultural traditions (tools, social organization, worldview). It would seem then that language developed over a long period of time in accordance with, or parallel to, the social, cultural, and neurobiological development of the species. Some aspects of language and cognition are wired into the neurobiological genetic apparatus. Other aspects are not so phylogenetically wired and are subject to environmental modification and adaptation. The latter would include the specifics of such things as categorizations of nature, systems of counting, concepts of time, states and processes, and causality. Or otherwise, the innate cognition may contain several possibilities, whose realization will depend on experiential factors. Thus, the recognition of states and processes/events is part of the human cognitive blueprint. But the exact relationship between state and process and more particularly the assignment of phenomena to one or the other, and even more particularly the way in which these are expressed linguistically, will depend on the specific cultural tradition as it relates to a conceptual view of the world. When did maturation occur, i. e., when did the basic blueprint come into effect, or when did the point arrive when further cognitive development was a function of phenotypic and environmental factors? This is difficult to determine. Has the genetic neurobiological make-up ended its development? Will future humans become wired for reading or calculus?

It is not difficult to see that the linguistic/cognitive development of the child recapitulates this phylogenetic sequence. As a matter of fact, child language provides useful insights into, if not confirmation of, the phylogenetic scenario: progressive maturation of the areas of the motor cortex which control the vocal tract and physiological maturation of the tract itself. Thus, back consonants appear first, before front consonants. And on the cognitive/linguistic plane, hypotheticals, counterfactuals, and conditionals are reported as developing later in child language acquisition, just as presumably they enter late in the phylogenetic scenario.

How does creologenesis fit into all this? There have been myriad claims about the relationship between child language (acquisition) and creole language (genesis). Beyond the often convoluted rationalist argumentation that concludes that creole syntax and child language both reflect directly the human language bioprogram, the empirical evidence is not very convincing. First of all, the mere coincidence of surface structures in creole syntax and some utterances of some children surely could not constitute evidence. The prevailing strategy of biophiles, where a similarity can be shown between a creole and child language, is to construct implicitly the following syllogism:

1. A feature F is found in one or several creoles and one or several children.
2. Speakers (learners) of the creoles were originally children.
3. Therefore F was acquired by creole languages from speakers of child language.

However, if no similarity exists, it is claimed that a whole series of ad hoc factors are responsible for the exceptional lack of similarity. Biophiles have never attempted to compare whole systems, but have picked out and compared isolated rules and features from creole and child language. No child so far recorded has ever spoken anything remotely approximating a creole. One might also add that you cannot compare sentences, taking a sentence here from child language and another sentence there from creole language; that you must compare the grammars that generated these sentences, or at least fragments of such grammars. This has not been done even by those who possess the pompous vocabulary of INFL, subjacency, + T, − T, and so on. Unfortunately, even if this were done, it would still prove nothing. Matching grammar against grammar as static sets of abstract rules will say nothing about the dynamic processes involved in language acquisition or language change.

Although developmentally there are clear universals in the process and stages of child language acquisition, specific features such as serial verbs are certainly not universally found. The appearance of serials in some children, but not in others, leaves open the question as to not only why these turn up in creole languages but other features do not, but also why they do not show up in all, or most, children. To conclude this introduction, it seems plausible to assume that the human neurobiological equipment has become specialized to include something one might call "innate linguistic knowledge", but surely more likely a capacity to acquire such knowledge at some point in maturation. It would really be absurd to suggest that the fertilized egg has the particular instance of knowledge of the form "serial verbs", certainly not the complex syntactic and cognitive structures of serial verbs in creole languages.

In one of the earliest comments on the Bickertonian language bioprogram hypothesis (already at the St. Thomas conference in 1979), I noted that it is difficult to see what aspect of the neurobiological structure of *homo sapiens* could lead to perfectives being marked by zero. I continued to be intrigued by this phenomenon which seems to be the foundation of the creole tense/modality/aspect (TMA) system, whereas it has been reported that the perfective is a relatively late acquisition in child language (Slobin's Operating Principle 2.6). I wish to propose a purely internal linguistic solution based on proximate causation, rather than a mentalistic solution based on ultimate causation. At least Slobin's Operating Principle 11.2 of child language ("there is a preference not to mark a semantic category by zero morpheme") will obviously not account for the creole perfective.

There are still a number of commonplace facts about creole languages which are still inadequately accounted for. There are also a number of creole commonplaces that have been accepted as fact quite uncritically, and are repeated quite often in the literature, but which, on closer scrutiny, are not all facts, but merely approximations to facts, simplifications that do not do justice to the historical and synchronic complexity of creole language structure. The examples that I wish to deal with here are:

i.   the zero marking of perfective, and
ii.   the alleged invariable verbal theme.

They are both approximations to facts, simplistically true in those cases where they seem to hold (and indeed it is true that these cases are probably in the majority).

I wish to present a possible (tentative) scenario for the development of these creole features within one group: French-based creoles. I do not think that there is any French creole in which the verbal theme is absolutely invariable. In trying to account for this, let me say without elaboration that I begin with the contact situation in which all the major forms of French verb morphology and syntax were used. This includes both the forms of standard French and of *le français populaire*, which favored a set of periphrastic forms for some aspectual categories over the inflectional forms of standard French. However, the dominant verbal forms were:

1. the past participle used in the *passé composé*, i. e., the perfective; in the stative or resultative; or adjectivally: *la porte est fermée.*
2. the infinitive, which gains from the use of periphrastic expressions.

In several cases, these are homophonous. The past imperfect and the second person plural of the present are also homophonous:

(1)   a. *la butik e ferme*
        'The shop is closed.'
    b. *yn butik ferme*
        'A closed shop.'
    c. *il e apre ferme la butik*
        'He is closing the shop.'
    d. *il va ferme la butik*
        'He will close the shop.'

The other favored form is the virtually single form used for the present tense, which in many cases ends in a consonant:

(2)   *je, ty, il, on, ferm la butik*
        'I, you, he, one close(s) the shop.'

We therefore have the beginnings of what is called in the literature "truncation of final vowel" or "long and short form" (*ferm* − *ferme*, *sort* − *sorti*).

Truncation is not the best term if it implies the existence of one single form which then loses a final vowel. Beginning with the different types and levels of verb morphosyntax in the contact situation, with obviously a lot of code mixing going on, we move to the exploitation of the two major forms for different syntactic and stylistic purposes in different French-creole dialects. The complex processes which occur may all be subsumed under the rubric of syntactic reanalysis, a strong motive force especially in Haitian where we find much in evidence the kind of drastic phonological wearing away which usually accompanies desemanticization in the process of syntactic reanalysis.

Le Réunionnais has inherited virtually all the forms of French verb morphosyntax from all the different dialectal levels of French, but, as far as I can gather from the literature on le Réunionnais, it has not restructured these forms or systematized them in a new semantic system, as the other French creoles have done.

The long and the short form in most cases can be explained etymologically and semantically in terms of French verb morphology: the short form derived from the French present, the long form going back to the infinitive, past imperfect, or past participle. But already in le Réunionnais, we also find the beginnings of a new stylistic exploitation of the long and the short form based apparently on the phonotactics of the phrase: the long form used before pause, the short form used if the verb is followed by another constituent of VP.

Restructuring becomes more evident in Mauritian and Seychellois, although even there the system seems still to be in transition. On the one hand, there is evidence that the long and the short form are related etymologically and semantically to the two dominant forms of French:

(3)   a. *labutik i ferm siz er*
          'The shop closes at six o'clock.'
       b. *labutik i ferme ozordi*
          'The shop is closed today.'
       c. *labutik i n ferme komela*
          'The shop has now been closed.'

But this seems to be fast becoming a relic of the past, giving way apparently to phonotactic conditioning for their occurrence. In Haitian, the two forms exist, but the situation is even freer than in the Indian Ocean, although there may again be a slight statistical favoring of the long form before a pause. But the dominant process in Haitian is the reanalysis, at different stages and degrees of completion, of a whole series of verbs by which they are being reanalysed as verbal auxiliaries or as tense-mood-aspect markers. In this process, they undergo quite drastic phonological reduction, and these reduced forms only occur in a preverbal position:

(4)   a. *kapab > kap > ka > k-* = 'can'
       b. *genyen > geny > gen > g-* = 'have to'
       c. *soti > sot* = 'have just'

This leads me to look at how the tense/aspect system typical of creole languages emerges within this group of languages; and the central issue is the marking of the perfective. One major principle underlying the emergence of this particular feature is the epistemological relationship between the completion of an event or process on the one hand, and the resultant state on the other. This relation is marked in human language by different means, including the absence of any overt marker. In some languages resultative constructions take the same form as the perfect although there is evidence in languages for an increasing distinction to be made (E *he is gone* → *he has gone*). In other languages, resultative constructions continue to be marked formally by the perfective marker (cf. Chinese). The logical links are obvious. It is a matter of perspective: the resultative focuses on the state that is the result of a previous, but completed, event or process, while the perfect emphasizes the event or process itself. This suggests that states are not viewed as independent or autonomous, but are linked conceptually to events or processes which cause them.

In the development of French creole languages, the key to the understanding of the emergence of the verbal system is the use of the French past participle in resultative phrases (*la boutique est fermée*). With the loss of the auxiliary, this participle becomes a finite verb; and the event that precedes and produces the state of closure, expressed by the perfective, becomes fused with the resultant state: *labutik ferme* means both 'la boutique a été fermée' ('the shop has been closed': event) and 'la boutique est fermée' ('the shop is closed': state). The completed event and the resultant state carry the same mark, in this case zero marking.

There is, however, also evidence of a tendency to formally express a distinction between the two categories through the syntactic reanalysis of the verb *finir*. The reduced phonological forms which accompany this reanalysis (*fin*, *in*, *n*) become obligatory aspect markers of the perfective in the Indian Ocean, but remain optional in the Caribbean. This allows Indian Ocean dialects to distinguish formally between the completion of an event or process and the resultant state, while in the Caribbean there is no obligatory overt distinction.

The next motive force in the restructuring is the link existing between event or action and active voice, and between state and passive voice. The event which on completion results in *labutik ferme* comes to be expressed actively by *yo* (or *zot*, etc.) *ferme labutik*, thus spreading the zero (or *fin*) marking of the perfective:

(5)   *labutik (fin) ferme* →   *yo (fin) ferme labutik*
        'The shop has been   'They have closed the shop.'
        (is) closed'

Incidentally, this suggests that the verbal theme is historically more closely related to the French past participle than to the infinitive. It also explains why a form of *être* rather than a form of *avoir* triumphs as the marker of past tense (le Réunionnais does have a form of *avoir*] in French creoles:

(6)   *labutik te ferme*   → *yo (zot,* etc.) *te ferme labutik*
       'The shop was closed'   'They closed the shop.'

It begins first of all with the resultative forms, then spreads to events in the active voice.

This link between completed events and resultant states also affects so-called adjectives or statives. Adjectives in French only express states and do not imply in any way the events which produced them. In French creoles, a development got underway by which stativity is not a semantic trait inherent in certain lexemes, as it may be in French, but it is rather a feature which is realized syntactically or pragmatically. In this development, adjectives are not statives, but can have a stative interpretation in certain phrases, but also (completed) event or process in others, in cases where, pragmatically, the lexemes are compatible with the notion of event or process. This emerges most clearly in a language like Seychellois, where completed events are marked by *fin* (as against those where there is zero marking of perfective and *fin* is optional). In Seychellois, the use of the overt marker *fin* with so-called adjectives or statives indicates transparently an event/process interpretation (which can also be indicated by the progressive aspect marker), while zero marking indicates a stative interpretation:

(7)   a. *tu pu mwa i n mir*
          'All of mine have ripened.'
       b. *tu pu mwa i ankor ver*
          'All of mine are still green.'

The relationship between active and passive, expressed by *yo ferme labutik* → *labutik ferme*, is sometimes called lexical diathesis and is assumed to be built on a base form in the active voice: *yo ferme labutik* is assumed to be the base, and *labutik ferme* is assumed to be derived. But for French creoles, the process is apparently the reverse. Hence a reverse diathesis begins to affect first of all the adjectives derived from French past participles. Thus, *uver, kuver, pendi*, past participles in French, become also active transitive verbs in French creole:

(8)   a. *uver* (< *ouvert* 'open', 'opened') = 'to open'
       b. *kuver* (< *couvert* 'covered') = 'to cover'
       c. *pendi* (< *pendu* 'hanged', 'hanging') = 'to hang'

The process then begins to affect primary French adjectives, but only few members of this class (according to my present knowledge) have so far completed the process. One examples is the following:

(9) a. *sinema plen*
     'The cinema is full.'
    b. *sinema fin plen*
     'The cinema has filled up.'
    c. *sinema pe plen*
     'The cinema is filling up.'
    d. *dimun fin plen sinema*
     'People have filled the cinema.'

Many so-called adjectives do not inherently express states, but may syntactically express either process or state; but they do not complete the process of reanalysis like *plen*. They express process syntactically by taking the progressive aspect marker, or, in the case of the Indian Ocean dialects, the overt perfective-aspect marker, to express the duration and completion respectively of the process/event:

(10) a. *li pe malad*
     'He is getting sick.'
    b. *li fin malad*
     'He is sick.' (Really: 'He has become sick.')
    c. *li malad*
     'He is sick.'

but not:

(10) d. **dimun fin malad li*
     'They have made him sick.'

I may point to two related phenomena to complete this paper. The historical development of this verbal system is continuing in French creoles where there are efforts to distinguish process/event from state by means of a passive auxiliary realized in most cases by a form derived etymologically from the French verb *gagner*:

(11) a. *zot pa envite*
     'They are not invited.'
    b. *zot pa n envite*
     'They have not been invited.'
    c. *zot pa n gany envite*
     'They have not been invited.'

And finally, there are quite obvious parallels with some English-based creoles, which I can only briefly point at. Several English past participles occur as verbal themes (*lost, left, broken*). Note also that even where the verbal theme seems to be the English infinitive, it is also derivable from the English past participle through the remodeling of final consonantal clusters to single consonants. The other parallel is that in English-based creoles a form of *to be* is used as a general past-tense marker. As in the French-based creoles, it seems to have started with resultatives and passives and then was generalized to actives.

This treatment of states and process does not seem to me to be referrable to the cognitive blueprint; even less likely to the linguistic blueprint. It seems to me to be a function of the world view of the population(s) among whom these language developments took place. We seem to be dealing with concepts of causality and its role in the universe. States are derived from processes; in other words, states are not perceived neutrally or abstractly, independent of the processes which give rise to them. In English or French, words like *thick, sick, mad*, etc., express states which can be viewed independently of any process. In fact, in the structure of English, process verbs like *thicken, sicken, make mad* (or *madden*) are derived, at least historically, from the state adjectives. By contrast, in the populations which generated creole languages like those of the Indian Ocean, nature is not a set of inert states, but a world of dynamic forces and processes. States are caused and are potentially explicable. There is an intricate network of causality involving humans, nature and the supernatural. This contrasts with the automatic determinism implicit in the structure of English or French.

References

Alleyne, Mervyn C.
    1982   *Theoretical issues in creole studies.* Kingston: UWI.
Bickerton, Derek
    1981   *Roots of language.* Ann Arbor: Karoma.
Lamendalla, Joseph (ed.)
    1978   *The early growth of language and cognition.* San Jose: California State University.
Slobin, Dan
    1977   "Language change in childhood and history", in: J. Macnamara (ed.), *Language learning and thought.* New York: Academic Press.

The making of a language from a lexical point of view

Geert Koefoed—Jacqueline Tarenskeen

1. Introduction

Our contribution to the Leiden workshop is in a way only negatively related to its theme: creole languages and language acquisition. This is because our paper is concerned with one aspect of the genesis of Sranan which — in our view — has little to do with language acquisition: its vocabulary.

As far as we know, no one has proposed that, besides the rules of syntax, the creole lexicon could also be ascribed to the innate creative potential of language-learning children. One could ask why not, for that matter; as many parents know, children do invent words; we return to this in the last section of this paper. For the moment, we take it for granted that a vocabulary is not created by some innate language acquisition device.

On the other hand, a creole lexicon could be the result of second-language acquisition or relexification as one of the constituent processes of language shift. What one would expect in such a case, is a majority of lexical items from the superstratum language, together with a number of relics from the substratum language, especially in some culturally significant domains (like religion, ritual food, and traditional crafts). Since every language community adds new items to its lexicon in the course of time, one would also expect a certain number of autonomous innovations (neologisms) and loans from languages with which the community, after the shift, has been in contact.

What one would not expect, however, is a very large number of such innovations, "self-made" linguistic expressions, in many semantic domains, and certainly not a number of such innovations that outweighs the number of words taken from the superstratum language. Yet this is exactly the picture that the Sranan lexicon shows.

We consider a Sranan word to be an autonomous innovation if it cannot be derived from a word in one of the lexifier or source languages. Two examples are *bak'anu* 'elbow' and *dek'ati* 'courage'. Though *baka* and *anu* are both (creolized) English words (*back* and *hand*, respectively), the compound as a whole has not been borrowed from English; it has been "made" by the Sranan speaking community. The same holds for *dek'ati*, composed of *deki* (from Dutch *dik* 'thick') and *ati* (from English *heart*).

The actual numbers and percentages of African, Portuguese, English, Dutch, and self-made innovations in the *Woordenlijst Sranan–Neder-lands–Engels* [Word list Sranan–Dutch–English] (1980) are shown in Table 1.[1] The remaining part of 12.7 percent (listed as "Other" in Table 1) consists of words from other languages (among these Kaliña and Arawak, Hebrew, Sarnami, and Javanese) and of words that have not yet been traced. The total number of words in the *Woordenlijst* is approximately 3050.

Table 1. Origins of Sranan words in the *Woordenlist Sranam–Engels*

Language	Approximate number	Percentage
African (A)	130	4.3
Portuguese (P)	100	3.2
English (E)	550	18.0
Dutch (D)	650	21.5
(English or Dutch	130	4.3)
Innovations (I)	1100	36.0
Other	390	12.7
Total	3050	100

If one then finds that most of these innovations were already part of the language in about 1780, we must conclude that early in the development of the language there must have been a period of explosive lexical expansion by means of lexical innovation. This in turn suggests that the community – which was still in development – was at the time not involved in second-language acquisition, but in something quite different: they were making a language of their own.

2. Lexicon archeology

Let us first take a look at the cardinal numerals of present-day Sranan:

(1) *wan* 'one'   *erfu* 'eleven'   *tutenti* 'twenty'   *ondro* 'a hundred'
      tu 'two'   *twarfu* 'twelve'   *dritenti* 'thirty'   *dusun* 'a thousand'
      dri 'three'   *tinadri* 'thirteen' etc.
      fo 'four'   *tinafo* 'fourteen',
      feyfi 'five'   etc.
      siksi 'six'
      seybi 'seven'
      ayti 'eight'
      neygi 'nine'
      tin 'ten'

Of these, the words *wan, tu, fo, siksi, ayti* stem from English; *dri* is of English or Dutch origin;[2] *feyfi, seybi, neygi, tin, erfu, twarfu* stem from Dutch. From then on, the words are innovations, "self-made" by the members of the speech community on the basis of the words from *wan* to *tin*: *tinadri, tinafo, tutenti, tutentiwan* (21), etc.; exceptions to this are *ondro* from English and *dusun* from Dutch. It is a fascinating distribution, a kind of layered structure: an English layer, a Dutch layer and a layer of autonomous innovations.

In many languages the lexicon does indeed show such a layered structure, which can be seen as a key to its development and to the cultural history of the language community. Cultural influences typically manifest themselves in certain portions or layers of loanwords within the lexicon. On the other hand, a large number of neologisms within certain semantic domains is often the result of a period of conscious language building, when the language community develops an attitude of cultural autonomy.[3]

To draw historical conclusions from lexical data, we need a theory, or at least a number of plausible generalizations about the nature of the lexical influence of one language an another in different contact situations. One such generalization is used by Norval Smith, in his reconstruction of the genesis of Sranan's creole languages (Smith 1987). He observes (1987: 145) that in Saramaccan the proportion of English-derived words to Portuguese-derived words within the category of function words is about 63 : 17, while in the Swadesh 200-word vocabulary it is about 50 : 35. From this he infers that the English layer is older than the Portuguese layer, and that Saramaccan is not a Portuguese-based creole, which stopped halfway in a process of relexifying towards English, but – on the contrary – an English-based creole, relexified towards Portuguese. Clearly, this argument is based on the following generalization: function words belong to the more conservative parts of a language, relatively resistent to replacement by words from other languages.

We will need more of such generalizations to interpret the data of the Sranan lexicon. But let us first present some of the data.

3. The distribution of words from different sources in the lexicon of Sranan

We focus our attention on the distribution of African, Portuguese, English, Dutch and self-made words within the Sranan vocabulary. African words seem to be concentrated in some specific semantic domains, as is to be expected: religion, traditional food, music, diseases. As nonspeakers of the language we have to rely on published word lists and dictionaries, which are clearly far from complete. Moreover, as non-Africanists we are unable to assess the "Africanness" of the words ourselves. We can only make use of those etymological data that are available in the literature. Undoubtedly there are many more words of African origin, precisely in those parts of the lexicon that are not covered by dictionaries.[4] We also find African words, however, within a common domain like body parts, among English, Dutch, and self-made words.

As regards the English, Dutch and self-made parts, one cannot speak of dominance in one particular semantic field; never do English-derived words dominate in one specific semantic area and Dutch words in another, or are self-made words conspicuously absent in a third. As indicated, one often finds all three types within one domain. The numerals already showed that, and so do the days of the week: *sonde* (English), *munde* (English), *tudewroko* (self-made), *dridewroko* (self-made), *fodewroko* (self-made), *freyda* (Dutch), *satra* (English).

Yet the distribution is not arbitrary; one feels that there is some kind of system in it. By and large, we think it is safe to assume that the probability of English-derived words increases as concepts are more basic; conversely, the more specific a word is, the greater the chance is that we are dealing with an autonomous innovation. It is in the area between the more basic and the more specific parts of the lexicon that we find most Dutch-derived words.

Such a generalization requires independent criteria or indications as to what counts as more basic and what counts as more specific. Frequency is one indication, but not the only one. In itself it is the outcome of a number of semantic, pragmatic, social, and cultural factors. Therefore, one should try to define "basic" versus "specific" in terms of perceptual, semantic, cultural, and communicative prominence. Most probably, the outcome will be that there is not one scale, but a multidimensional continuum. And one has to consider the possibility that "prominence of concept" will not always correlate with "frequency of word".

For the time being, we take "more or less basic" as an intuitive notion. According to this notion, "belly" is more basic than "stomach", and "back" is more basic than "shoulder". Our experience is that people reasonably agree on this notion. Readers may check this by comparing their judgments with ours in Table 2.

Table 2. Examples of "basic" vs. "specific" terms

More basic	More specific
hand	*arm*
arm	*armpit*
breast ('*mamma*')	*nipple*
red	*yellow*
yellow	*brown*
Monday	*Tuesday, Wednesday*
twelve	*thirteen*
day, night	*afternoon, evening*

It will be clear that different factors are involved in determining the more or less basic character of the concepts. Most of these judgments, however, correlate with data on word frequencies.

One word must be said about the "basicness" of function words in relation to content words. The prototypical basic content words are both concrete and general; they refer to tangible objects or perceptible states and events but in a rather unspecific way, like *chair* (versus *armchair*), *tooth* (versus *eyetooth*), *rain* (versus *drizzle*), and *walk* (versus *saunter*). Function words, on the other hand, abstract meanings. Of course, they are "basic" in semantic and pragmatic respects; quite a few of them are also very frequent. But in many situations one can do without function words and both in first- and second-language acquisition function words are acquired rather late. When below we talk about "basic words", we refer to basic content words, not to function words.

We consider a Sranan word to be of English origin if by some phonological process, i. e., (phonological) creolization, the Sranan word can be derived from the alleged English base. The regular sound correspondences between English and Sranan can be found in Norval Smith's study on the development of the Surinamese creoles (Smith 1987). The processes by which the words from English were creolized are different from those by which the words from Dutch were creolized; as a rule, the former were more "drastic" than the latter, in the reduction of both consonant clusters and diphthongs. These differences between the two sets of creolization rules sometimes enable us to decide between an English and a Dutch word as the ancestor of a Sranan word. *Lanti*, for example, must stem from Dutch *land* (pronounced as [lant]), because the English word *land* would have become *landi* or *lani* (compare *beni* < *bend*). *Troto* must probably be derived from English *throat*, not from Dutch *strot*, because in that case one would expect *stroto* (compare *strey* < D *strij(d)en* and *tranga* < E *strong*). One cannot be quite sure, however, since Dutch *strijken* did lose its initial *s-* and became Sranan *triki.* Then there are words for which both an English and a Dutch origin are equally possible, for example *(h)iri*, from English *heel* or Dutch *hiel.*[5]

As to the African words, we rely on work by others;[6] that is, if an author claims to have found an African source for a Sranan word and this claim seems not too farfetched, we consider that word "African". The same holds for the Portuguese part of the vocabulary. As far as we know, the ancestry of quite a few words has not yet been traced. Clearly, there is still a great deal of etymological work left to be done.

In section 2 we already gave an indication of our criteria with regard to the category of self-made innovations, with two examples. A more explicit definition of this category reads as follows: a Sranan word is considered as a self-made innovation when it is clearly neither African nor Portuguese and there is no English or Dutch word that can be "phonologically creolized" in such a way that it yields the Sranan word. A few more examples are: *bobimofo* 'nipple', *trnaga-yesi* 'disobedience' and *soso-skin* 'naked', which are obviously self-made. Although the elements (except *soso*) can be derived from English, the words are no creolizations of English models. On the other hand, *yarabaka* (the name of a fish) is a creolization of English *yellow back*; *yara* does not occur as a free word in Sranan, the word for "yellow" (*geyri*), being derived from Dutch. *Aytifi* 'eyetooth' and *ambeyri* 'small axe, hatchet' are dubious cases. Sranan has the words *ay* and *tifi*, so it could be considered as a self-made compound; but one cannot rule out that it is a creolization of English *eye teeth.* Similarly, *ambeyri* could be a compound of *anu* and *beyri* or a creolization of Dutch *handbijl.* In all such dubious cases we have decided, sometimes against our intuition, to consider the words not as innovations but as creolizations of English or Dutch words. We do not want to overstate the case for the autonomous character of the language; as a matter of fact, the evident cases of innovation are numerous enough to state that case.

Many of these self-made innovations (mostly compounds) may turn out to be calques (relexifications) from West African languages (see Huttar 1975 and the contributions of Claire Lefebvre and John Lumsden to this volume). This does not diminish, however, their innovative character (see note 3). The important fact is that the Sranan speakers did not take the English or Dutch word for "elbow" or "lip", nor did they borrow words from one of the African languages that were spoken by imported slaves. Rather, they considered their common language as it had already been developed as the stock of material from which new expressions could be made. So they created words like *bak'anu, mofobuba* 'mouth-skin', compare Haitian *po-bouch*); for these, words from African languages only served as models.[7] Apparently, the community had stopped looking for words and taking them over from other languages. They were not involved in a process of accommodation to other groups. There was no other language nor any other group of speakers that served as a target; the "target", so to speak, was their own community and their own language.

As said before, the global impression of the Sranan vocabulary of content words is that the more basic words are predominantly English, while the more specific ones are autonomous innovations; words from Dutch are typically found in the area in between. Of course, these are tendencies only, not exceptionless laws. We will illustrate this with the names of body parts. The following list is based on the *Woordenlijst*, but supplemented with words from the dictionaries by Schumann (1783), Focke (1855), Wullschlägel (1856), indicated by (Sch), (F), and (W) respectively:

(2) a. English:

skin 'body'	*ede* 'head'
fesi 'face'	*ai* 'eye'
yesi 'ear'	*noso* 'nose'
mofo 'mouth'	*tongo* 'tongue'
tifi 'tooth'	*aitifi*(?) 'eyetooth'
bakatifi 'back tooth'	*neki* 'neck'
troto 'gullet'	*bohi* 'breast', "mamma"
bere 'belly'	*priki* 'penis' (Sch)
baka 'back'	*lasi*(?) 'bottom'
anu 'arm/hand'	*finga* 'finger'
futu 'foot', leg'	*iri*(?) 'heel'
honyo 'bone'	*ati* 'heart'
brudu 'blood'	

b. Dutch:

kakumbe 'jaw'	*borsu* 'chest'
skowru 'shoulder'	*doin* 'thumb'
nangra 'nail'	*pols, polsu* (W) 'wrist'
bowtu 'thigh'	*kindi* 'knee'

koyti 'calf'   *enkel* 'ankle'
lebriki 'rib'   *krabnari* 'rib'
lefre 'liver'   *niri* 'kidney'
muru 'uterus'   *senwe* 'nerves'[8]

c. Innovations:

fes'ede 'forehead'   *bak'ede* 'back of head'
seifesi 'check'   *seimofo* (F) 'cheek'
bropresi 'temple'   *aiw'wiri* 'eyelash'
blaka fu ai (Sch, W, F) 'pupil'   *mama fu ai* (Sch) 'pupil'
aibuba 'eyelid'   *yesibuba* 'earlobe'
bakayesi 'back of ear'   *yesimama* 'eardrum'
nos'oro 'nostril'   *mofobuba* 'lip'
pikintongo 'uvula'   *festifi* 'front tooth'
matatifi 'back tooth'   *bobimofo* 'nipple'
kumbatitei 'umbilical cord'   *ondrobere* 'underbelly'
mindrifutu 'genitals'   *manplesi* (Sch) 'penis'
umanplesi (Sch) 'vagina'   *umansani* (Sch) 'vagina'
seibere (W) 'loin'   *bakatingi* W, F) 'coccyx'
sturupe 'anus', 'arse'   *kaolo* 'anus', 'arse'
bakadan 'bottom'   *anuskrufu* (W) 'wrist'
tapusei-anu (W) 'upper arm'   *bak'anu* 'elbow'
ondr'anu 'armpit'   *gronfutu* 'foot'
skrufu fu futu (W) 'ankle'   *bakafutu* 'heel'
ondrofutu 'sole of foot'   *bakabon* 'spine'
mindri-bakabon (W) 'spine'   *kalabasi fu ede* (Sch) 'skull'
ede tonton 'brains'   *mama fu bele* (Sch) 'stomach'
nyansaka (W) 'stomach'   *brudutitei* 'vein', 'artery'

d. African:

buba(?) 'skin'   *kumba* 'navel'
toli(?) 'penis'   *pima*(?) 'vagina'
bombo(?) 'vagina'   *gogo* 'bottom'
dyonku 'hip'   *fokofoko* 'lungs'
kuku 'spleen'

e. Portuguese:

tripa 'intestines'

If we restrict ourselves to the clear cases, present-day Sranan has 21
names of body parts from English, 16 from Dutch, one from Portuguese

and between five and nine of African origin. As for the innovations, one has to consider the possibility that some of these were coined by German missionaries in order to solve problems in translating the bible into Sranan. If we therefore disregard those words that only occur in the "German" dictionaries by Schumann and Wullschlägel (Focke was a native speaker of the language), the number of self-made words is still 32, that is at least 31 percent of the total number of mentioned names of body parts.

The truly basic character of the 21 English words will be clear. These basic words are remarkably constant; Schumann's dictionary had exactly the same 21 words (plus one: *priki*, seemingly the only "dirty word" that has been taken from a European language). Generally speaking, the self-made words are more specific than the words from Dutch. We see a concentration of possible "African" words, at least words that cannot be traced to one of the European languages, in the domain of sex. *Kumba* has a strong religious meaning. There is furthermore a small concentration of Dutch words in the medical sphere (names of inner organs, like liver and kidney).

4. Types of contact processes and lexical influence

How did this distribution come about? As said before, we need generalizations about the different types of lexical influence of one language upon another in different situations.

There is a general opinion that basic (content) words are conservative. The Swadesh 200-words list, intended as a tool to determine historical relations between languages, is based on this idea. When a language community undergoes cultural influence from another community (a present-day example is the influence the Frisian language community is undergoing from the Dutch language community), we do not expect that it starts with the replacement of basic words like *head, eye, foot*.[9]

On the other hand, in both first- and second-language acquisition basic words are learned first. In those situations where a contact language may emerge, one would expect basic words, taken from the superstratum language, to be the first words "agreed upon" in the emerging jargon or pidgin. When this contact language, by a process of language shift, becomes a community's first language, these basic words constitute the lexical core of the new language.

The basic vocabulary, therefore, is both conservative and progressive, dependent on the nature of the contact processes. We have to distinguish between:

i. cultural borrowing in different degrees of intimacy, but without language shift;
ii. language shift towards a dominant language without creolization (such a process may result in an ethnic variety of the target language, not in a new language);[10]
iii. pidginization the emergence of a jargon or contact language;
iv. creolization that is: language shift towards a "new" language.

In the case of cultural borrowing, basic words are conservative: they are seldom replaced by words from the dominant language. In processes of language shift, pidginization, and creolization, however, they are the most "progressive" words of the vocabulary: they constitute a kind of bridgehead towards the newly acquired language, or − in the case of creolization − they constitute the lexical core of the newly formed language.

Besides the basic and generally rather frequent words, there are other parts of the lexicon that are resistant to replacement by loans in cultural borrowing. A plausible condition on cultural borrowing from a culturally dominant language seems to be that only words that have a certain relevance and therefore a certain currency in the intergroup communication will be borrowed and eventually replace words from the recipient language. This could be called the "frequency condition". Words that play only a marginal role in intergroup communication will not be replaced. Among them one finds taboo words and words that are specifically linked to aspects of the intragroup cultural life. But also in this group are words that are simply too specific and therefore too infrequent to be replaced by a word from the prestige language. In a sense the "frequency condition" protects the more specific words against replacement by loans.

In a process of language shift, however, the frequency condition works unfavorably for infrequent words: there is a fair chance that very infrequent words are not learned by a generation already more fluent in the new language than in the language of their parents. Relics of the abandoned language are therefore mainly to be expected among those words that relate to aspects of the culture that the group wants to maintain (in spite of the language shift). Such words then function in a way as ethnicity markers.

If we divide the lexicon of a language roughly into three components – basic content words (rather frequent), specific words (taboo words, culturally specific and rather infrequent words) and the middle group of "not too specific words" – then language-contact situations of the kinds we distinguished earlier will each affect the three components differently:

i. In the case of cultural borrowing, basic, elementary words constituting the core vocabulary and the very specific words will remain unaffected by replacements from a prestige language;

ii. Pidginization: the rudimentary contact language upon which a linguistically heterogeneous community has reached agreement, consists primarily of elementary words taken from the superstatum language, adapted to substratum phonology. Specialized terminology is absent; ad hoc improvizations and circumlocutions will be resorted to in order to meet referential needs;

iii. Language shift: the superstatum language that has been adopted as a group's new language, provides for the elementary as well as the specific portion of the lexicon. If, however, the group that has made the shift, wishes to maintain an ethnolinguistic identity of their own, a number of words of the substratum language(s) are likely to be retained, especially those referring to culture-specific concepts. Such residues of abandoned languages then come to serve as markers of ethnic identity and group solidarity.

The distinctions between different parts of the lexicon, on the one hand, and the processes occurring in different situations of language contact, on the other, enable us to describe what is involved in creolization. The subordinate group, linguistically heterogeneous, is more or less forced to undergo a process of language shift. The original native languages have lost their function in the new social context, since they are no longer sustained by any homogeneous community; consequently they will not be learned by future generations. The emerging community is still without a single language that could support and demonstrate the consolidation of their new sociocultural unity. Therefore, the direction of the shift is not towards the superstratum language. What happens in the case of creolization, then, is that the shift is directed inward: the "target" is sought within the community itself. While regular language shift is a centrifugal process, directed towards a fully developed language which exists outside of the shifting group, creolization is a process which is essentially centripetal.[11] The target is being created in and by the shift itself. The linguistic means and expression already in common use among those forming the community will function as the foundation of the language. The type of language that will emerge under the sociolinguistic conditions just sketched could be properly called an "autonomous creole". That is, a creole that has expanded within the developing community of its speakers, not just to meet growing communicative needs but also in function of a growing cultural unity and autonomy.

This type of creole shows the effect of language shift in its relics from the substratum language and the effect of pidginization in its basic vocabulary; the most salient characteristic, however, is the number of autonomous (self-made) innovations in the section of the lexicon between the basic vocabulary and the most specific vocabulary, as a result of the fact that the vocabulary has expanded from within.

When after or during its formation period, a creole is affected by cultural borrowing, lexical additions and replacements are expected to be found in the same area as in other cases of cultural borrowing, that is in the "not too specific" part of the lexicon. Both the basic vocabulary and the more specific vocabulary are conservative and resistant to the effects of cultural contacts.

This is — not exactly, but roughly — the picture shown by the Sranan vocabulary, with its English-derived elementary part, relics from African languages in its most specific part, and in between, Dutch words, and innovations — self-made words created from basic (therefore predominantly English) material. Of course, the dividing lines between the English part, the Dutch part, the self-made part and the African part are not always clear. Innovations may find themselves competing with loans from Dutch, which has been and still is the principal donor of loans after the language's formation period. In fact, it seems that some Dutch words have actually "percolated" down into the basic vocabulary. We refer once again to the cardinal numbers in Sranan. One would at least have expected an English word for 10. The Dutch layer seems to start with 5, but 6 and 8 are still from English. As yet, we have no explanation for these facts.

What we do know, however, is that many Dutch elements only entered the language between 1783 (the year of Schumann's *"editio tertia"* [third edition]) and 1856 (when Wullschlägel was published), replacing English elements. The numerals in Schumann are:

(3) *wan* 'one' (English)   *seben* 'seven' (English)
     tu 'two' (English)   *aiti* 'eight' (English)
     dri 'three' (English)   *neni* 'nine' (English)

fo 'four' (English)	*tin* 'ten' (Dutch)
feifi 'five' (Dutch)	*hondro* 'a hundred' (English)
sik(i)si 'six' (English)	*dusent* 'a thousand' (Dutch)

And, while present-day Sranan has *erfu, twarfu*, Schumann still has *tinna wan, tin na tu*.[12] The entry which reads "*tin hondro* (da wan dusent)" is also illustrative of the competition between autonomous innovations and loans from Dutch.

We now examine yet another domain, the different parts of the day: *dey* 'day', *neti* 'night', *musudey* 'dawn', *mamanten* 'morning', *brekten* 'noon', *bakadina* 'afternoon', *mofoneti* 'evening', *sapaten* (obsolete) 'suppertime', *mindrineti* 'midnight'. Besides the basic words for day and night, only one of the more specific words is of English origin, *sapaten*. Not even one word from Dutch origin has entered this domain.

5. Sranan as an autonomous creole

We refer again to Table 1 which shows the actual numbers and percentages of African, Portuguese, English, Dutch and self-made innovations in the *Woordenlijst*. Of course, not all words from Dutch are replacements of African, Portuguese, English, or self-made words. As a matter of fact, many of them are just loans, added to the lexicon without replacing existing words. For example, Schumann does not have *borsu*, but translates *hatti* not only as 'Herz' but also as 'Brust', Focke (1855) does the same, but Wullschlägel (1856) gives for 'Brust', besides *hatti, borst/borsoe*. In present-day Sranan *ati* means only 'heart' (apart from the three homonyms *ti*, meaning 'hurt', 'pain'; 'hot'; and 'hat'). Here, as in many other cases,[13] we see the Dutch word enter the language as an expansion of the existing lexicon. Nevertheless, we may assume that self-made words constitute a larger part of the Sranan vocabulary in, say, 1770 than in present-day Sranan. What does this mean with regard to the genesis of Sranan?

Paraphrasing a remark made by Salikoko Mufwene at the previous Creole Workshop in Amsterdam (spring 1989), we would like to say that there are languages without syntax but no languages without words. Moreover, syntactic constraints, syntactic constructions and even some concepts may be innate, in that they may emerge spontaneously as a consequence of cognitive and linguistic maturation; but words are definitely not innate. Words are social objects by definition.

Chomsky considers language to be primarily a psychological object. In his *Knowledge of language* (1986) he argues that I-language, that is, the internal representation of linguistic knowledge, is the only real object of linguistics. Of course, people within a community share language, so their "I-languages" must be rather similar, otherwise they could not function socially. But their sociality is secondary, as it were. It is not due to processes of interaction, but to the fact that all individual learners are endowed with the same device and construct similar rule systems, when presented with similar data.

This, however, cannot apply to words. Words are conventional signs and therefore primarily social objects. It is, of course, an individual who coins or creates a particular new word; but for a word to become a sign, part of a language, it must be shared by members of a community (however small). It is not that children do not invent words − they are rather creative in this respect, as many parents know. Some of their inventions may gain currency and so become words within the small community of their family or peer group. But that is precisely the point: an individual activity alone can never yield a social product, the individual creation must be accepted and come into use by members of the community. A vocabulary is the product of interaction; in this respect a language is − as Sapir (1949: 225) puts it − a collective work of art. Children can participate, of course, in this communal activity; but so can adults − their Universal Grammar may be extinct, but their linguistic creativity is not. The bulk of lexical innovations must undoubtedly be ascribed to the adult members of the community, not because children are less creative but because they do not take part in those processes of interaction from which the community's language arises. In final instance, it does not matter who invents a particular new verbal expression, because it is not its invention but its use in interaction that makes it into a word of the community's language. As soon as one considers the lexicon as an essential component of any language, one has to acknowledge the fact that languages are not only psychological but also social objects that arise from and are learned by interaction, just like any other aspect of culture.

Only one-fifth of the lexicon of Sranan consists of words taken from the original lexifying superstratum language, and more than one-third of autonomously created expressions. Confronted with such facts, one must conclude that any acquisitional and therefore essentially psychological account of creole genesis can only tell us one part of the story. We think that it is justified to say that the Africans in Suriname created their own language, just as they have made their own culture. Indeed, the making of a language of their own was just one — essential — part of their efforts to become a people, a community. After all, creolization is a wider — not purely linguistic — sense, means cultural adaptation by maintenance, transformation, and creation.

A number of questions may arise with respect to this view. First: what about the large number of *sowtwatra-nengre* 'salt-water negroes', the newly imported slaves? At least till 1760 the imported slaves outnumbered the "creoles" (slaves born in the colony). Can one speak of one culture-and-language community, when the majority of the population consists of newcomers who all speak their own language? It is true that, for example, in 1768, 51 percent of the slave population on the plantation Roosenburg (roughly 100 persons) were imported slaves. But of course these hundred slaves did not arrive at the same time. Oostindie (1989: 77) gives the numbers of slaves at Roosenburg: 90 in 1720; 132 in 1733; 221 in 1762 (the highest number in the history of the plantation). The average growth in this — most expansive — period of the plantation and of the colony as a whole is not more than three slaves per year. The high death rate, means that, on average, more than three slaves had to be bought, but not many more. It seems safe to assume that newly acquired slaves usually arrived in small groups of six to twelve persons and that this did not happen on a yearly basis (Oostindie 1989: 97). The group to which they were added, consisted of 130 to 200 slaves, of whom the great majority — whether or not born in the colony — had lived on the plantation for more than four to five years. Of course, many of them were bilingual: they knew *nengre-tongo* 'negro-language' and their own *kondre-tongo* 'country-language' (their first language from Africa). Their knowledge of African languages was possibly a source of "new relics" — if we may use this contradictio in terminis — for specific registers.[14] But it seems reasonable to assume that within two or three years such a small group of newcomers had learned the language of the plantation and had become integrated into the community.[15]

Another question is whether the great number of innovations must be seen as the manifestation of an attitude of cultural autonomy. Wasn't it caused by pure necessity? Wasn't the society so segregated that the negroes had no opportunity to borrow from Dutch? We do not think so. In spite of the extremely cruel oppression and the politics of apartheid, there must have been many contacts between Europeans and Africans. The slave population had its own stratification: there were *basya* 'overseer', craftsmen, and houseslaves, who all must have had frequent contacts with the white population. Then there were freed slaves (numbering probably three to four hundred around 1740) with contacts in both "worlds". And finally, there was the system of concubinage. Besides, we know from Stedman (1796) that the white population, even the young ladies, spoke Sranan, not only with their slaves but also among themselves. This Sranan of the Europeans could also have functional as a channel through which Dutch words were able to enter the language. After all, "Neger-Engels" was from the beginning the lingua franca of the colony. Yet we see that in the expansion of the basic vocabulary, innovations play a much greater role than loans from Dutch.

As is well known, Schumann's informant makes a distinction between *bakratongo* 'whiteman's language' and *nengretongo*. There are sixteen words in Schumann list that are characterized as *bakratongo*, mostly followed by the equivalent word in *nengretongo*. One of the informant's remarks suggests that the two varieties were at that time (around 1780) converging: "*adjossi, da bakkratongo:* Ningre takki *kroboi;* ma, pikin morro, alla Ningre njusu *adjossi* tu" [*adjosse*, that is *bakratongo*; the negroes say *kroboi*; but almost all negroes use *adjossi* too].[16] We do not know objectively how different the two varieties may have been; the important thing, however, is that for the slaves the lingua franca was something different from their own language.

In short, there must have been ample opportunity to borrow expressions from Dutch; but the African population was involved, not just in expanding their verbal means of expression, but also in making their own language.

A final question, which, however, we cannot answer, at least, not yet. We have spoken of an explosive expansion by means of innovation. When and where did this take place? In Suriname, between 1670 and, say, 1760 or prior to this in Barbados, where the English colonists came from with their slaves? Or even earlier, in Sierra Leone, when Krio came into existence? To solve this problem we have a lot more comparative work to do. This paper is thus a first report of work in progress.

Notes

1. The percentages within the Swadesh 200-word list are (according to Smith 1987: 139): English 77.14 percent, Dutch 17.58 percent, Portuguese 1.59 percent, African 1.59 percent. The category "innovations" is either absent in this vocabulary or has not been distinguished from English. The number of African words would increase if one took more words into consideration, especially words from the secret religious languages. See also note 4. The Swadesh 200-word vocabulary was developed by Morris Swadesh and Sarah Gudschinsky in order to establish the "time-depth" of genetic relationships between languages. See Gudschinsky (1956).

2. English voiceless *th* generally corresponds with *t* in Sranan, not with *d*: compare *throw away* > *trowe, thrust* > *trusu*. Therefore, Sranan *dri* seems to derive from Dutch *drie*. There are, however English dialects, including the dialect of Bristol, that have a retro-flex *d* in this position.

3. All Dutch terms of traditional grammar (*onderwerp, werkwoord, voornaamwoord*, etc.) and of mathematics, for example, were coined during the period of nation-building (the sixteenth to the eighteenth century). Many of these were loan translations from Latin words, but that does not deminish the deliberate effort of the language-making com-munity to make Dutch into a language that could stand on its own feet and was not inferior to any other language.

4. This may be inferred from Turner's experiences:
   When talking to strangers the Gullah negro is likely to use speech that is essentially English in vocabulary. When he talks to his friends, however, or to the members of his family, his language is different. My first recordings of the speech of the Gullahs contain fewer African words by far than those made when I was no longer a stranger of them. (Turner 1949: 12)
   Price (1975: 462) suspects "that a dictionary which included *all* of the words in Saramaccan would show a proportion of African-derived words closer to 50%". The existing word list by Donicie−Voorhoeve (1963) is, according to Price, "a very partial dictionary, weakest in many of those semantic domains (e. g., religion, sex) which include a particularly high proportion of African-derived terms."

5. A comparison of Schumann's *Wörter-Buch* with present-day Sranan shows that at least in some cases phonological creolization of Dutch words has been a gradual process. In Schumann we find for example *geel, helpi, kool, koors*, where present-day Sranan has *geyri, yepi, koro, korsu* (meaning 'yellow', 'help', 'cabbage', and 'fever', respectively). Wullschlägel often gives variants: *helpi/jrepi/jerepi, kool/koro*. This enables us to estab-lish a chronological order between different Dutch words: a noncreolized word from Dutch has entered the language later than a creolized word.

6. We have consulted the following works: Alleyne 1980; Cassidy−LePage 1980; Daele-man 1972; Echteld 1961; Herskovits−Herskovits 1969; Lichtveld 1928−1929; Rens 1953; Schuchardt 1979; Smith 1987; Turner 1949; Voorhoeve 1970.

7. Huttar (1975) demonstrates the striking similarity between Sranan and West-African manners of verbal expression, for instance in using the word for "mouth" in its meta-phorical meaning: *mofoyari* 'final period of the year', *mofoneti* 'beginning of night, evening'.

8. Wullschlägel also mentions *maag* 'stomach' and *darm* 'intestine', 'guts', but marks them as (*h*), indicating that these words are *holländisch* [Dutch] and only used in Paramaribo.

9. Another example: the community of Dutch linguists is quite willing to replace parts of the Dutch linguistic vocabulary with English terms, so we talk about *complementizers* and *nouns*, but basic terms like *woord* 'word' and *zin* 'sentence' remain intact.

10. The distinction between culture contact without language shift and processes of lan-guage shift is not unproblematic and probably in itself a matter of degree rather than a clear-cut distinction.

11. We owe the terms *centrifugal* and *centripetal* to characterize this difference in orienta-tion to Hein Eersel (personal communication).

12. Schumann's dictionary also contains *twalf*, but only in the name of a coin, *pisitwalf* (three guilders or 12 Schilling).

13. A comparison of the color terms in Schumann, Focke, and Wullschlägel yields the following results:

Schumann: *blakka, brakka* 'black', 'blue'; *redi, ledi* 'red', 'yellow', 'light brown'; *weti* 'white'; *grun, lala* 'green', 'fresh', 'unripe'; *geel* 'yellow', "*bakratongo; ningre takki redi*" [*bakratongo*; the negroes say *redi*]. Focke adds to these: *blau, brau* 'blue' and *broin* 'brown' and gives *geel* in a creolized form: *geeri*.

Wullschlägel gives for '*gelb*' [yellow]: *geeli, redi* (obsolete) and adds: *aranja* 'orange' and *grys* 'grey'.

It is remarkable how the order of additions follows the pattern of basic color terms established by Berlin and Kay (1969).

14. Schumann gives two examples in his lemma *kondre-tongo*: "*Mi vergeti mi kondre-tongo kaba*" 'I have already forgotten my country-language', and "*da de takki hem kondre-tongo*" 'he speaks his country-language'. Both may be seen as significant with respect to the language situation.

15. Focke (1855) describes the way newcomers were introduced to plantation life. Each one of them was assigned a kind of "mentor", preferably from the same language group; an important task of this mentor was to teach his new fellow-slave the language of the country, i. e., *Neger-Engels* 'Negro-English'.

16. Around 1855 the distinction seems to have disappeared. Wullschlägel mentions both expressions, but as two different names for the same language. Most words that were characterized as *bakratongo* in Schumann are included without comment in the dictionaries of Focke and Wullschlägel.

References

Alleyne, Mervyn C.
  1980   *Comparative Afro-American.* Ann Arbor: Karoma.
Berlin, Brent—Paul Kay
  1969   *Basic color terms: Their universality and evolution.* Berkeley—Los Angeles: University of California Press.
Cassidy, Frederic G.—Robert B. Le Page
  1980   *Directionary of Jamaican English.* Cambridge University Press.
Chomsky, Noam
  1986   *Knowledge of language: Its nature, origin and use.* New York: Praeger.
Daeleman, Jan
  1972   "Kongo elements in Saramacca Tongo", *Journal of African Languages* 11: 1—44.
Donicie, Antoon—Jan Voorhoeve
  1963   *De Saramakaanse woordenschat* [The Saramaccan lexicon]. Amsterdam: Bureau voor Taalonderzoek in Suriname, Universiteit van Amsterdam.
Echteld, Johannes Julius M. M.
  1961   *The English words in Sranan.* Groningen: Wolters.
Focke, Hendrik C.
  1855   *Neger-Engelsch Woordenboek* [Negro-English dictionary]. Leiden: Van den Heuvell.
Gudschinsky, Sarah C.
  1956   "The ABC of Lexicostatistics". *WORD* 12: 2, 175—210.

Herskovits, Melville J. – Francis S. Herskovits
1969   *Suriname folklore.* New York: AMS Press.
Huttar, George' L.
1975   "Sources of creole semantic structures", *Language* 51: 684–695.
Johnson-Laird, Philip N. – Peter C. Wason (eds.)
1977   *Thinking: Readings in cognitive science.* Cambridge: Cambridge University
           Press.
Kramp, André A.
1983   Early creole lexicography: A study of C. L. Schumann's manuscript dictio-
           nary of Sranan. [Unpublished Ph. D. dissertation, University of Leiden.]
Lichtveld, Lou
1928–1929 "Afrikaansche resten in de creolentaal van Suriname" [African elements in
           Surinamese creole], *West-Indische Gids* 10: 391–402, 507–526; 11: 72–84,
           251–262.
Oostindie, Gert
1989   *Roosenburg en Mon Bijou: Twee Surinaamse plantages, 1720–1870* [Roosen-
           burg and Mon Bijou: Two Suriname plantations, 1720–1870]. Dordrecht:
           Foris.
Price, Richard
1975   "Kikoongo and Saramaccan: A reappraisal", *Bijdragen tot de taal-, land- en
           volkenkunde* 131: 461–478.
Rens, Lucien L. E.
1953   *The historical and social background of Surinam Negro-English.* Amsterdam:
           North-Holland.
Rosch, Eleanor
1977   "Classification of real-world objects: Origins and representations in cogni-
           tion", in: Philip N. Johnson-Laird – Peter C. Wason (eds.), 212–222.
Sapir, Edward
1949   *Language: An introduction to the study of speech.* New York: Harcourt, Brace
           and Company.
Schuchardt, Hugo
1979   *The ethnography of variation: Selected writings on pidgins and creoles.* Edited
           and translated by T. L. Markey. Ann Arbor: Karoma.
Schumann, C. L.
1783   *Neger-Englisches Wörter-Buch.* MS, published with annotations in Kramp
           (1983).
Smith, Norval S. H.
1987   The genesis of the creole languages of Surinam. [Unpublished Ph. D. disserta-
           tion, University of Amsterdam.]
Stedman, John G.
1796   *Narrative of a five years' expedition against the revolted negroes of Surinam ...
           from the year 1772 to 1777.* Vols. 1–2. London: Pall Mall.
[1972]   [Reprinted Amherst: University of Massachusetts Press.]
Turner, Lorenzo D.
1949   *Africanisms in the Gullah dialect.* Chicago: University of Chicago Press.
Voorhoeve, Jan
1970   "The regularity of sound correspondences in a creole language", *Journal of
           African Languages* 9: 51–69.

1980   *Woordenlijst Sranan-Nederlands-Engels* [Word list Sranan—Dutch—English].
            Paramaribo: Bureau Volkslectuur/Vaco.
Wullschlägel, H. R.
1856   *Deutsch-Negerenglisches Wörterbuch.* Löbau.
[1965]   [Reprint Amsterdam: S. Emmering.]

Creolization and the acquisition of English as a second language

Herman Wekker

In this paper I want to discuss the process of creolization in terms of second-language acquisition. Who were the learners? What was their social and linguistic background? What language or dialect were they learning? For what purposes? And, how effective were they, linguistically, at what they were doing?

There is considerable confusion about terminology. Let me begin therefore by briefly defining two of the terms I will be using in my paper. Definitions always contain implicit theoretical claims.

In the first place, the terms "creole" and "creolization" will be used here to include "pidgin" and "pidginization", unless specific reference is required to the traditional distinction. It is often difficult to draw a clear dividing line between pidginization and creolization, and it may not be very useful to make the distinction. I will define creolization as the process of the emergence of "new languages", including newly acquired second (inter)languages. What distinguishes creoles from other natural languages is that, in general, the date of their birth can be easily established, often within the last 350 years (Sranan, Saramaccan, Barbadian, and Jamaican belong to the oldest English-related creoles in the Caribbean). I regard creolization as a continuous process of second-language acquisition by adults, often extending over several generations. I suggest that the terms "creole" and "creolization" are more felicitous, because (i) their etymology stresses the newness of the languages involved, and (ii) they have few negative connotations.

Secondly, I will use the term "second-language acquisition" to include "foreign-language acquisition" and other types of nonprimary acquisition, including creolization, and the term "acquisition" to include "learning", unless I specifically want to refer to the distinction that is sometimes made between these processes in the applied-linguistics literature. Although the terminological distinction may be of some practical importance, it does not seem crucial to the argument of my paper.

I believe that creolistics and historical linguistics are intrinsically related disciplines (even though creolistics has challenged some of the basic assumptions of the traditional comparative method), and the time has now come for further study of the earliest creole texts that have become available. The work done by Arends (1989), Rickford (1987), Schneider (1989), D'Costa and Lalla (1989, Lalla–D'Costa 1990), and a few others, are excellent examples of diachronic linguistic research on early creole texts. There is a need for detailed linguistic analysis of such early documents in the history of creole languages.

I also think that creolists have so far put too much emphasis on the presumed morpho-syntactic influence of substrate languages on creole genesis; the role of superstrate influence and the structural convergence of substrate and superstrate input features have been underestimated. Further systematic study of the grammar of certain English dialects of the seventeenth, eighteenth, and nineteenth centuries could help to determine what its influence has been on English-related Atlantic creoles.

And, finally, I believe that L1 acquisition is intrinsically different from L2 acquisition, but we have to find out what the relevant differences are for the purposes of creole studies. I will argue that there are two main reasons for the presumed difference between L1 and L2 acquisition: (i) the operation of cross-linguistic transfer, and (ii) the existence of certain universal principles in L2 acquisition (I will argue that these are, in fact, no more than surrogate Universal Grammar principles, to which the second-language learner has access only through his or her L1). In another paper, with Pieter Seuren (Seuren–Wekker 1986), we discussed one of these universal principles, i. e., the tendency in creole genesis to strive for greater analyticity and an optimal one-to-one correspondence between linguistic form and meaning (the notion of "semantic transparency"). I will return to these points below.

According to Bickerton (1981, 1984), as we know, creolization is the realization of the language bioprogram by the children of pidgin-speaking parents: first-language acquisition with restricted non-native input. This view has now been challenged, and Bickerton seems recently to have shifted his position quite considerably on this point. What I want to do in this paper is discuss further historical and applied linguistic evidence in support of the so-called gradualist (or transgenerational) model of creolization, proposed by Carden and Stewart (1988), and by Arends (1989). The claim I want to make is that creolization is best described as a gradual process of language formation, involving a period of bilingualism in which substrate features will be transmitted. Nativization is not a necessary condition for the emergence of creoles. At least in the case of the Surinamese creoles, creolization was a process of collective second-language acquisition, mainly by adult learners, based on heterogeneous linguistic input, and taking place at individually differential rates. As far as I know, "abrupt creolization" (in Thomason and Kaufman's [1988] sense, may also occur when learners have extremely limited access to the target language, but this situation will be the exception rather than the role. I see no reason why creoles should develop more rapidly than other human languages, apart from the fact that in their formative stages creoles are created under pressure, by people who know the grammar of at least one other natural language.

In recent years a great deal of research on the theory of language and language acquisition has centred around the question to what extent learners have access to Universal Grammar. There is now a substantial body of data on various aspects of the acquisition of first and second languages (L1/L2). Second-language acquisition researchers and creolists have recognized points of mutual interest in their work and emphasized the need to learn from one another. The general research effort over the past two decades has been referred to as that of the logical problem of language acquisition, i. e., explaining how acquisition takes place, given the gap between the limited available input and the quality of the competence attained (Chomsky 1981; Bley-Vroman 1989). We can assume that young children confronted with the task of learning their native language have at their disposal a set of language universals and specific language-learning procedures, with which they are genetically endowed. This innate capacity somehow compensates for the fact that children lack the cognitive ability to deal with complex abstract systems like language. Universal Grammar theory assumes that the child's knowledge of language is constrained by a set of abstract principles and parameters. But can the same be said of adult second-language learners?

Whether Universal Grammar is still actively operative in second-language acquisition and creolization is an interesting research question (cf. Romaine 1988; Odlin 1989; Mufwene 1990). My own view about the role of Universal Grammar is that there are too many obvious differences between child language acquisition and second language acquisition to equate the two. Adult second-language learners have lost the child's knowledge of Universal Grammar and also the child's specific language-learning capability. On the other hand, adults possess not only a general problem-solving ability which can deal with complex systems, but also previous experience with at least one natural language (Bley-Vroman 1989: 53–54). To some extent this knowledge enables adult learners to cope with situations in which their mastery of the second language is insufficient, through general reasoning procedures and compensatory strategies. It is well known that in general adults utterly fail to acquire perfect knowledge of a second language. This is a striking difference with child language acquisition, where full success is normally guaranteed. To account for children's uniform success, it is reasonable to presuppose the reality of the operation of Universal Grammar in child language acquisition, but this is not necessarily the case in second-language acquisition. It cannot be taken for granted that Universal Grammar is still available in second-language acquisition in the same form. The object of research is to assess to what extent the adult L2 learner is guided by the same kind of Universal Grammar principles and parameters. To demonstrate that, it would be necessary to show that in second-language acquisition, just as in child language acquisition, the learner's output is underdetermined by language input. Can L2 learners possess knowledge of the L2 which goes beyond L1 input and which cannot be acquired on the basis of general learning strategies or the mother tongue? In that case, the observed phenomena would have to be ascribed to a form of Universal Grammar. There is some historical evidence that the learners of Surinamese pidgins and creoles were predominantly (male) adults, who acquired the pidgin or creole as a second language. In other words, pidginization/creolization in that situation was a special case of nonprimary language acquisition.

For an account of creole genesis from a historical second-language acquisition perspective, as proposed here, we need a methodological framework which stringently formulates which factors and prerequisites will be involved. It seems to me that there are at least four interrelated conditions which are crucial to such an approach: (i) identifying the substrate languages whose speakers shifted to the target language in the relevant period, (ii) detailed structural and sociolinguistic information about the substrate and adstrate languages in the relevant period, (iii) similar information about the target language (e. g., English) before the shift, and (iv) a theory of second-language acquisition rich enough to provide an explanation for the outcomes of such language shifts; such a theory would also have to account for phenomena which historical linguists and sociolinguists are commonly concerned with, such as diffusion, convergence and divergence, social networks, dialect continua, and waves of linguistic innovations (cf. Holm 1983, 1988; Thomason–Kaufman 1988). It is evident that, given the current scarcity of diachronic data and a full-fledged acquisition theory, these conditions are difficult to satisfy. Still, it strikes me that what we have here is an exciting research program for historical linguists, language-acquisition researchers, and creolists to follow through. And significant progress has already been made in some of these areas.

I adopt the view that creoles are mixed languages resulting from extended language contact. Creolization is a continuous but individually differential process of language acquisition, involving linguistic reduction (but not necessarily simplification), followed by its mirror-image process, linguistic expansion. The input is heterogeneous, but at the same time constitutes a linguistically rich repertoire of codes. The term "acquisition" — in its conventional sense — may be misleading in this context, since what we witness in these situations is a community's collective attempt to cope with a form of linguistic deprivation, in which a "non-native currency of convenience" (Jordan 1985: 123) has to be agreed upon and established. I will regard this kind of linguistic negotiation as an important aspect of the language-acquisition process.

Most creoles have no single parent language, and are instances of what Thomason and Kaufman (1988) have called "interrupted transmission", in the sense that there is no normal genetic continuity from one generation of speakers to the next. On the other hand, I would not go so far as to claim that there is no continuity at all in the origin of creoles: for example, Sranan, Saramaccan, and Jamaican Creole are more or less distant relatives of their lexifier language, English, but none of these creoles is a completely new and genetically unrelated language. There is just too much English vocabulary in them to deny the relationship (cf. Thomason–Kaufman 1988; Trudgill 1990).

Creolization involves, among other things, massive borrowing of lexical and grammatical elements, grammaticalization, reanalysis, loss of iconicity, and a high degree of multifunctionality, in response to the communicative needs of the speakers. The generally accepted view is that, apart from universal features, the creole lexicon comes from one source (the lexifier or superstrate language) and the creole grammar from one or more other sources (the substrate languages). However, these are broad generalizations. The sociolinguistic histories of each of these languages must be examined individually, because factors like intensity of contact, group size, and availability of the target language are likely to have considerable influence on the outcome of any contact-induced linguistic change.

In the substrata-versus-universals debate (cf. Muysken–Smith 1986), creolists have tended to adopt either of two extreme positions: one that is associated with the Universal Grammar, or language bioprogram, hypothesis (Bickerton's language bioprogram hypothesis) and the other with the substratum, or language transfer, hypothesis. The first assumption emphasizes the essential difference in kind between pidgins and emerging creoles, and addresses the fact that many of the striking similarities observed between creoles cannot be traced back to their pidgin ancestors; in this view, new language features must be ascribed to innate language universals. Whether these universals should be of the Greenbergian or the Chomskyan type, is a matter of dispute. The other view, which is equally extreme and untenable, is that pidgins and creoles rely exclusively on substrate and superstrate languages as sources for their expansion. In any case, the two hypotheses probably complement each other (Mufwene 1986).

Creolization can be regarded as an extreme case of contact-induced language shift, where communities completely or partially abandon their own native languages, and create a "new" medium for communication. The original language system may become distorted and subsystems are sometimes entirely lost. The process in question is one of imperfect second-language acquisition, predominantly by adults, involving the usual language transfer from the learners' L1. It is second-language acquisition taking place under exceptional sociolinguistic circumstances, with restricted access to the target language. In Suriname and the English Caribbean, for example, successive cohorts of African slaves arriving on the plantations must have acquired some imperfect version of English as a second (or third) language. In the emergence of these (inter)languages grammaticalization and reanalysis had a crucial role to play, resulting in considerable indeterminacy of categories and multifunctionality. The widely held view that it is only unmarked language features which get transferred, is incorrect. To determine and account for the different outcomes of these types of language contact, one will also have to examine the sociolinguistic and demographic histories of each of the speech communities involved. Apart from looking at the structures of the languages in contact, it will be necessary to emphasize the role of the individual histories of the communities, on the assumption that language change is not only driven by language-internal factors, but also by language-external factors like relative group size, degree of homogeneity in the (African) substrates, the ages of the learners, the number of children and women in the community, the length and intensity of language contact, and the availability of the (European) superstrate languages. I propose that further study of Early Modern English dialects is needed to establish the extent of their lexical and grammatical influence on the formation of

English-related creoles in West Africa, the Caribbean, the Pacific, and elsewhere.

The gradualist second-language acquisition hypothesis is supported by the different social histories and the demographic data concerning slave populations in the Caribbean, including Suriname, in the seventeenth, eighteenth, and nineteenth centuries. In the case of Suriname, Price (1976) has shown that during the first century of the colony's existence (between roughly 1650 and 1750) more than 90 percent of the slave population was born in Africa, and that there were constantly new imports of "salt water" slaves into the colony. In that period the number of children was extremely low: probably no more than one or two per plantation. It was not until about 1750 that the number of locally born slaves (adults and some children) began to rise to about ten per plantation. The fresh cohorts of predominantly male adult slaves from overseas probably outnumbered the Suriname-born "Creoles" by ten to one. It is clear that this demographic situation lends no support to the instantaneous creolization hypothesis.

Arends (1989) and Carden and Stewart (1988) have provided linguistic evidence for the gradual and differential, rather than the instantaneous and monolithic, character of creolization. Arends has demonstrated that, at least in the case of Sranan, creolization cannot have been a uni-generational process, but must have extended over several generations. His conclusion is based on a diachronic study of three syntactic constructions in Sranan between 1700 and 1950: the copula, comparison and clefting constructions. In each case it could be shown that it took one or two centuries, rather than one or two generations, for relatively stable systems to get established, and also that syntactic developments can take place at differential rates. The reason why clefting was established comparatively early in Sranan, i. e., around 1750, may be due to the fact that the superstrate and substrate languages involved have no conflicting systems on this point (except predicate clefting). The copula and comparative constructions, on the other hand, are very different in the languages in contact, so in those cases it was to be expected that it would take longer to negotiate a linguistic compromise. In the past decade, starting with Mervyn Alleyne's work *Comparative Afro-American* (1980), we have seen the publication of some pioneering comparative studies of the history of Caribbean creoles, for example Rickford (1987) on nineteenth-century Guyanese Creole (see also D'Costa−Lalla [1989], Lalla−D'Costa [1990]). What these studies have shown is the significant role of Barbados in the migration of the first English-speaking settlers, the poor whites, and the

African slaves and their families. I agree with Lalla and D'Costa (1990: 1) that

> further work on the varieties of EModE as well as the contribution of African languages other than the Kwa group is of utmost importance in view of the nature of the data collected ... and the implications of linguistic and historical research now available.

Viewing creolization as a gradual process of imperfect second-language acquisition by successive cohorts of adult slaves, extending over generations, makes it possible to account for the process in terms of (i) transfer from the learners' L1s (i. e., substrate influence), and (ii) innate language learning strategies (i. e., indirect access to Universal Grammar).

If we look at the earliest Sranan texts (e. g., the "Herlein fragment" of 1718 and Nepveu's corrections of 1765), written more than three generations after first European settlement in Suriname, we find that they contain very few of the typical creole features (see Arends 1989: 122–130). Several authors have commented on the unreliability of the 1718 Herlein fragment in particular, but it remains a useful historical text for our purposes. The Herlein fragment lacks, for example, copulas, tense-modality-aspect marking, articles and serial verb constructions in positions where in later stages of Sranan they would be obligatory.

It is generally assumed that in English-related creoles it is mainly the lexicon which is English, and that the phonology and the syntax will be typically non-European, the almost complete loss of marked features and bound morphology being ascribed to the reduction process. There are numerous exceptions to each of these assumptions. At the level of syntax, for example, the creole nature of the preverbal tense-modality-aspect markers *ben, sa/wi/o/go, e/de*, etc. has been exaggerated (cf. Jones 1990). Not only are these particles etymologically derived from English auxiliaries, they also share some of their syntactic and semantic properties. If this is an example of the convergence of substrate and superstrate influences, there is no explanation for the late development of this system in creoles. My conjecture would be that this has to do with the internal complexity of the English tense and aspect system; this is a notoriously difficult area of English syntax, which foreigners usually take a relatively long time to master. A universal language-acquisition theory must explain the primacy of aspect in L2 learning and the interdependence between grammatical and lexical aspect. Other acquisition phenomena that second-language acquisition theory must account for include the following four:

i. The early development of *wh*-questions in many creoles. The 1718 Herlein fragment, for example, contains several examples of transparent phrases like *oe fasse* 'what fashion', 'how', *oe som bady* 'what person', 'who', and *oe tem* 'what time', 'when'. Arends (1989: 129) calls this a creole feature in an otherwise pidgin-like text. The occurrence of these question words can indeed be regarded as evidence against the gradualist view, unless an alternative explanation is offered. It seems to me that in this case the superstrate influence from English is clear, and so is one universal learning strategy adopted, viz. striving for optimal semantic transparency (Seuren−Wekker 1986, Muysken−Smith 1990).

ii. Word-order phenomena. Is there a principled explanation for the canonical SVO word order of most creoles, irrespective, it sometimes seems, of the substrate and superstrate input? I must make two brief comments here: I assume that generally in second-language acquisition research one must not be concerned with underlying word order; the transparency of superficial word orderings and the degree of convergence of the learners' input data seem much more relevant. Nor is it certain that English, at the time, uniformly possessed a fixed SVO order, as is always claimed. It may well be that after the Middle English period the relevant dialects of English still contained remnants of the Old English SOV order; modern Standard English, in any case, still has constructions which are reminiscent of the old SOV order.

iii. The absence of periphrastic *do* in English-related creoles.

iv. The position of the negative marker, and the occurrence of multiple sentence negation.

These are just a few examples of areas in early creole syntax where language-acquisition research could be usefully conducted. In this paper I have tried to demonstrate that in my view creolists must continue to repeat to themselves the questions: Who were they? What was their linguistic background? What language were they learning? For what purposes? And, how good were they at what they were doing? Creole history and second-language acquisition theory should provide at least some of the answers.

References

Alleyne, Mervyn
  1980   *Comparative Afro-American.* Ann Arbor: Karoma.
Arends, Jacques
  1989   Syntactic developments in Sranan. Creolization as a gradual process. [Unpublished Ph. D. dissertation, University of Nijmegen.]

Bickerton, Derek
1981   *Roots of language.* Ann Arbor. Karoma.
1984   "The language bioprogram hypothesis", *The Behavioral and Brain Sciences* 7: 173—221.
Bley-Vroman, Robert
1989   "What is the logical problem of foreign language acquisition?", in: Susan-Gass—Jacquelyn Schachter (eds.), 41—68.
Byrne, Francis
1987   *Grammatical relations in a radical creole. Verb complementation in Saramaccan.* Amsterdam: John Benjamins.
Carden, Guy—William Stewart
1988   "Binding theory, bioprogram, and creolization: Evidence from Haitian Creole", *Journal of Pidgin and Creole Languages* 3: 1—67.
Chomsky, Noam
1981   *Lectures on Government and Binding: the Pisa Lectures.* Dordrecht: Foris.
D'Costa, Jean—Barbara Lalla (eds.)
1989   *Voices in exile: Jamaican texts of the 18th and 19th centuries.* Tuscaloosa: University of Alabama Press.
Gass, Susan—Jacquelyn Schachter
1989   *Linguistic perspectives on second language acquisition.* Cambridge: Cambridge University Press.
Givón, Talmy
1982   "Tense-aspect-modality: The creole prototype and beyond", in: Paul Hopper (ed.), 114—163.
Holm, John
1983   "On the relationship of Gullah and Bahamian", *American Speech* 58: 303—318.
1988   *Pidgins and creoles.* Vol. 1. Cambridge: Cambridge University Press.
Hopper, Paul (ed.)
1982   *Typological studies in language.* Vol. 1. Amsterdam: John Benjamins.
Jones, Frederick
1990   "The grammatical items *bin, fo,* and *mos* in Sierra Leone Krio", *Linguistics* 28: 845—866.
Jordan, June
1985   *On call: Political essays.* Boston, MA: South End Press.
Lalla, Barbara—Jean D'Costa
1990   *Language in exile: Three hundred years of Jamaican Creole.* Tuscaloosa: University of Alabama Press.
Mufwene, Salokoko
1986   "The universalist and substrate hypotheses complement one another", in: Pieter Muysken—Norval Smith (eds.), 129—162.
1988   "English pidgins: Form and function", *Word Englishes* 7: 255—267.
1990   "Transfer and the substrate hypothesis in creolistics", *Studies in Second Language Acquisition* 12: 1—23.
Mühlhäusler, Peter
1986   *Pidgin and creole linguistics.* Oxford: Blackwell.
Muysken, Pieter (ed.)
1981   *Generative studies on creole languages.* Dordrecht: Foris.

Muysken, Pieter – Norval Smith
1990   "Question words on pidgin and creole languages", *Linguistics* 28: 883 – 903.
Muysken, Pieter – Norval Smith (eds.)
1986   *Substrata versus universals in creole genesis.* Amsterdam: John Benjamins.
Odlin, Terence
1989   *Language transfer: cross-linguistic influence in language learning.* Cambridge: Cambridge University Press.
Price, Richard
1976   *The Guiana Maroons: a historical and bibliographical introduction.* Baltimore: John Hopkins University Press.
Rickword, John
1987   *Dimensions of a creole continuum: History, texts and linguistic analysis of Guyanese Creole.* Stanford: Stanford University Press.
Romaine, Suzanne
1988   *Pidgin and creole languages.* London: Longman.
Schneider, Edgar W.
1989   *American Earlier Black English: Morphological and syntactic variables.* Tuscaloosa – London: University of Alabama Press.
Seuren, Pieter – Herman Wekker
1986   "Semantic transparency as a factor in creole genesis", in: Pieter Muysken – Norval Smith (eds.), 57 – 71.
Thomason, Sarah Grey – Terrence Kaufman
1988   *Language contact, creolization, and genetic linguistics.* Berkeley: University of California Press.
Trudgill, Peter
1990   Review of Sarah Grey Thomason – Terrence Kaufman (1988), *Journal of Linguistics* 26: 513 – 517.

Part III
Creolization as relexification

The functional category "agreement" and creole genesis

Claire Lefebvre

The research reported on in this paper is part of an ongoing project which seeks to test the theory that Haitian Creole was created through relexification.[1] The general methodology of the project consists of a detailed comparison of the grammar of Haitian Creole and the grammar of its source languages, French and Fon, a language of the Kwa family, chosen among the languages of the substratum of the basis of external factors (cf. Lefebvre 1986 and 1993).

My paper is divided into three parts. First, I present our theory of relexification. Second, I present a case study showing that, in the genesis of Haitian Creole, the AGR of Fon has been relexified. This explains the remarkable parallelism between the structure of the clause in Haitian and in Fon. It follows that the structure of the clause in Haitian and in Fon differs in a similar way from the structure of the clause in French. Third, I discuss the relevance of the results of this case study for the theory of relexification, for theories of creole genesis in general, and for acquisition.

1. Relexification and creole genesis

1.1. Our theory of relexification

Our hypothesis on the genesis of creole languages is based on the notion of relexification (cf. Lefebvre–Lumsden 1989; Lefebvre 1986 and 1993). By relexification we mean the use of the units of their native language lexicon(s) by speakers of the substratum language(s) as a basis for the incorporation of the phonetic strings produced by speakers of the superstratum language. Hence, for each unit already established in their lexicon, speakers of the substratum languages searched for a corresponding phonetic sequence in the superstratum language. In the process of relexification, then, phonetic sequences produced by the speakers of the superstratum language were associated with lexical units of the substratum languages.

Our theory predicts that a close examination of the source languages will show a systematic division of the properties of the creole language: while the superstratum language provides the phonetic strings, the substratum languages provide the semantic/syntactic properties of words, with certain exceptions generally motivated by the need to generate the surface word order of the lexical categories of the superstratum languages.[2] This division between the phonetic and semantic properties of lexical entries is illustrated in (1) below. The data in (1), which contain a sample of compound nouns in Haitian Creole (from Brousseau 1989), provide us with a clear example of the respective contribution of the source languages to Haitian. These Haitian compound nouns correspond to noncompound nouns in French. Hence, the compound *pye-bannan* 'banana tree' in Haitian corresponds to *bananier* 'banana tree' in French. The compounds in (1) are composed of two lexical units, each of which corresponds to a French word. Hence, *pye* 'tree' corresponds to French *pied* 'foot' and *bannan* 'banana' corresponds to French *banane* 'banana'. But as can be observed in (1), there is a systematic correspondence between the semantic units of compound nouns in Haitian and those of Fon. Haitian *pye* 'tree' corresponds to Fon *tín* 'tree' and Haitian *bannan* 'banana' corresponds to Fon *kwékwé* 'banana'.

(1)　　*Haitian*　　　　　　　*Fon*　　　　　　　　　　*French*
　　　　pye-bannan (tree-banana)　*kwékwé-tín* (banana-tree)　*bananier* 'banana tree'
　　　　pye-palmis (tree-palm)　　*dè-tín* (palm-tree)　　　　*palmier* 'palm tree'
　　　　po-bouch (skin-mouth)　　*nùe-fló* (mouth-skin)　　　*lèvre* 'lip'
　　　　po-je (skin-eye)　　　　　*nùekún-fló* (eye-skin)　　　*paupière* 'eyelid'
　　　　twu-nen (hole-nose)　　　*àɔntín-dó* (nose-hole)　　　*narine* 'nostril'
　　　　plim-je (hair-eye)　　　　*wuèn-ɖà* (eye-hair)　　　　*cil* 'eyelash'

The theory of relexification accounts for the division observed in (1). The Fon speakers searched for French phonetic strings corresponding to each of the lexical units of the compound words in Fon. This explains why Fon speakers did not simply adopt the French words *bananier* 'banana tree' or *paupière* 'eyelid'. Given the fact that word order within constituents is given as part of phonological sequences, it is to be expected that, in the relexified language, word order within constituents will pattern on the order found in the superstrate language rather than on the order found in the substrate language. Hence in (1), the Haitian compounds are left-headed, as in French, whereas the Fon compounds are right-headed (cf. Brousseau 1989).[3]

Our theory of relexification is formulated in terms that are sufficiently specific, so that it is possible to test its validity. We predict a systematic division in the lexical properties of a creole in comparison with its source languages. While phonetic strings are provided by the superstrate language, the syntactic/semantic properties are predicted to be derived from the substratum languages. If we were to find an arbitrary division of these properties in the lexicon of a given creole, the theory of relexification would be falsified.

1.2. How different is relexification from other approaches to creole genesis?

The systematic division between the respective contribution of the source languages to a given creole, predicted by our theory, is in agreement with Sylvain's (1936) claim that Haitian Creole consists of French phonetic matrices in a West African mould. It sets it apart, however, from the substratum theory proposed in Alleyne (1980). Alleyne's theory stipulates that creole languages have emerged through gradual transformation of West African languages spoken by the slaves under the influence of colonial languages. While this approach explains why creole languages present features of both African and European languages, it does not make any predictions as to the respective contribution of the source languages. The particular systematic division between the respective contribution of the source languages to a given creole also sets our theory apart from the proposal which advocates that creole languages correspond to a crystallized stage in the "imperfect" acquisition of a second language (e. g., Valdman 1978; Anderson 1983; Thomason 1983). The latter proposal does not explain why nor how creole languages crystallized in the form they have.

In our theory, the substratum languages contributed to almost all of the syntactic and the semantic properties of the creole. This accounts for the fact that the grammar of Haitian has all the typical properties which characterize the grammar of West African languages (e. g., verb serialization, predicate clefting, verb doubling, etc.).[4] From a typological point of view, then, Haitian is best classified as a West African language. This is in direct contrast with the claim that Haitian Creole is a Romance language (e. g., Faine 1937; Hall 1950; Hyppolite 1949; Pompilus 1955; Valdman 1978; Wittman – Fournier 1983). This is also in direct contrast with Seuren and Wekker's (1986) semantic transparency theory. Under the relexification hypothesis, the structure of creole languages does not reflect a "universal semantic structure" anymore than West African languages do.

Under the relexification hypothesis, the relexified language is created by speakers in possession of a mature grammar. Whatever name we give to this language variety (pidgin or creole), it constitutes the first instantiation of a new language, in this case, Haitian. Hence in our view, the creole is not created by people deprived of a model for language, as is advocated in Bickerton (1981). In the theory of relexification, the relexified language, the creole, consists of a mature adult grammar, which is parallel to the non-relexified original grammars of the substratum languages. This aspect of our theory is in direct opposition to the "foreigner" or "baby talk" approach to creole genesis (e. g., Göbl-Gáldi 1934; Ferguson 1964, 1971). It is the relexified language which is presented to a first generation of children who learn the creole as their native language. The grammar is not impoverished in any way; it is simply relexified. Consequently, under the theory of relexification, there is no break in the natural transmission of language from parents to children. This aspect of our theory is in direct contrast with Bickerton's (1981) "universalist" theory. Bickerton claims that in situations where creole languages are created, the children are deprived of an adult model for language and that this situation creates a break in the normal transmission of language from generation to generation. The lack of an adult model activates the potential or capacity for language (the bioprogram). This results in the invention of a new language, a creole, by these children.

1.3. How different is Haitian Creole from other reported cases of relexification?

Media Lengua, documented in Muysken (1981), is characterized by a Quechua syntax and by a lexicon drawn from two sources. While lexical items defined by major features, $[\alpha \text{ N}, \beta \text{ V}]$, are almost entirely of a Spanish form, affixes and functional lexical items are of the Quechua form. This is shown in (2), taken from Muysken (1981).

(2)   *no sé*   (Spanish)
       mana yacha-ni-chu (Quechua)
       no   sabi- hi- chu (Media lengua)
       NEG know 1   VAL
       'I do not know.'

It thus appears that, in this case, only major lexical items have been relexified.

The case of Métif, spoken by the French Métis of Canada (cf. Papen 1988; Bakker 1989), differs from Media Lengua in the following way. While verbs and verbal affixes are of the Cree form, the lexical categories related to the noun phrase, major as well as minor, are of the French form. This is illustrated in (3), taken from Papen (1988).

(3)   *Li soldad de amêrik li nabimâ zun   ver   kulör*
        The soldiers of America the clothes yellow green color
        kiskam-wak.
        wear-3PL
        'The American soldiers wear a khaki uniform.'

In this case, both major and minor lexical items appear to have been relexified, but relexification has applied only to lexical elements related to the projection of nouns.

We consider that Haitian Creole constitutes a third case of relexification. In Haitian, all lexical categories, minor as well as major, have been relexified, regardless of the nature of the projection. This will be illustrated by the case study that follows.

2. The clausal determiner is the head of AGRP in Fon and in Haitian

In the second part of my paper I show that the structure of the Haitian clause is remarkably parallel to the structure of the Fon clause. Both languages exhibit a clausal determiner, which I will argue is the head of AGRP. The difference between Haitian/Fon and French is that in the former the head of AGRP is defined by the feature [α deictic] whereas in the latter it is defined by the features [α person, β number].[5]

2.1. Preliminary remarks

In the recent literature on the decomposition of INFL, it has been proposed that AGR-S and T each head a separate projection rather than a single projection (Pollock 1989). On the basis of data drawn from past-participle agreement in French, Kayne (1989) argues for a projection of AGR-O. Chomsky (1989) further argues that there are two AGR projections in a tensed clause in languages like French and English: AGR-S which is defined by the features corresponding to the morphology of agreement between a tensed verb and its subject, and AGR-O which is defined by the features corresponding to the morphology of agreement between a past participle and its object. Furthermore, it is proposed that AGRP-S and AGRP-O constitute domains for Case assignment where Case is assigned through Spec-Head agreement. According to this proposal, the structure of the clause for languages like French and English is as in (4).

(4)   French/English

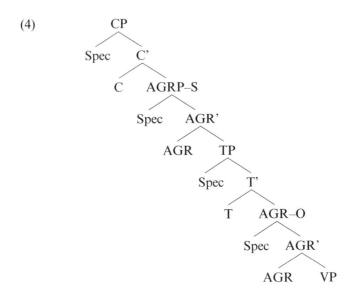

In the following sections, I present four arguments showing that the clausal determiner in Haitian and Fon is the head of AGRP. Under this proposal, the structure of the clause in Haitian and in Fon is as in (5), which except for the fact that AGRP is head final, is parallel to (4).

(5)   Haitian/Fon

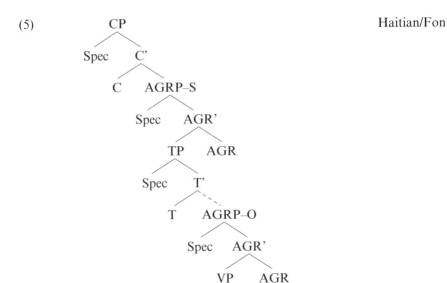

Before presenting the arguments, I present a short introduction to the determiner in these languages.

The determiner has the following allomorphs: *la, (n)an, a* in Haitian and *lɔ́, ɔ́n, ɔ́* in Fon. The determiner may occur with NPs as in (6).

(6) *lari a* (Haitian)
     àlì ɔ́ (Fon)
     street DET
     'The street (that we see or that we know of)'

While the determiner in French is defined by the feature [α definite], the determiner of Haitian and Fon is best characterized by the feature [+ deictic], as has been suggested in Fournier (1977), Lefebvre–Fournier (1978), and Lefebvre (1982) for Haitian, and in Lefebvre (1986) for Fon. The determiner can be used in one of the three following situations: when the NP has already been mentioned in discourse, when reference to the NP is made explicit by the situational context, or when the NP in question refers to what is part of shared knowledge. Following the analysis in Lefebvre–Massam (1988), and in Lumsden (1989, 1990) for Haitian, and the analysis in Brousseau–Lumsden (1990) for Fon, I will assume that in the context of a noun phrase the determiner heads a projection DP. As can be seen in (6), DP is head final. DET takes the NP as its complement. The head of DP remains lexically unfilled in a [– deictic] context. With Lefebvre–Massam (1988), I will assume that the lexical determiner is in complementary distribution with a phonologically null determiner.

(7) *lari ∅* (Haitian)
     àlì ∅ (Fon)
     street
     'a/any street'

In both languages, the [+ deictic] determiner may also occur in the context of a clause as in (8).[6] Crucially, the clause containing a determiner may be assigned two meanings, a fact which will be shown to follow from the theory that there are two positions for the clausal determiner.

(8) a. *Jan rive Pòtoprens la.* (Haitian)
        Kɔkú wá Kútɔ̀nù ɔ́. (Fon)
        J/K arrive P/K   DET
        'Actually Jan/Koku has arrived at Port-au-Prince/Cotonou'
        or 'Jan/Koku has arrived at Port-au-Prince/Cotonou as we knew he would.'

Like with noun phrases, the determiner occurring in clauses is in complementary distribution with a phonologically null determiner. Observe the contrast in meaning between (8) and (9).

(9)   *Jan   rive   Pòtoprens ∅.*   (Haitian)
        Kɔkú   wá   Kútɔnù   ∅.   (Fon)
        J/K   arrive P/K   DET
        'Jan/Koku has arrived at Port-au-Prince/Cotonou.'

In light of this preliminary information about the determiner in the two languages, I now turn to the arguments showing that the clausal determiner is the head of AGRP.[7, 8]

2.2. The semantics of clauses in the context of a clausal determiner

In the context of a clausal determiner, the clause may be assigned two interpretations. I will argue that these correspond to two positions for the determiner in the clause.

First, the interpretation of the clause entails an assertion or an emphasis on the truth value of the clause. In this case, the meaning of the clause is rendered as 'actually', 'really'. Examples are provided in (10) and (11).

(10)   *Ròb   la   blan   an*   (Haitian)
        Àvɔ   ɔ   wé   ɔ   (Fon)
        dress   DET   be-white   DET
        'The dress is really white.'

(11)   *Jan   rive   Pòtoprens la.*   (Haitian)
        Kɔkú   wá   Kútɔnù   ɔ.   (Fon)
        J/K   arrive P/K   DET
        'Actually Jan/Koku has arrived at Port-au-Prince/Cotonou.'

Second, in the context of a clausal determiner, a clause like *John has arrived at X* may be interpreted as 'John has arrived at X, the arrival that is known of or 'the arrival that is expected'. In this case, the presence of the [+ deictic] determiner entails that the event referred to is part of shared knowledge, in the sense that participants know that the event took place, or expect it to have taken place at the moment of speech. Informants of both languages render this interpretation by 'as expected/ as we knew event x would happen'. Examples are provided in (12) and (13).

(12)   *Jan   rive   Pótoprens la.*   (Haitian)
       Kòkú wá   Kútɔ̀nù   ɔ́.   (Fon)
       J/K   arrive P/K   DET
       'Jan/Koku arrived at Port-au-Prince/Cotonou as expected.'

(13)   *Jan   vòle   manchin nan   an.*   (Haitian)
       Kɔ̀kú fìn   mɔ́tò   ɔ́   ɔ́.   (Fon)
       J/K   steal car   DET DET
       'Jan/Kɔ̀kú stole the car as expected/as we knew.'

The two interpretations assigned to a clause containing a clausal determiner are not unrelated. In both cases deixis is involved.[9] The difference
between the two appears to be a difference in scope. In the first case, the
determiner has scope over the clause; the interpretation of the clause is
speaker-oriented. In the second case the determiner appears to have scope
over a projection of V; the interpretation is event-oriented. In (10) and
(11) the determiner heads AGRP-S, yielding a wide-scope interpretation
(i. e., on the clause). In (12) and (13) the determiner heads AGRP-O
yielding a narrow-scope interpretation (i. e., on a projection of V).

   In the next section, I argue that these two positions are independently
motivated.

2.3. Spec-Head agreement in deixis within AGRPs

2.3.1. Agreement facts within AGRP-S

In the context of a [− deictic] subject, the determiner cannot appear as
the head of AGRP-S as is shown by the ungrammaticality of the sentences in (14). Notice that this fact is independent of whether or not the
objects is [+ deictic].

(14)   a. **Nèg   vòle   manchin (nan)   an.*   (Haitin)
          *Súnù fìn   mɔ́tò   (ɔ́)   ɔ.   (Fon)
          man   steal car   DET   DET
          ['Literally: 'Actually a man stole a/the car.']
       b. **Nèg   wè   vòlè   (yo)   a.*[10]   (Haitian)
          *Súnù mɔ̀ àjòtɔ́ (lέ)   ɔ́.   (Fon)
          man   see thief PL   DET
          [Literally: 'A man really saw (the) thieves.']
       c. **Nèg   kònnèn kreyòl   la.*   (Haitian)
          *Súnù sè   fɔ̀ngbè   ɔ́.   (Fon)
          man   know   Haitian/Fon DET
          [Literally: 'A man really knows Haitian/Fon.']

    d. **Ròb blan   an.*   (Haitian)
       *Àvɔ̀ wé   ɔ́.   (Fon)
       dress white DET
       [Literally: 'A dress is really white.']

    e. **Moun rive   Pòtoprens la.*   (Haitian)
       *Súnù wá   Kútɔ́nù   ɔ́.   (Fon)
       man   arrive P/K   DET
       [Literally: 'Actually a man has arrived at Port-au-Prince/Cotonou.']

By contrast, in the context of a [+ deictic] subject the determiner can appear as head of AGRP-S, as shown in (15).

(15)   a. *Nèg la   vòle machin (nan) an.*   (Haitian)
       Súnù ɔ́   fin mɔ́tò (ɔ́)   ɔ́.   (Fon)
       man DET steal car   DET DET
       'Actually the man stole a/the car.'

    b. *Jan   wè vòlè (yo) a.*   (Haitian)
       Kɔ̀kú mɔ̀ àjòtɔ́ (lé) ɔ́.   (Fon)
       J/K   see thief PL   DET
       'Jan/Koku really saw (the) thieves.'

    c. *Jan   kònnèn kreyòl   la.*   (Haitian)
       Kɔ̀kú sè   fɔ̀ngbè   ɔ́.   (Fon)
       J/K   know   Haitin/Fon DET
       'Jan/Koku really knows Haitian/Fon.'

    d. *Ròb la   blan   an.*   (Haitian)
       Àvɔ̀ ɔ́   wé   ɔ́.   (Fon)
       dress DET white DET
       'The dress is really white.'

    e. *Moun nan   rive Pòtoprens la.*   (Haitian)
       Súnù ɔ́   wá   Kútɔ́nù   ɔ́.   (Fon)
       man   DET arrive P/K   DET
       'Actually the man has arrived at Port-au-Prince/Cotonou.'

The fact that the subject of the clause must be [+ deictic] in the context of an overt determiner is evidence for the projection AGRP-S.

Notice from the examples in (15) that the clausal determiner as head of AGRP-S is compatible with various types of predicates: (15 a) contains an affectedness verb, and (15 b) an unaffectedness verb; (15 c, d) exhibit individual-level predicates; (15 e) contains an ergative verb. While the clausal determiner as head of AGRP-S is compatible with various types of predicates, the clausal determiner as head of AGRP-O is not, as will be shown below.

From the data discussed in this section, we can see that a cluster of properties is associated with the determiner as head of AGRP-S. The determiner can appear in the context of a [+ deictic] subject. Semantically, the truth value of the clause is asserted or emphasized, an interpretation which follows from agreement in deixis between the subject of the clause and the head AGRP-S. Finally, the determiner in head of AGRP-S is compatible with various types of predicates.

2.3.2. Agreement facts within AGRP-O

Just as there is agreement within AGRP-S, there is agreement within AGRP-O. In the context of a [− deictic] object, the determiner cannot appear as head of AGRP-O. This is illustrated by the ungrammaticality of (16) in which the object is [− deictic]. Example (16) also shows that this result is obtained regardless of whether or not the subject is [+ deictic].

(16)   a. *Nèg (la) vòle manchin nan. (Haitian)
          *Súnù (ó) fin mótò ó.   (Fon)
          man (DET) steal car   DET
          [Literally: 'A/the man stole a car as expected.']

    b. *Nèg (la) manje pen an. (Haitian)
          *Súnù (ó) ɖù bléɖì ó.   (Fon)
          man DET eat   bread DET
          [Literally: 'A/the man has eaten bread as expected.']

    c. *Nèg (la) bay ti-moun liv la. (Haitian)
          *Súnù (ó) ná vǐ   wèmá ó. (Fon)
          man DET give child   book DET
          [Literally: 'A/the man gave a child a book as expected.']

    d. *Moun (nan) pati mache a. (Haitian)
          *Súnù (ó) yì àxì   ó.   (Fon)
          man the go market DET
          [Literally: 'A/the man went to a market as expected.']

By contrast, in the context of a [+ deictic] object, the determiner can appear as head of AGRP-O.

(17)   a. Nèg (la) vòle manchin nan an. (Haitian)
          Súnù (ó) fin mótò ó ó. (Fon)
          man the steal car   DET DET
          'A/the man stole the car as expected (the theft of the car would take place).'

b. *Nèg (la) manje pen   an   an.*   (Haitian)
   Súnù (ɔ́) ù   bléɖì ɔ́ ɔ́.   (Fon)
   man DET eat   bread DET DET
   'A/the man has eaten the bread as expected (the eating of the
   bread would take place).'

c. *Nèg (la) bay ti-moun nan liv   la.*   (Haitian)
   Súnù (ɔ́) ná vǐ ɔ́   wèmá ɔ́.   (Fon)
   man DET give child   book DET
   'A/the man gave the child a book as expected (the giving [of
   a book] to the child would take place).'

d. *Moun (nan) pati gran-mache   a.*   (Haitian)
   Súnù (ɔ́) yì dàntókpá   ɔ́.   (Fon)
   man the go   central-market DET
   'A/the man went to the central market as expected (he would
   go to the central market).'

On the basis of the contrast in grammaticality between (15) and (16), one
could be led to the conclusion that [+ deictic] objects are sufficient for
the determiner to appear as head of AGRP-O.

   This is not the case, however. Consider the ungrammatical sentences
in (18), in which the object is [+ deictic].

(18)   a. **Jan wè vòlè yo a.*   (Haitian)
          *Kɔ̀kú mì àjòtɔ́ lέ ɔ́   (Fon)
          J/K   see thief PL DET
          [Literally: 'Jan/Koku saw the thieves as expected.']

       b. **Jan kònnèn kreyòl   la a.*   (Haitian)
          *Kɔ̀kú sè   fɔngbè   ɔ́ ɔ́.   (Fon)
          J/K   know   Haitian/Fon DET DET
          [Literally: 'Jan/Koku knows Haitian/Fon as expected.']

How can we account for the difference in grammaticality between the
sentences in (17) and the sentences in (16) and (18)?

   The sentences in (17) contain a verb with an affected object (e. g., *steal,
eat, give*). The affected object is [+ deictic]. It delimits (in the sense of
Tenny 1987) the event denoted by the verb. In *X ate the bread* (cf. [17 b],
for example, the [+ deictic] affected object imposes an end point to the
event of eating. When all the bread has been eaten, the event is over. The
sentences in (16) differ minimally from those in (17). In (16) the affected
objects of the same verbs are [− deictic]. [− deictic] objects do not delimit
the event denoted by an affectedness verb. In *X ate bread* (cf. [16 b]), for

example, the [− deictic] affected object does not entail an end point to the event of eating. The minimal difference between the data in (16) and the data in (17) thus appears to be that in the latter case there is a delimiter of event, while in the former there is not. In the sentences in (17) the determiner in head of AGRP-O can appear, while in the sentences in (16) it cannot. This suggests that it is the delimiter (which is obligatorily [+ deictic]) which makes it possible for the determiner to appear in head of AGRP-O.

In light of this analysis, the ungrammaticality of the data in (18) is easily explained. In (18 a) the internal argument of the verb *see* is [+ deictic]. However, the internal argument of *see* is not an affected object, and even though it is [+ deictic], it does not delimit the event denoted by the verb. The clause in (18 b) contains an individual-level predicate. Individual-level predicates denote a permanent property of an individual. By defitinition, individual-level predicates are not delimited.

The proposal that it is the delimiting argument which is crucial to the fact that the determiner in head of AGRP-O is permitted, is supported by the following data.[11] In a clause containing an affectedness verb like *give*, but in which the goal, which is the delimiting argument for such a verb, is not overtly manifested, the clausal determiner is not permitted. This holds even in the context of [+ deictic] theme.[12]

(19)   *Jan   te   bay   [liv   yo]   a.   (Haitian)
         *Kɔ̀kú   kó   ná   [wèmá   lɛ́]   ɔ́.   (Fon)
         J/K   T   give   book   PL   DET
         [Literally: 'Jan/Koku gave the books away as expected.']

A cluster of properties is associated with the determiner in the head of AGRP-O. The determiner is permitted in the context of a delimiting argument of the predicate of the clause. Consequently, the determiner is only compatible with a delimited predicate. Semantically, the presence of the determiner induces an interpretation which entails shared knowledge of the event or an expectation that the event will have taken place at the moment of speech. This interpretation follows from the fact that, in this context, there is agreement in deixis between the delimiter and the head of AGRP-O.[13]

2.3.3. Spec-Head agreement in deixis

The facts described in sections 2.3.1 and 2.3.2 can be accounted for by Spec-Head agreement. I assume that by S-Structure, the position Spec of AGRP-S will be filled by the subject of the clause.

(20)

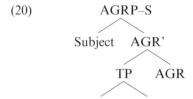

I assume that delimiting arguments are base generated in the node sister to the verb. Regardless of the thematic role that they bear, these arguments share the following property: they impose an end point to the event denoted by the verb. I further assume that the position sister to the verb is restricted to delimiting arguments. Under this proposal, all other arguments will be associated with specifier positions in the syntactic tree. This dichotomy is represented in (21).

(21)

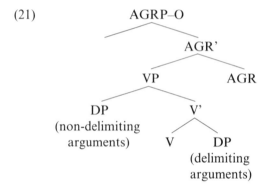

By S-Structure, delimiting arguments will have moved from their basic position to the specifier position of AGRP-O as in (22).

(22)

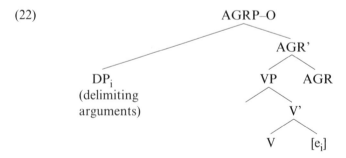

By S-Structure, both projections of AGR will contain a DP in their specifier position, hence exhibiting an appropriate configuration for Spec-Head agreement.

Since the feature of the head of the projection is [α deictic], Spec-Head agreement has to be formulated in terms of this feature.[14] Following the general proposal that Spec-Head agreement is the means by which Case is assigned to the noun phrase in Spec of AGRP, I assume that nominative Case and objective Case are assigned within AGRP-S and AGRP-O, respectively. The specifications concerning Spec-Head agreement (and case assignment within these projections) in Haitian and Fon are discussed in Lefebvre (to appear).

The fact that the subject of the clause and the head of AGRP-S agree in deixis and the fact that the delimiting argument and the head of AGRP-O agree in deixis, provide strong evidence for the proposal that there are two positions for the clausal determiner in Haitian and in Fon. Under an analysis where there would be only one syntactic position for the clausal determiner, it would be impossible to account for the agreement facts.

Furthermore, the fact that the determiner as head of AGRP-S is compatible with a wide range of predicates, whereas the determiner as head of AGRP-O is compatible with a very specific type of predicates, namely delimited predicates, constitutes another argument supporting the proposal that there are two syntactic positions for the clausal determiner. Again, under an analysis where there would be only one syntactic position for the clausal determiner, it would be impossible to account for these facts.

On the basis of the data discussed in this section, I conclude that there are two independently motivated positions for the clausal determiner.

Additional data involving the distribution of the clausal determiner in the context of negation provide further evidence that there are two syntactic positions for the clausal determiner. In this context, the two positions for the clausal determiner are directly accessible from the distribution of functional lexical items at surface structure.

2.4. The clausal determiner in the context of negation

In Fon, negation can be encoded by the marker *má* (cf. (23)) or by the counterfactual marker *ǎ* (cf. (24)).

(23)   *Kòfí má   sà   mɔ̀tɔ̀ ɔ́.*   Fon
         Kofi NEG sell car   DET
         'Kofi did not sell the car.'

(24)   *Kòfî wá   ǎ.*   Fon
          I   arrive CFM
          'I believe that Koku has not arrived.'

As can be seen from the above examples, while *má* occurs between the subject and the verb, *ǎ* occurs after the verb. Following the analysis in da Cruz (1994) I will assume that *má* is the head of the projection NEGP. Following the analysis in da Cruz (1994) I will assume that *ǎ* is the head of a functional category hosting markers which give the point of view of the speaker on the proposition. This is shown in (25).

(25)   AGRP–S   Fon

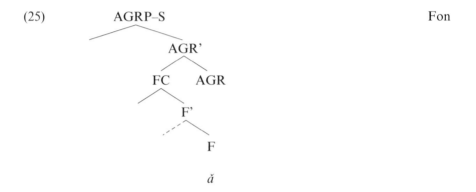

In Haitian, negation is expressed with *pa* as in (26).

(26)   *Jan   pa   rive.*   Haitian
          John NEG   arrive
          'John has not arrived.'

Following the analysis in DeGraff (1993) I will assume that *pa* is the head of NEGP. To the best of my knowledge, in Haitian, there is no counter-factual marker corresponding to Fon *ǎ*.

I now turn to the discussion of the clausal determiner in the context of negation. The Fon and the Haitian data will be discussed in turn.

There are two surface positions in Fon for the determiner with respect to the counter-factual marker. The determiner can precede it, as in (27), or it can follow it, as in (28). In (27) the determiner is assigned the interpretation which corresponds to its position as AGR-O. It precedes the counter-factual marker and hence it does not have scope over that marker. The interpretation is that the event denoted by the verb would have taken place at the moment of speech.

(27)   *Súnù ɔ́ fìn mɔ́tò ɔ̀ ɔ̀ ǎ.*   (Fon)
           man   DET steal car   DET DET NEG
           'The man did not steal the car as expected.'

In (28) the determiner is assigned the interpretation which corresponds to its position as AGR-S. The determiner has scope over the counter-factual marker.

(28)   *Súnù ɔ́ fìn mɔ́tò ɔ̀ ǎ ɔ́.*   (Fon)
           man   DET steal car   DET NEG DET
           'Actually the man did not steal the car.'

This distribution suggests that when the determiner precedes the negation particle, it is in the head of AGRP-O and that when it follows the negation particle, it is in the head of AGRP-S. This suggestion is confirmed by agreement phenomena.

When the determiner precedes the counter-factual marker, it is permitted only in the context of a [+ deictic] delimiting argument. In (29), where the affected object is [− deictic], the determiner is not licit. In (30) where the affected object is [+ deictic], the determiner is licit.

(29)   **Súnù (ɔ́) fìn mɔ́tò ɔ̀ ǎ.*   (Fon)
           man   DET steal car   DET NEG
           [Literally: 'A/the man did not steal a car as expected.']

(30)   *Súnù (ɔ́) fìn mɔ́tò ɔ̀ ɔ̀ ǎ.*   (Fon)
           man   DET steal car   DET DET NEG
           'A/the man did not steal the car as expected.'

The fact that the determiner preceding negation is permitted only in the context of a [+ deictic] affected object shows that when the determiner precedes the negation marker, it must be the head of AGRP-O.

Similarly, when the determiner follows the counter-factual particle, it is permitted only in the context of a [+ deictic] external argument as is illustrated by the contrast in grammaticality between (31), where the subject is [− deictic] and (32) where the subject is [+ deictic].

(31)   **Súnù (ɖé) fìn mɔ́tò (ɔ́) ǎ ɔ́.*   (Fon)
           man   a   steal car   DET NEG DET
           [Literally: 'Actually a man did not steal a/the car.']

(32)   *Súnù ɔ́ fìn mɔ́tò (ɔ́) ǎ ɔ́.*   (Fon)
           man   DET steal car   DET NEG DET
           'Actually the man did not steal a/the car.'

The fact that the determiner following the counter-factual marker is permitted only in the context of [+ deictic] external argument shows that when the determiner follows that marker, it is in head of AGRP-S.

The distribution of the determiner with respect to the counter-factual marker further supports the hypothesis that there are two positions for the clausal determiner. There are two surface positions for the clausal determiner with respect to the counter-factual marker. For each of these surface positions, the meaning conveyed by the presence of the clausal determiner and the agreement phenomena correspond to those associated with AGRP-O and AGRP-S, respectively.

Since Haitian does not have a counter-factual marker, the distribution discussed for Fon is not directly accessible in word order in this language. Nonetheless, the same interpretive facts obtain. The clause in (33) contains a [+ deictic] subject and a delimiting argument. It may be assigned an interpretation in which the determiner has scope over negation, (as in the first alternative in [33]), and an interpretation in which the determiner does not have scope over negation, (as in the second alternative in [33]).

(33)   *Nèg la   pa vòle manchin nan   an.*   (Haitian)
        man DET not steal car   DET DET
        'Actually the man did not steal the car' or,
        'The man did not steal the car as expected.'

In the context of a [− deictic] subject, the first interpretation does not obtain.

(34)   **Nèg pa   vòle manchin (nan) an.*   (Haitian)
        man DET not steal   car   DET
        'Literally: 'Actually a man did not steal a/the car.']

In the context of a non-delimited predicate, the second interpretation does not obtain.

(35)   **Nèg (la)   pa vòle manchin nan.*   (Haitian)
        man DET not steal car   DET
        [Literally: 'A/the man did not steal a car as expected.']

These facts can be derived from the analysis that there are two positions for the determiner. The first interpretation in (33) follows from the analysis that the clausal determiner heads AGRP-S, and the second interpretation follows from the analysis that the determiner heads AGRP-O.[15]

2.5. Deixis and finiteness

The distribution of the clausal determiner is related to the finite character of the clause. The clausal determiner is not overtly manifested in [− T] clauses. In both Haitian and Fon, the verb *want* may take an infinitival complement as in (36). Infinitival complements have neither a [+ T] complementizer nor a tense marker.

(36) *Li vle   ale Pòtoprens.* (Haitian)
      É jló   ná yì Kútɔ́nù.   (Fon)
      he want to go P/K
      'He wants to go to Port-au-Prince/Cotonou.'

The clausal determiner is excluded from the infinitival complement of *want*. In (37) the determiner cannot be associated with either of the two AGR positions within the infinitival complement.[16]

(37) **Li vle   ale Pòtoprens la.*   (Haitian)
      È   jló ná   yì Kútɔ́nù   ɔ́.   (Fon)
      he   want to go P/K   DET

   Tense expresses deixis in time, since it situates an event/state with respect to the moment of speech (prior to, subsequent to, or coinciding with, the moment of speech). The data in (36) and (37) show that a clause or an event cannot be the object of a deictic functional category if they are not situated in time. Hence the [+ deictic] feature of the clausal determiner is incompatible with the [− T] feature of the clause. Finite clauses are temporal R-expressions (cf. Chomsky 1981). Suppose that the fact that finite clauses are R-expressions allows them to be the object of a [+ deictic] determiner (as head of AGRP-S). Similarly, suppose that the fact that an event is part of an R-expression (a tensed clause) allows it to be the object of a [+ deictic] determiner (as head of AGRP-O). Conversely, a clause or an event which is not an R-expression could not be the object of a [+ deictic] determiner. This explanation would account for the fact that the clausal determiner will not be manifested in a [− T] clause in either AGR-S or AGR-O.

   Finally, there can be only one instantiation of the determiner per clause as is shown by the ungrammaticality of (38), in which both AGR positions are being filled.

(38) **Li pa rive   Pòtoprens la   a.* (Haitian)
      **É   wá   Kútɔ́nù   ɔ́   ǎ   ɔ́.* (Fon)
      he   not arrive P/K   DET NEG DET

The surface distribution of the [+ deictic] determiner in Haitian and Fon may be related to the structure of events as discussed in Van Voorst (1988). In Van Voorst's analysis, the subject marks the starting point of an event and the delimiter the end point of that event. The fact that there can be only one overt determiner per clause follows from the fact that deixis cannot bear on both the starting point of an event (the subject) and the end point of that event (the delimiter). This is analogous to the fact that there can be only one tense per clause. An event cannot be situated (hence be the object of tense deixis) at two different points in time with respect to the moment of speech.

The fact that there is a correlation between the distribution of the clausal determiner and the finite character of the clause constitutes another aspect of the parallelism of this functional category with AGR in languages like French and English.

2.6. Summary

There are three arguments supporting the theory that there are two independently motivated positions for the clausal determiner in Haitian and in Fon: 1) two interpretations; 2) two domains of agreement; and 3) two surface positions with respect to negation. AGR-S/O in French and the projection of the clausal determiner in Haitian and Fon are parallel with respect to the following features: 1) the two positions for AGR have the same distribution; 2) the projections of AGR in both types of languages are projections within which Spec-Head agreement takes place; 3) in both types of languages there is a relationship between overt agreement and the finite character of the clause. These facts provide ample arguments for an analysis of the clausal determiner in Haitian/Fon as head of AGRP-S/O.

The similarity in the structure of the clause of Haitian and Fon follows from the fact that in both languages the head of AGRP is defined by the feature [α deictic]. Hence, Haitian and Fon do not lack agreement. It is simply that in these languages, the feature which defines the terms of the agreement is different from those which define agreement in French: [α person, β number].

An analysis holding that the clausal determiner is not AGR in Haitian/ Fon imposes a big burden on the language learner. Under such an analysis, the Haitian/Fon child would have to figure out whether his language has AGR or not. This decision-making process leads him to the conclusion that his language does not have AGR but some other functional category. Which one? Why two positions? Why agreement within these projections? How is case assigned? Why is it that the determiner does not occur in [− T] clauses?

If, however, we posit that the clausal determiner heads AGR, it reduces the burden of the language learner. If AGR is given by universal grammar, the Haitian/Fon child only has to figure out the feature(s) of the head on the basis of the morphology available in its language. When he has discovered that AGR is specified for the feature [+ deictic], he immediately knows that there are two positions for the clausal determiner and that agreement proceeds according to the feature he has identified. Case assignment under Spec-Head agreement follows from general principles of Universal Grammar. So does the fact that the determiner is not overtly manifested in [− T] clauses.

What are the consequences of the facts discussed above for a theory of creole genesis?

3. Back to creole genesis

3.1. AGR in Haitian/Fon and the theory of relexification

The structure of the Haitian clause is identical to that of Fon: both languages exhibit a head-final [+ deictic] determiner heading the projection AGRP-S/O. The fact that the distribution and function of the clausal determiner in Haitian is identical to the distribution and function of the clausal determiner in Fon, strongly suggests that the clausal determiner of Fon has been relexified by *la*. What is the phonetic source of *la*?

Suppose that with Fournier (1977: 8), Wittman and Fournier (1983: 193) and Valdman (1978), we assume that the deictic French adverb *là* 'there' is the phonetic source of the Haitian determiner *la*.[17] The deictic adverbial *là* may occur after major constituents in nonstandard varieties of French. This usage of the deictic adverb has been attested since the seventeenth century (cf. Flutre 1970: 141, 146; Hull 1975: 2). This is exemplified in (39).

(39)   a. *L'homme là* ... (Wittman−Fournier 1983: 193; Hull 1975: 2)
         The man there ...
         'The man in question ...'

  b. *L'homme là,   qui   a fait ça   là, .../ Un homme*
     The man there, who did   that there   A   man
     là, ...   (Québec French)
     there, ...
     'The man in question, who did that .../A man there, ...

First, this deictic adverbial comes at the end of constituents and hence it is in the right position to relexify the head-final determiner of Fon.[18] Second, the deictic adverbial *là* shares the feature [+ deictic] with the clausal determiner of Fon, which makes it a good candidate to relexify the Fon clausal determiner.[19] Under this proposal then, the deictic adverbial *là* of French would have contributed the phonetic matrix of the clausal determiner of Haitian.[20] The syntactic properties of the determiner as head of AGRP, however, are provided by Fon, as was evidenced in the second part of this paper. The phonological processes undergone by this lexical item are also given by the Fon grammar. While the Haitian determiner presents the allomorphs in (40 a), the Fon determiner presents the allomorphs in (40 b). The French adverbial *là* presents no allomorphs.

(40)   a. *la, (n)an, a*
        b. *lɔ́, ɔ́n, ɔ́*

Assuming that the above scenario is correct, I take the data discussed in the second part of this paper to strongly support the theory of relexification presented in the first part of this paper.

As is predicted by the relexification hypothesis, there is a principled division in the Haitian data with respect to its source languages. French contributed to the phonetic matrix of the clausal determiner, and Fon contributed to the semantics as it is tied to the syntax of AGR (and phonological processes).

The fact that AGRP may be headed by a [+ deictic] determiner is a specific property of Fon, and presumably of other West African languages. Hence, Haitian is best characterized as a West African language rather than as a Romance language. In Romance languages the head of AGRP is defined by the features [α person, β number]. Similarly, the very specific property of AGR in Haitian, which corresponds to the property of AGR in Fon, that of being headed by a [+ deictic] determiner, does not support the proposal that creoles reflect a semantic universal structure.

The remarkable parallelism between the structure of the clause in Haitian and in Fon, due to the specific property of AGR in both languages supports the proposal that Fon was relexified by West African speakers in possession of a mature grammar. The data discussed above strongly support the claim that it was the relexified variety of Fon which was offered as a model to the first generation of native speakers of Haitian. Given the striking parallelism between the Haitian and the Fon clause structure, it would be quite a remarkable coincidence if children had created the Haitian clausal system (equivalent to the Fon clausal system) in the absence of an adult model. Hence, the data support a theory where no break in regular transmission of language is postulated. The data rather suggest that the first generation of Haitian native speakers acquired AGR the same way other children do.

The facts presented on the determiner as head of AGR in Haitian show Haitian speakers' competence in the "grammar of Fon" so to speak, not Haitian speakers' competence in an intermediary stage between Fon and French as would be the case under a L2, hypothesis of creole genesis. This claim is further supported by ongoing research on constructions such as predicate cleft, verb doubling, and by facts discussed in published work by members of our team.[21] When we look at the phonological strings which constitute the Haitian words, it is evident that the creators of Haitian did not have much access to French and certainly no formal instruction in the language. Examples are *dlo* 'water', which corresponds to three words in French, i. e., *de l'eau* 'water', *lari* 'street', which corresponds to two words in French, i. e., *la rue* 'the street', etc.

The fact that the head of a functional category like AGR has been relexified is a direct counterexample to Muysken's (1988) claim that functional categories do not relexify.

> [Functional categories] do not have a meaning outside the linguistic system that they are part of, since their meanings are paradigmatically defined within that linguistic system. So when you relexify a system of function words, automatically the semantic organization of the target language comes in, and the result is at best a compromise between source and target language systems. This conclusion is relevant to the substrate debate in creole studies as a whole. If the argument is correct, we must conclude that the only African features that could have been transmitted more or less intact through relexification are those dependent on properties of content words. This means: lexically determined-semantic distinctions and subcategorization features, but no syntactic properties related to function words. This consequence seems to me more or less on the right track, given the conflicting evidence for substratum so far. The strongest cases involve lexical properties of content words. (Muysken 1988: 15)

The situation that we hypothesize prevailed when Haitian Creole was created is the following. There were speakers of several West African languages speaking languages with relatively compatible grammars (cf. Singler 1986; Koopman, 1986), but with no common lexicons. If the slaves needed to communicate with the colonizers, more importantly, they needed to communicate among themselves. In order to do so, they needed a common lexicon. I suggest that this is what the creators of Haitian were busy trying to establish. Relexification was a means of creating this common lexicon in a relatively short period of time. This could be achieved without much direct exposure to French, and certainly without formal instruction in the language. Hence, the creators of Haitian were not concentrating on learning the syntactic and semantic properties of French words and certainly they were not trying to figure out what the features of AGR were in French. They were only using the French phonetic strings in order to provide new phonetic matrices for a common lexicon. Nonetheless, the grammatical properties which where associated with the relexified lexical entries were determined, on the one hand, by the distribution of French phonetic sequences, and on the other hand, by the properties already established for the corresponding lexical entries in the lexicon of West African languages. This enabled the first inhabitants of Haiti to produce clauses which were phonetically and semantically similar to French clauses and to decode the general meaning of the sentences produced by the French speakers (cf. Lefebvre–Lumsden 1989: 267).

Notes

1. The project is entitled "La genèse du créole haïtien: Un cas particulier d'investigation sur la forme de la grammaire universelle". The project is financed by CRSH, FCAR and FIR (Université Québec à Montréal). I would like to thank John Lumsden, Robert Papen, Elizabeth Ritter, Elizabeth Cowper, Lisa Travis, Lydia White, and the participants in the workshop held in Leiden for their comments on an earlier version of this paper. I thank the native speakers of Haitian and Fon who provided me with the data analysed in this paper: Jean-Robert Placide and Ange-Marie Clerjeune from Haiti, and Maxime Dacruz and Irénée Fandohan from Benin.

2. For a preliminary discussion on word order in Haitian, see Lefebvre–Lumsden (1989). For a more elaborate discussion on word order in relexification, see Lefebvre–Lumsden (in preparation).

3. For discussions on the position of the morphological head, see Brousseau–Filipovich–Lefebvre (1989).

4. For serialization, see Déchaine (1988), Lefebvre (1989). For predicate cleft, see Lumsden–Lefebvre (1990), Lefebvre (1990), Lefebvre–Larson (1991). For verb doubling constructions, see Piou (1982), Lefebvre–Ritter (1989) and Lefebvre–Ritter (to appear).

5. The data and analysis presented in this section are drawn from a more extensive study on the clausal determiner in Haitian and Fon as head of AGRP (cf. Lefebvre, to appear).

6. Cf. Lefebvre (1982), Lefebvre (1986) and Lefebvre−Massam (1988) where it is shown that the clausal determiner may occur in a wide range of matrix clauses (e. g., declarative, interrogative, direct questions) and subordinate clauses (e. g., indirect questions, relative clauses, adverbial clauses).

7. The clausal determiner is similar to the nominal determiner in both languages with respect to the following features. First, in both environments the projection of the determiner is head final (cf. [6] and [8]). Second, in both environments the determiner undergoes the same phonological processes yielding numerous variants: *la, (n)an, an* (cf. Tinelli 1970; Valdman 1976 and Fournier 1978) for Haitian, and *ló, ó, ón* (cf. Lefebvre 1986) for Fon. Third, in both cases, the syntactic feature which defines the determiner is [+ deictic] (as will become clear in section 1). Fourth, in both environments, the determiner is in complementary distribution with a phonologically null determiner (cf. [7] and [9]). Finally, in both contexts there appears to be a surface filter, preventing the succession at S-Structure of several determiners presenting the same phonological shape. There is a lot of variation among speakers with respect to this surface filter. For some Haitian speakers the filter applies to any two contiguous determiners (cf. Lefebvre 1982). For other speakers, the filter applies when two contiguous determiners appear with the same number specification and it does not apply in the context where determiners appear with different number specification (cf. Lumsden 1989). Finally for another group of speakers (those who were informants for this paper), the filter applies only when two consecutive determiners have the same phonological shape. For Fon no extensive study of this phenomenon has been conducted as yet. In the course of doing fieldwork in Benin (November 1989, August 1990), I noticed that the patterns found for Fon speakers of Cotonou are parallel to those found for Haitian speakers. Speakers from Abomey, however, do not seem to have that filter since they accept and produce several determiners in a row, regardless of their number and phonological form.

8. The following facts dismiss the possibility that the clausal determiner be analyzed as a complementizer. In both languages, the clausal determiner occurs in embedded clauses (as in [i] and [ii]), as well as in matrix clauses (cf. [8]).

    (i)   *M kwè (ke) li rive   Pòtoprens la.* (Haitian)
            Ùn ɖì   ɖò   wá Kútónù   (Fon)
            I believe COMP he arrive P/K DET
            'I believe that he has actually at Pòtoprens/Kút' or,
            'I believe that he has arrived at Pòtoprens/Kút as expected.'
    (ii)   *M vle pou u vini   an.* (Haitian)
            Ùn jló nú   à ná wá ó. (Fon)
            I want COMP you to come DET
            'I want you to come as expected.'

As can be seen in (i) and (ii), the determiner may occur in a clause containing a complementizer. In (i), the complementizer is *(ke)/ɖò* 'that'. In (ii), the head of CP is filled by the complementizers *pou* and *nú*, respectively. The fact that the determiner appears in clauses containing a lexical complementizer shows that the clausal determiner is not the head of CP (cf. Lefebvre 1991). In the following sections, I will show that the clausal determiner either TP or some projection of V.

9. Note that the semantics of the clausal determiner is not unrelated to the semantics of the determiner in the context of an NP (cf. section 2.1).

10. In the context of a plural marker, the determiner is generally not overtly manifested in both languages, as shown in (i) (from Lefebvre 1986).

(i)   Haitian   Fon
             (la) yo   ((l)ɔ́) lɛ́ɛ́
             DET PL   DET PL

11. For a discussion of the clausal determiner in the environment of ergative verbs, see Lefebvre (to appear).

12. Note that the clause in (19) is grammatical when the clausal determiner is associated with the head of AGRP-S.

    (i)   *Jan   te   bay liv   yo   a.*   (Haitian)
           Kɔkú kó   ná   wèmá lɛ́   ɔ́.   (Fon)
           J/K   PA   give book PL   DET
           'Actually Jan/Koku gave the books (away).'

13. The fact that the determiner as head of AGRP-O has scope only over the internal arguments of the verb strongly suggests that AGRP-O is inside the complex VP rather than outside of it. Hence, the position of AGRP-O within a complex VPs would be as in (i). Arguments supporting this structure are provided in Lefebvre (in preparation).

    (i)

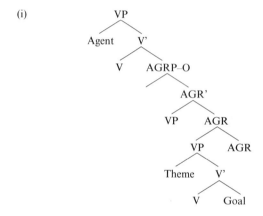

This constitutes independent evidence for a proposal along these lines in Travis (in preparation).

14. As can be observed from the following examples there is no agreement in number in the context of a [+ plural] DP in Spec of AGRP.

    (i)   **Ròb la yo blan (an) yo.* (Haitian)
           *Àvɔ̀ ɔ́ lɛ́ wé (ɔ́) lɛ́. (Fon)
           Dress DET PL white DET PL
           [Literally: 'The dresses are really white.']

    (ii)   **Nèg (la) vòle manchin yo (a) yo.* (Haitian)
           *Súnù (ɔ́) fín mɔ̀tò lɛ́ (ɔ́) lɛ́. (Fon)
           Man (DET) steal car PL DET PL
           [Literally: 'A/the man stole the cars as expected.']

    The sole feature involved in Spec-Head agreement is thus [α deictic]. The fact that the feature number is not involved in Spec-Head agreement in Haitian and in Fon follows from the fact that, unlike the determiner occurring with a noun phrase, the clausal determiner does not select a number phrase (cf. Ritter, 1992). It selects either TP, when in head of AGRP-S, or a projection of V when in head of AGRP-O.

15. This distribution further suggests that the relative position of the determiner with re-spect to the particle of negation cannot be accounted for by head movement of the negation particle (cf. Pollock 1989).

16. Note, however, the grammaticality of (i) in which the determiner is associated with the subject of the main clause.

(i)　　　*Li vle　　ale　　Pòtoprens la.*　　(Haitian)
　　　　　É jló　ná yí　Kútónù　ɔ́.　　(Fon)
　　　　　He want to leave P/K　　DET
　　　　　'He really wants to go to Port-au-Prince/Cotonou.'

17. A variant of this proposal is found in Faine (1937), where it is suggested that the source of the clausal determiner is the deictic adverbial occurring with the demonstrative *ce*, as in *cet homme-là* 'that man'.

18. This position contrasts with that of the French article which is head-initial. Cf. Fournier (1977) and Sylvain (1936: 59) for a discussion pertaining to the fact that the determiner of noun phrases cannot be the source of the clausal Haitian determiner.

19. Cf. Muysken (1988) for a discussion of the necessity of common semantic features between lexical items in relexification.

20. It is also possible that conflation (cf. Kihm 1989) played a role in the relexification of the clausal determiner. Pending more information on the other languages of the sub-stratum, I do not discuss this question further.

21. Work by various members of our team reveals that the grammars of Haitian and Fon are extremely parallel in crucial areas of their grammar. Cf. Lefebvre − Lumsden (1989), Lefebvre − Brousseau − Filipovich (1989), Brousseau (1989), Ndayiragije (1989), Lefebvre (1989).

References

Alleyne, Mervyn C.
　　1980　　*Comparative Afro-American: An historical-comparative study of English-based Afro-American dialects of the New World.* Ann Arbor: Karoma.

Anderson, Roger W.
　　1983　　*Pidginization and creolization as language acquisition.* Rowley, MA: Newbury House.

Bakker, Peter
　　1989　　"Relexification in Canada: The case of Metif-Cree". *Canadian Journal of Linguistics* 34: 339−350.

Benincà, P.
　　1989　　*Dialect variation and the theory of grammar.* Dordrecht: Foris.

Bickerton, Derek
　　1981　　*Roots of language.* Ann Arbor: Karoma.

Boretzky, Norbert − Werner Enninger − Thomas Stolz (eds.)
　　1988　　*Beiträge zum 4. Essener Kolloquium über Sprachkontakt, Sprachwandel, Sprachwechsel, Sprachtod vom 9. 10. − 10. 10. 1987 an der Universität Essen.* Bochum: Studienverlag Dr. N. Brockmeyer.

Brousseau, Anne-Marie
　　1989　　"De 'nù-fló' à 'po-bouche': Hypothèse sur l'origine des composés en haïtien", *Canadian Journal of Linguistics* 34: 285−312.

1990   "Panorama de la morphologie du Fongbe", *Journal of West African Languages* 20: 27–44.

Brousseau, Anne-Marie–Sandra Filipovich–Claire Lefebvre
1989   "Morphological processes in Haitian Creole: The question of substratum and simplification", *Journal of Pidgin and Creole Languages* 4: 1–37.

Brousseau, Anne-Marie–John Lumsden
1990   "Nominal structure in Fongbe", in: *La genèse du créole haïtien: Un cas particulier d'investigation sur la forme de la grammaire universelle. Etudes syntaxiques, phonologiques et lexicales*. Vol. 1. Rapport de recherche pour l'année 1989–1990. Montreal: Université du Québec à Montréal, 1–32.

Byrne, Francis–Alexander Caskey (eds.)
to appear   Proceedings of the conference on focus and grammatical relations in creole languages, Chicago.

Chomsky, Noam
1981   *Lectures on government and binding*. Dordrecht: Foris.
1986   *Knowledge of language: Its nature, origin and use*. New York: Praeger.
1989   "Some notes on the economy of derivation and representation". *MIT Working Papers* 10: 43–74.

Da Cruz, Maxime
1994   "Contribution à l'étude de la négation en Fongbè", in: Claire Lefebvre (ed.), Research Report, Université du Québec à Montreal, 69–111.

Déchaine, Rose-Marie
1988   "Opérations sur les structures argumentales: Le cas des constructions sérielles en créole haïtien", in: Claire Lefebvre (ed.), Travaux de recherche sur le créole haïtien 1. Université du Québec à Montréal.

DeGraff, Michel Anne Frederic
1993   Creole grammar and acquisition of syntax: the case of Haitian. Doctoral Dissertation, University of Pennsylvania.

Faine, Jules
1937   *Phonologie créole: Études historiques et étymologiques sur la langue créole d'Haïti*. Port-au-Prince, Haïti: Imprimerie de l'État.

Ferguson, Charles A.
1964   "Baby talk in six languages", in: John J. Gumperz–Dell Hymes (eds.), 103–114.
1971   "Absence of copula and the notion of simplicity: A study of normal speech, baby talk, foreigner talk, and pidgins", in: Dell Hymes (ed.), 141–150.

Flutre, Louis-Ferdinand
1970   *Le moyen picard, d'après des textes littéraires du temps (1560–1660): Textes, lexique, grammaire*. Paris: Presses du Palais-Royal.

Fournier, Robert
1977   *N ap fè yun ti-kose su la* (La grammaire de la particule la en créole haïtien). [Mémoire de maîtrise, Université du Québec à Montréal, Montréal.]
1978   "De quelques anomalies dans le traitement de l'article défini par H. Tinelli 1970", *Amsterdam Creole Studies* 2: 101–115.

Göbl-Gáldi, L.
1934   "Esquisse de la structure grammaticale des patois français-créoles", *Zeitschrift für französische Sprache und Literatur* 58: 257–295.

John J. Gumperz—Dell Hymes (eds.)
1964   "The ethnography of communication", *American Anthropologist* 66.
Hall, Robert A. Jr.
1950   "The genetic relationships of Haitian Creole", *Recherche lingustique* 1: 194—203.
Hull, Alexander
1975   On the origin and chronology of the French-based creoles. [Paper presented at the international conference on pidgins and creoles, University of Hawaii.]
Hymes, Dell (ed.)
1971   *Pidginization and creolization of languages.* Cambridge: Cambridge University Press.
Hyppolite
1949   *Les origines des variations de créole haïtien.* Port-au-Prince: Collection Haïtiana.
Kayne, Richard
1989   "Facets of Romance past participle agreement", in: P. Benincà (ed.), 85—103.
Kihm, Alain
1989   "Lexical conflation as a basis for relexification", *Canadian Journal of Linguistics* 34: 351—376.
Kihm, Alain (ed.)
1991   *Revue linguistique de Vincennes.* Numéro spécial: "Les langues créoles".
Koopman, Hilda
1986   "The genesis of Haitian: Implications of a comparison of some features of the syntax of Haitian, French and West African languages", in P. Muysken—N. V. Smith (eds.), 231—258.
Lefebvre, Claire
1982   "L'expansion d'une catégorie grammaticale: Le déterminant *la*, in: Claire Lefebvre et al. (eds.), *Syntaxe de l'haïtien.* Ann Arbor: Karoma, 21—63.
1986   "Relexification in creole genesis revisited", in: Pieter Muysken—Norval Smith (eds.), 279—301.
1989   "Instrumental '*Take*-Serial' constructions in Haitian and in Fon", *Canadian Journal of Linguistics* 34: 319—337.
1990   "On the interpretation of predicate cleft", *Linguistic Review* 6. Foris: 169—194.
1991   "La distribution du déterminant et des complémenteurs en créole haïtien", in: Alain Kihm (ed.), 21—47.
1992   "AGR in languages without overt agreement: The case of the clausal determiner in Haitian and Fon", in: Claire Lefebvre—John Lumsden—Lisa, Travis (eds.), 137—157.
1993   "Relexification and syntactic reanalysis in creole genesis: Methodological aspects of a research program", in: Salikoko S. Mufwene (ed.), 254—280.
in prep.   "Arguments for AGR-O within VP". Université du Québec à Montréal.
Lefebvre, Claire (ed.)
1988   *Travaux de recherche sur le créole haïtien.* Vol. 1. Université du Québec à Montréal.
Lefebvre, Claire—Anne-Marie Brousseau—Sandra Filipovich
1989   "Haitian Creole morphology: French phonetic matrices in a West African mold", *Canadian Journal of Linguistics* 34: 273—283.

Lefebvre, Claire–Robert Fournier
1978   "La particule *la* en créole haïtien", *Les cahiers de linguistique de l'Université du Québec* 9: 37–73.
Lefebvre, Claire–Richard Larson
1991   "Predicate clefting in Haitian Creole", *Proceedings of the North Eastern Linguistic Society (1990):* 247–263.
Lefebvre, Claire–John Lumsden
1989   "Les langues créoles et la théorie linguistique", *The Canadian Journal of Linguistics* 34: 249–272.
in prep.   "Precision on word order in relexification".
Lefebvre, Claire–John Lumsden–Lisa Travis (eds.)
1992   *Functional categories.* Special Issue of the *Canadian Journal of Linguistics* 37.2.
Lefebvre, Claire–Diane Massam
1988   "Haïtian creole syntax: A case for DET as head". *Journal of Pidgin and Creole Languages* 3: 213–243.
Lefebvre, Claire–Elisabeth Ritter
1989   "Note sur le redoublement verbal", *Revue québécoise de linguistique* 18: 173–182.
1993   "Two types of predicate doubling adverbs in Haitian Creole", in: Francis Byrns–Alexander Caskey (eds.). *Focus and Grammatical Relations in Creole Languages:* 65–95. The Netherlands: Benjamins.
Lumsden, John
1989   "Constraints on functional categories: Haïtian noun phrases and beyond", *Revue québécoise de linguistique* 18. Université du Québec à Montréal: 65–93.
1990   "The biclausal structure of Haitian clefts", *Linguistics* 28 (308): 741–759.
Lumsden, John–Claire Lefebvre
1990   "Predicate-cleft constructions and why they aren't what you might think", *Linguistics* 28: 761–782.
Meisel, Jürgen M. (ed.)
1976   *Langues en contact – pidgins – créoles.* Tübingen: Narr.
Mufwene, Salikoko S. (ed.)
1993   *Proceedings of the conference on Africanisms in Afro-American language varieties.* Amsterdam: John Benjamins.
Muysken, Pieter
1981   "Halfway between Quechua and Spanish: The case for relexification", in: Albert Valdman–Arnold Highfield (eds.), 52–78.
1988   "Lexical restructuring in creole genesis", in: Norbert Boretzky–Werner Enninger–Thomas Stolz (eds.).
Muysken, Pieter–Norval Smith (eds.)
1986   *Substrata versus universals in creole genesis.* (Creole Language Library volume 1.) Amsterdam: John Benjamins.
Ndayiragije, Juvenal
1989   "La source du d'éterminant agglutiné en créole haïtien", *Canadian Journal of Linguistics* 34: 313–317.
Papen, Robert
1988   Convergence et divergence linguistique en métif. [Paper presented at the Département de linguistique, Université du Québec à Montréal, May 1988.]

Piou, Nanie
1982   "Le redoublement verbal", in: Claire Lefebvre et al. (eds.), 122−152.
Pompilus, Pradel
1955   "Quelques traces du moyen français et du français classique dans le créole
            haïtien", *Optique* 16: 27−30.
Pollock, Jean-Yves
1989   "Verb movement, Universal Grammar, and the structure of IP", *Linguistic
            Inquiry* 20: 365−424.
Ritter, Elizabeth
1992   "Cross-linguistic evidence for number phrase", in: Claire Lefebvre−John
            Lumsden−Lisa Travis (eds.), 197−219.
Seuren, Pieter−Herman Wekker
1986   "Semantic transparency as a factor in creole genesis", in: Pieter
            Muysken−−Norval Smith (eds.), 57−71.
Singler, John
1986   Caribbean creoles and West African languages. [Unpublished MS, Summer
            Institute, Linguistic Society of America, City University New York.]
Sylvain, Suzanne
1936   *Le créole haïtien: Morphologie et syntaxe.* Wetteren, Belgique: Imprimerie de
            Meester.
Tenny, Carol
1987   Grammaticalizing aspect and affectedness. [Unpublished Ph. D. dissertation,
            MIT, Cambridge, MA.]
Thomason, Sandra
1983   "Chinook Jargon in areal and historical context", *Language* 59: 820−870.
Tinelli, Henri
1970   *Generative phonology of Haitian Creole.* [Unpublished Ph. D. dissertation,
            University of Michigan, Ann Arbor.]
Travis, Lisa
in prep.   "Specifiers". McGill University, Montreal.
Valdman, Albert
1976   "Créolisation sans pidgin: Le système des déterminants du nom dans les
            parlers franco-créoles", in: Jürgen M. Meisel (ed.), 105−136.
1978   *Le créole: Statut et origine.* Paris: Klincksieck.
Valdman, Albert−Arnold Highfield (eds.)
1981   *Historicity and variation in creole studies.* Ann Arbor: Karoma.
Van Voorst, Jan
1988   *Event structure.* (Current Issues in Linguistic Theory 59.) Amsterdam: John
            Benjamins.
Wittman, Henri−Robert Fournier
1983   "Le créole c'est du français coudon", *Revue de l'Association québécoise de
            linguistique* 3: 187−202.

On the acquisition of nominal structures in the genesis of Haitian Creole

John S. Lumsden

1. On creole genesis

Since creole languages are natural languages, the study of creole grammars must be a particular instance of the study of the grammar of natural languages in general. That is, creoles must be the product of the same cognitive faculties which produce any other natural language. Therefore, a synchronic study of a creole language in itself has no properties which distinguish it from studies of non-creole languages.

Yet creoles do differ from other natural languages in their historical evolution. Where most languages evolve slowly, responding mainly to pressures which are interior to a largely unilingual population group, creoles are the result of the social confrontation of several languages, and the genesis of a creole language is relatively abrupt. Creoles differ massively from any single one of the source languages which contribute to their origin and, moreover, they develop these differences in a relatively brief period and in a particular social context. Therefore, the comparison of a creole grammar with the grammars of the source languages to which it is historically related does have a special interest. The particular historical circumstances of creole genesis offer the possibility of observing the results of drastic linguistic changes in a relatively unusual context.

The superstratum language is dominant in the social context where the creole is formed, and it is (in some sense) the target language of those language learners who develop the creole. Thus, the phonological shape of the majority of words in the creole lexicon normally corresponds to the sound of words in the superstratum language. Other aspects of the superstratum grammar may also contribute to the formation of the creole, although the exact nature of this contribution remains a matter for discussion.

It has also been argued that the substratum languages make a substantial contribution to the creole grammar. In the relexification theory of creole genesis, for example (cf. Lefebvre 1986; Lefebvre–Lumsden 1989), it is argued that adults who are already equipped with a fully developed grammar of one of the substratum languages generate the creole by systematically adapting certain aspects of the superstratum grammar (notably the phonological shape of words and the word order of lexical categories) while otherwise retaining the grammar of the substratum language. Since the creole is developed by adults, it follows from this perspective that the genesis of a creole language is a function of second-language acquisition. But here, the relexification theory offers a significant degree of precision: creole languages are developed in communities which have relatively few contacts with native speakers of the superstratum language. One might call this "second-language acquisition at a distance".

Of course, Universal Grammar must also play a role in determining the creole grammar. But the extent of the role of Universal Grammar in creole genesis is a matter of some controversy. The universalist theory (cf. Bickerton 1981) would have it that creoles are developed by children who are not given sufficient data to determine the grammar of the target (superstratum) language, so that they have recourse to their innate understanding of Universal Grammar to generate the creole grammar. From this perspective, the genesis of a creole language is a function of first-language acquisition. One might call this "first-language acquisition at a distance".

The universalist hypothesis makes the interesting prediction that creole languages will realize the unmarked values of any grammatical parameters which are not set at marked values by the data to which the original creole speakers were exposed. Since by hypothesis such data were largely lacking, we could therefore expect to find that the grammars of creole languages are quite generally unmarked; a phenomenon which would be an accident under the relexification hypothesis. On the other hand, the relexification hypothesis predicts that creole grammars will have properties which are parallel to the properties of the grammars of the source languages to which it is related and such parallels could only be accidental under the universalist hypothesis.

The test of these hypotheses and the special contribution which the study of creoles can make to our understanding of language acquisition will be found in detailed studies which compare the grammar of the creole with the grammars of the source languages to which it is related. In this paper, I will focus on the nominal phrase in Haitian Creole. I will argue that at least one aspect of this phrase must be considered a marked option in the repertoire of Universal Grammar. Therefore, this is a problematic case for the Universalist theory. On the other hand, I will show that the data can be explained naturally in the relexification theory.

I turn now to the examination of nominal structures in Haitian Creole (taken from Lumsden 1989). I will then compare the creole with the superstratum and one of the substratum languages. Since the syntax of relative clauses and prepositional phrases is similar in all three languages, this discussion will concentrate on arguments and adjectives in nominal phrases.

2. Nominal structures in Haitian Creole

The nominal phrase in Haitian Creole may appear with a singular deictic determiner (realized in various surface forms, *la/a/[n]an*, depending on the phenological context) or with a plural marker (*yo*). These elements always follow the head noun, as in (1).

(1)   a. *timoun   nan*
              child   the
              'the child'
         b.   *yo*
              child PL
              'the children'
         c. *tab   la*
              table   the
              'the table'
         d. *bato   a   yo*
              boat   the   PL
              'the boats'

In some modern dialects, only one or the other of these forms may appear in a nominal phrase, but not both. In others, a combined form *a yo* is possible, as in (1 d).

Following Lefebvre and Massam (1988) and Lumsden (1989), I represent these examples in the format of the DP-hypothesis. That is, the determiner and the number marker are the head of a functional category phrase which dominates the lexical category phrase (i. e., the NP which provides the principal semantic content of the phrase). Thus in Haitian Creole, an nominal phrase with a determiner or a number marker would have the structure shown in (2).

(2) 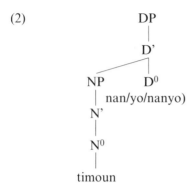   Haitian

In the creole, the arguments of nominal phrases (including possessive pronouns) also follow the head noun, as illustrated in (3).

(3)   a. *timoun Mari*
         child   Mari
         'Mari's child'
      b. *bato pèche   yo*
         boat fisherman PL
         'the fishermen's boat'
      c. *papa   m*
         father my
         'my father'

Haitian Creole nouns may have a complex argument structure as is illustrated in (4).

(4)   a. *pòtre   pèche   a*
         portrait fisherman the
         'the portrait of the fisherman'
      b. *pòtre   pent   sa   a*
         portrait painter this the
         'the portrait by this painter'
      c. *repons kesyon   mwen nan*
         answer question my   the
         'the answer to my question'
      d. *repons pwofèse   a*
         answer professor the
         'the answer of the professor'

But it is a notable property of these nominal phrases that they permit only a single NP argument in any one phrase, as we see in (5 a−c).[1] If a second argument is required in a nominal phrase, it must be expressed as a PP or in a relative clause, as in (5 d−f).

(5) a. **pòtre pèche   pent   sa   a*
        portrait fisherman painter this the
     b. **pòtre   pent   sa pèche   a*
        portrait painter this fisherman the
     c. **repons kesyon   mwen nan pwofèse   a*
        answer question my   the professor the
     d. *pòtre   pèche   a   pent   sa a   te   pentire*
        portrait fisherman the painter this the PAST paint
        'the portrait of the fisherman which this painter painted'
     e. *repons pwofèse   a   sou kesyon   mwen nan*
        answer professor the on question my   the
        'the professor's answer to my question'
     f. *repons kesyon   mwen pwofèse   te   fèt*
        answer question my   professor PAST make
        'the answer to my question which the professor gave'

Moreover, a nominal phrase which has an NP argument cannot appear in construction with an overt number marker or determiner. When a number marker or determiner does appear in such a phrase, it must be interpreted as part of the embedded argument phrase and not as part of the matrix nominal phrase, as is shown in (6).[2]

(6) a. *jouet timoun yo*
        toy   child   PL
        'the toy(s) of the children'
        (not 'the toy(s) of the child')
     b. *bato peche   yo*
        boat fisherman PL
        'the boat(s) of the fishermen'
        (not 'the boat(s) of the fisherman')

Thus, it is not possible to have two determiners or number markers in these constructions (i. e., one which is pertinent to the argument and one which is pertinent to the matrix phrase), as can be seen in (7).

(7) a. **manchin dokte yo a*   (cf. *manchin dokte yo*)
        car   doctor PL the
        ('the car of the doctors')
     b. **liv   nèg yo yo* (cf. *liv nèg yo*)
        book man PL PL
        ('the men's books')

    c. **manchin dokte   a   a*   (cf. *manchin dokte a*)
       car   doctor the the
       ('the car of the doctor')
    d. **liv   nèg   la   yo*   (cf. *liv nèg la*)
       book man the PL
       ('the man's books')

Nonetheless, functional categories can be linearly adjacent in certain constructions. This fact is illustrated in (8). However, this is possible only in structures involving a relative clause, etc. (but not when the structure involves a nominal phrase with an NP argument, as in [7]).[3]

(8)   *Ou te   wè [nèg [ki   te   vini an] yo]?*
        you PAST see man who PAST come the PL
        (Frantz 1988, p. 205)
        'Did you see the men who came (as we knew they would)?'[4]

Lumsden (1989) argues that these constraints can be explained in an account of genitive Case assignment, and in this regard, the grammar of Haitian Creole is very similar to that of other languages. Recent analyses of Hungarian (cf. Szabolsci 1987) and English (cf. Abney 1987), for example, have proposed that Case can be realized in the specifier position of a functional category projection which dominates the NP of the nominal phrase. The surface structure of a complex nominal-phrase construction in English, for example, can be represented as in (9). The theme argument (*of the queen*) is realized within the NP projection, with an inserted Case marker (*of*). The possessor or agent argument *the king's* is realized outside of the NP, in the specifier position of a functional category phrase (XP).

(9)   *the king's portrait of the queen*

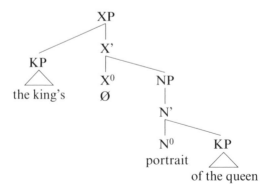

The functional category has a phonologically null head (i. e., Ø). Genitive Case is realized in the specifier of this functional category phrase and this realization is signalled by a Case-marker (i. e., *'s*). Since specifier positions in general allow only a single element (a constraint which follows from the binary branching hypothesis of Kayne 1984), only one item can appear in this position (e. g., one can say *Claire's conference* or *yesterday's conference*, but not **Claire's yesterday's conference*). Moreover, since English permits only a single functional category to appear in the structure of a nominal phrase, the presence of the null functional category prevents any other determiner from appearing in the matrix nominal phrase (i. e., the two determiners are incompatible; e. g., **the the king's hat*).

The parallel with the facts of nominal phrases in Haitian Creole is striking. Lumsden (1989) argues that Haitian nominal phrases can also have a (phonologically null) functional category which permits the realization of genitive Case in its specifier position. Thus, except for a difference in directionality, the Haitian nominal phrase illustrated in (10) is quite similar to the prenominal genitive construction of English.

(10)   *jouet   timoun   nan*
        toy   child   the
        'the child's toy'

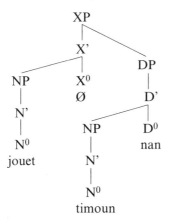

The explanation of the properties of the Haitian phrase parallels the account of English. Because this is a specifier position, only one item can appear. Because Haitian allows only a single functional category projection in a nominal phrase, the use of the null functional category is incompatible with the use of the overt determiner or the number marker. These elements cannot appear in construction with the same noun phrase.

There is a class of exceptions to this pattern which provides further support for this view of genitive Case realization in Haitian nominal phrases. Frantz (1988) has noted that in Haitian Creole proper names (and certain nouns)[5] seem to be exempt from the Case realization constraints which apply to ordinary nouns. Thus, for example, these nouns may appear as the complement of a verb of motion without the Case marker which is obligatory for ordinary nouns in this context, as illustrated in (11).

(11)   a. *Alsi al *(nan) rivyè*
           Alsi go   to   river
           'Alsi went to the river.'
        b. *Alsi al Rivyè Panyòl*
           Alsi go River Panyol (< Spanish River)
           'Alsi went to Spanish River.'
        c. *Pol al *(nan) mache*
           Pol go   to   market
           'Pol went to market.'
        d. *Pol al Mache Pòspyewo*
           Pol go Market Pospyewo (< Poste-Pierrot)
           'Pol went to Pospyewo Market.'

Given this exceptional distribution in verb phrases, it is notable that this class of nouns also has an exceptional distribution in nominal phrases, as is shown in (12).

(12)   a. *timoun Jan yo*
           child   Jan PL
           'Jan's children'
        b. *manchin Mari yo*
           car   Mari PL
           'Mari's cars'

In contrast with the examples we have seen in (6), in (12) the plural marker is not pertinent to the embedded argument. Rather, it dominates the matrix noun. The structure of these phrases is illustrated in (13) (contrast this structure with that in [10]).

(13)

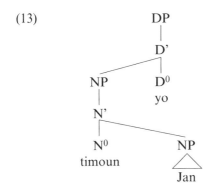

Since proper nouns are exempt from the need to appear in particular Case environments in VP, it follows immediately from the proposed analysis that these nouns will have an exceptional distribution in nominal phrases as well. Ordinary nouns must move to the specifier position of the null functional category phrase in order to realize genitive Case. But, as we have seen, proper nouns are exempt from Case realization requirements, so they do not have to obey this constraint. Therefore, proper nouns can appear as the argument of a nominal phrase which has an overt functional category. The exception, I would argue, proves the rule. I therefore conclude that genitive Case in Haitian Creole nominal phrases has many points in common with Case realization in the nominal phrases of languages like English and Hungarian, etc.

I turn now to a brief account of adjectives in the Haitian nominal phrase. Adjectives in the Haitian nominal phrase may follow or precede the noun depending on the particular adjective which is used (as in [14]).

(14)   a. *bèl   timoun nan*
          pretty child   the
          'the pretty child'
    b. *gran nèg la*
          big   man the
          'the big man'
    c. *ròb   rouj yo*
          dress red PL
          'the red dresses'
    d. *ide impotan   nan*
          idea important the
          'the important idea'

Those adjectives which follow the head noun must precede the argument phrase, as we see in (15).

(15)   a. *manchin blan   presidan*
        car   white president
        'the white car of the president'
    b. **manchin presidan   blan*
        car   president white

This summary of the Haitian nominal phrase will suffice for the purpose at hand. Now I would ask how this Haitian construction compares with the parallel constructions in the source languages of the creole. I turn to a brief account of nominal phrases in French, the superstratum language.

3. Nominal structures in French

French nominal phrases appear with a determiner which is marked for number, gender and definiteness and which precedes the head noun, as illustrated in (16).

(16)   a. *le livre*
       'the book'
    b. *les enfants*
       'the children'
    c. *la table*
       'the table'

The nominal arguments in French nominal phrases are typically realized after the head noun, with a Case marker (*de* or *à*). It is notable that, in contrast with the Haitian construction, more than one argument can be realized in a single phrase (cf. Milner 1978). This is illustrated in (17).

(17)   a. *le portrait d'Aristote de Rembrandt du Louvre*
       'the portrait of Aristotle by Rembrandt in the Louvre'
    b. *la réponse du professeur à la question de l'étudiant*
       'the answer of the professor to the question of the student'

An argument of a nominal phrase which is realized as a clitic pronoun must be realized in a position preceding the noun (cf. Tremblay 1990, for a more complete account). But this position allows the expression of only a single argument, as in (18).

(18)   a. *son portrait*
       'his/her portrait'

b. *ses enfants*
   'his/her children'
c. *ta table*
   'your table'

Since the form of the clitic pronoun reflects the number and gender of the head noun and since this prenominal position permits only a single element, it may be argued that the clitic is actually in the specifier of a functional-category projection. On the other hand, the reiterated position with *de* is within the NP projection. Thus, the basics of the French nominal phrase structure may be illustrated as in (19).

(19)   *son portrait d'Aristote*
         'his picture of Aristotle'

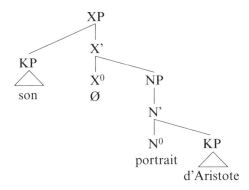

Turning to French adjectives, we see that they may precede or follow the head noun, depending on the adjective, as shown in (20).

(20)   a. *la robe rouge*
          'the red dress'
       b. *la belle jeune fille*
          'the pretty girl'

Adjectives which follow the head noun must precede any nominal argument, as in (21).

(21)   a. *la voiture rouge de mon père*
          'my father's red car'
       b. **la voiture de mon père rouge*

This brief survey of the French nominal phrase will suffice for the purpose of comparison with the Haitian creole phrase.

4. French and Haitian Creole compared

One may see at a glance that the creole has taken nothing from the French determiner system. Even the clitic possessive pronouns which precede the head of the French nominal phrase do not appear in the creole. Further evidence to support this conclusion is found in examples of determiner incorporation such as those shown in (22). The simple Haitian noun includes the phonological shape of the French noun and a French functional category.

(22)   a. *zanmi*
            'friend' (Fr. *les amis*)
        b. *lopital*
            'hospital' (Fr. *l'hôpital*)
        c. *lekol*
            'school' (Fr. *l'école*)

On the other hand, the word order of the lexical categories of the creole phrase follows the French quite closely. In both languages, adjectives precede or follow the head noun. In both languages, arguments of the head noun follow any postnominal adjectives. This is to say that the surface string of lexical words in Haitian Creole is parallel to the surface string of lexical words in French, as predicted in the relexification theory of creole genesis.

There are some aspects on the creole nominal phrase which find no parallel in the superstratum language. The most striking example is the postnominal determiner system (i. e., *la* and *yo*) and the postnominal possessive pronouns. These data can be explained in a theory based on a strong universalist hypothesis only if we can assume that this directionality is unmarked in natural languages. That is, the creators of the creole were children who were not exposed to enough French data to establish the French determiner and possessive pronoun system and so they instituted the unmarked option of Universal Grammar.

Of course, one may ask how the phonological forms were chosen in this process and, moreover, the markedness of this parameter setting is quite debatable. Are postnominal determiners really the default in Universal Grammar? Is the deictic interpretation of the creole determiner really less marked than the definite interpretation of the French determiner? I won't debate these points here. Rather, I would like to remark on another distinction which is illustrated in the data we have just seen.

Haitian nominal phrases have only one way in which nominal arguments can be realized and this one possibility allows only a single argument – but French allows iterated arguments in nominal phrases (compare [5] with [17]). Moreover, Indo-European languages in general allow the expression of more than one nominal argument in nominal phrases and as we will see below, this is also true of at least one African language. In fact, to my knowledge, most natural languages have some method of realizing more than one nominal argument in a nominal phrase. But for some reason, Haitian Creole nominal phrases allow only a single nominal argument. It seems to me to be very unlikely that this is an unmarked option of Universal Grammar. Therefore, this fact is surprising under the universalist hypothesis. I will show that there is a natural explanation for this fact in the theory of relexification.

I turn now to a brief account of nominal phrases in Fon (a Kwa language of the Niger-Congo group). This analysis is taken from Brousseau–Lumsden (1994).

5. Nominal structures in Fon

Fon is one of the substratum source languages for Haitian Creole and arguably the most important among the substratum languages in Haiti during the genesis of the creole, (cf. Singler 1989). The nominal phrase in Fon can appear with a definite (deictic) determiner (realized in various surface forms [*ló, ɔ́, ɔ́n*] depending on the phonological context) and with a plural marker (*lέ*). These elements aways appear after the head noun. In Fon, both the determiner and the number marker can appear in a single nominal phrase, as shown in (23).

(23)   a. *ɖiɖè   ɔ́   lέ*
         sketch the PL
         'the sketches'
    b. *wèmá ɔ́   ὲ*
         book the PL
         'the books'

Arguments in the Fon nominal phrase can be realized in two different ways. They either appear before the head noun with a Case marker *sín* or after the head with a Case marker *tɔ̀n*, as illustrated in (24).

(24)   a. *Kɔ̀kú sín ɖiɖè lὲ*
         Koku CASE sketch PL
         'sketches of Koku'

b. *ɖìɖè   Kɔ̀kú   tɔ̀n   lὲ*
sketch Koku CASE PL
'sketches of Koku'

But the symmetry of these two positions is not complete. The position
with *sín* (before the head) can be reiterated, as we see in (25).

(25)   a. *Kɔ̀kú   sín   Aristote   sín   ɖìɖè   lὲ*
Koku CASE Aristotle CASE sketch PL
'Koku's sketches of Aristotle'
    b. *yòvó   ɔ́   sín   Kanada sín   wìwέn   ɔ́n   lὲ*
stranger the CASE Canada CASE message the PL
'the stranger's messages from Canada'

By contrast, only one argument can be realized after the head, as is
shown in (26).

(26)   a. **ɖìɖè   Aristote   tɔ̀n   Kɔ̀kú   tɔ̀n   lὲ*
sketch Aristotle CASE Koku CASE PL

    b. **wìwέn   yòvó   ɔ́   tɔ̀n   Kanada tɔ̀n   ɔ́n   lὲ*
message stranger the CASE Canada CASE the PL

Brousseau and Lumsden argue that the positions with *sín* (before the
head noun) are dominated by a syntactic projection of the noun itself,
but the position with *tɔ̀n* (after the head noun) is the specifier of a functional category phrase. The proposed structure of the Fon nominal
phrase is illustrated in (27).[6]

(27)   *Báyí sín   ɖíɖe   Kɔ̀kú   tɔ̀n   ɔ́   lέ*
Bayi CASE sketch Koku CASE the PL
'(the) Koku's sketches of Bayi'

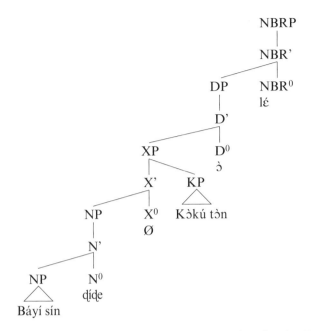

Turning now to adjectives, we can see in (28) that in the Fon nominal phrase, these modifiers must follow the head noun. But they may precede or follow a postnominal argument.

(28) a. *ɖìɖè   ɖàgbé Kɔkú tɔn   ɔ   lɛ̂*
          sketch good Koku CASE DET PL
          'Koku's good sketches'
      b. *ɖìɖè   Kɔkú tɔn   ɖàgbé ɔ   lɛ̂*
          sketch Koku good CASE DET PL
          'Koku's good sketches'
      c. * *ɖàgbé ɖìɖè*
          good   sketch
          'good sketch'

This brief survey of the Fon nominal phrase should suffice for the purposes of the comparison.

6. Fon and Haitian Creole compared

It is notable that the word order of the lexical words in Haitian Creole is not that which is found in Fon. The creole has no prenominal arguments in the nominal phrase, but Fon does. Fon has no prenominal adjectives, but the creole does. Fon allows adjectives before or after a postnominal argument, but Haitian Creole permits adjectives only before such arguments. In short, the surface order of lexical words is different in the two languages, a fact which is expected in light of the relexification hypothesis.

On the other hand, the functional category systems in the two languages do have something in common. Both Fon and Haitian Creole have deictic determiners and number markers which follow the head noun. Moreover, in both Fon and in Haitian Creole nominal phrases, only a single postnominal argument is allowed. As we have seen, this constraint on postnominal arguments is argued to follow from the independently motivated assumption that arguments in nominal phrases can be realized in the specifier position of a functional category. Thus the parallel between the functional category systems of the two languages is really quite striking.

On the basis of these facts, I would argue that the theory of relexification provides a direct account of the genesis of nominal phrases in Haitian Creole. Compare the nominal structures of the three languages given in (29).

(29)   a. Fon
        Báyí sín   ɖíɖe   Kɔkú tɔn
        Bayi CASE sketch Koku CASE
        'Koku's sketch of Bayi'

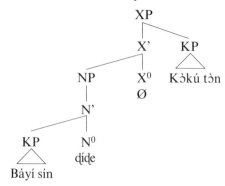

        b. French
        son portrait d'Aristote
        'his picture of Aristotle'

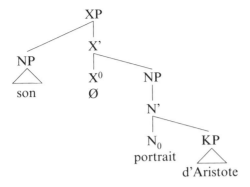

c. Haitian Creole
pòtre   *pèche*   *a*
portrait fisherman the
'the portrait of the fisherman'

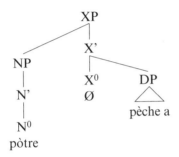

Our hypothesis is that the creole was created by adult speakers who had already acquired the nominal structure of Fon (or a similar language), as in (29 a). These speakers were ready to manipulate the order of lexical categories to parallel the word order of the target language (i. e., French), as in (29 b); but they continued to use the functional-category system of their native language and they ignored the functional-category system of the target language. Noting that in French, nominal arguments in nominal phrases follow the head noun, as in (29 b), these speakers abandoned the prenominal positions provided by the Fon grammar, shown in (29 a). But the Fon grammar allows only a single argument to appear after the head noun (also shown in [29 a]), and this constraint remained unchanged in the creole grammar, as in (29 c). In short, the creole structure can be derived by superimposing the French lexical-word order on the Fon structure, while pruning the tree of excess parts, etc. Since complex argument structures in nominal phrases are rather rare in daily usage, this

constraint would not disrupt the minimal interactions taking place between the bulk of the creole-speaking community and native speakers of
French.

The parallel between the functional-category system of Haitian Creole
and that of Fon is, as we have seen, quite striking. But there is at least
one significant distinction. In Fon, the entire inventory of functional categories can appear in a single nominal phrase, as in (27). Normally in the
creole, however, only a single functional category is realized. That is, if
there is a null functional category with an argument in its specifier position, then there can be no overt determiner nor a number marker, as was
shown in (7). Moreover, many speakers do not use the combined form
layo, so even the overt determiners do not appear in the same phrase.

I have the distinct impression that those dialects where it is possible to
use the combined form, as in (30), are more conservative dialects.

(30)   *timoun nanyo*
           child   the PL
           'the children'

Such examples can be found in the early works on Haitian Creole, and
my own informants tell me that although they never use these forms, it
might be something their "old uncle" or their grandmother would say. If
this is the case, then it suggests that the constraint (whatever it is) which
limits functional categories to one instance in any one nominal phrase of
Haitian Creole is a relatively new phenomenon. I suggest, therefore, that
the original grammar of the creole may have been even more like that of
Fon − individual nominal phrases could appear with the entire range of
functional categories.

I conclude that there is a systematic division to be seen in the comparison of Haitian Creole nominal phrases with similar phrases in the source
languages. The phonological shape of words roughly parallels the shape
of words in the superstratum language (although the origin of the form
yo, the number marker, is not clear to me). Moreover, the word order
for lexical categories is also related to the word order of lexical categories
in the superstratum. But there is strong evidence that the functional category system of Haitian Creole nominal phrases resembles closely the
functional category system of (at least one of) the substratum languages.
This systematic division of properties is predicted by the relexification
hypothesis. Under the universalist hypothesis, this systematicity is accidental. Therefore, I would argue that the relexification theory gives a
better account of the facts.

7. Relexification and syntactic categories

Although I would argue that creoles are formed through a very particular process of second-language acquisition (that is, second-language acquisition "at-a-distance"), this process must use the same mental faculties which are available for all other instances of the acquisition of natural languages. It is notable that the languages created by relexification show us that second-language acquisition involves a systematic revision of lexical entries, a revision which operates in domains defined by syntactic features.

At least two of the documented cases of relexification show a difference in the behavior or lexical versus functional categories. In the case of Media Lengua, a new language was created combining the functional categories of Quechua (including the phonological shapes of Quechua forms) with relexified lexical categories taken from Spanish (cf. Muysken 1981). As we have seen, in Haitian Creole, all words have relexified phonological shapes (taken generally from French). But while lexical categories conform to the word order of French, functional categories retain the syntactic properties and the structure of Fon functional categories. A third example of relexification makes a different cut. The Canadian Indian language Métif has a nominal-phrase system which takes its phonological shapes from French and a verbal-phrase system which retains the forms of Cree (cf. Papen 1988; Bakker 1989).

These examples indicate that second-language acquisition may proceed with reference to syntactic categories. That is, language learners can acquire information which is pertinent to one set of categories while ignoring the data which bear on other categories. Moreover, there seems to be a hierarchy of categories involved in this process. The minimal example is that of Métif, where only nominal phrases are relexified. Media Lengua goes a little further, relexifying all lexical categories (e. g., nouns and verbs) but no functional categories. Haitian Creole has relexified almost the entire vocabulary, but even in the creole, functional categories are less affected than lexical categories. The next stage might be a complete second-language acquisition.

Notes

1. But Lumsden (1989) observes that proper names and members of the "bare NP adverb" class may appear as multiple NP complements in nominal phrases.

   (i)   *respons Jan lendi   a*
          answer Jan Monday he
          'Jan's answer on Monday'

2. Lumsden (1989) points out that apparent exceptions to this statement can be found in noun-noun compounds. In the following example, the number marker is only pertinent to the complement when the structure is syntactic. But if the structure is morphological (when the two nouns are compounded) the number marker is pertinent to the whole. But, of course, the interpretation is different.

   (i)   *Mwèn te   pentire eskalye lekol   yo*
          I   PAST paint   stairs   school PL
          'I painted the stairs of the schools' or
          'I painted the school stairs.'

3. It should be noted that there is an additional constraint on the distribution of these functional categories, in that the same functional element can never appear twice, side by side (i. e., **yo yo*; **la a*), no matter what structure is involved (cf. Lumsden 1989).

4. The Haitian determiner may appear with a relative clause, giving the interpretation that the information presented in that clause is presupposed. See Lefebvre (1982), for discussion.

5. These include kinship terms and the class of "bare NP adverbs".

6. Brousseau and Lumsden point out that the number marker may originate in X^0 and be adjoined to D^0 at S-structure. If so, there is no number projection.

References

Abney, Stephen
   1987   The English noun phrase in its sentential aspect. [Unpublished Ph. D. dissertation, MIT, Cambridge, MA.

Bakker, Peter
   1989   "Relexification in Canada: The case of Métif (French-Cree)", *Canadian Journal of Linguistics* 34: 339–350.

Bickerton, Derek
   1981   *Roots of language.* Ann Arbor: Karoma.

Brousseau, Anne-Marie–John Lumsden
   1994   "Nominal structures in Fongbe", in: *The Journal of West African Linguistics* XXII; 1: 5–26.

Frantz, Joseph
   1988   "La détermination nominale en créole haïtien". [Unpublished Ph. D. dissertation (Thèse pour le doctorat de troisième cycle), Universitè Paris VII.]

Highfield, Arnold–Albert Valdman (eds.)
   1981   *Historicity and variation in creole studies.* Ann Arbor: Karoma.

Kayne, Richard
   1984   *Connectedness and binary branching.* Dordrecht: Foris.

Kenesei, (ed.)
   1987   *Approaches to Hungarian.* Volume 2: Szeged.

Lefebvre, Claire
  1982   "L'expansion d'une catégorie grammaticale: le déterminant LA", in: Claire Lefebvre, Hélène Magloire–Holly and Nanie Piou (eds.), *Syntaxe de l'haïtien.* Ann Arbor: Karoma.
  1986   "Relexification and creole genesis revisited: The case of Haitian Creole", in: Pieter Muysken–Norval Smith (eds.), 279–300.
Lefebvre, Claire–John Lumsden
  1989   "Les langues créoles et la théorie linguistique", *La revue canadienne de linguistique* 34: 249–272.
Lefebvre, Claire–Diane Massam
  1988   "Haitian Creole syntax: A case for Det as head", *Journal of Pidgin and Creole Languages* 3: 213–243.
Lumsden, John S.
  1989   "On the distribution of determiners in Haitian Creole", Revue québécoise de linguistique 18: 64–93.
Milner, Jean-Claude
  1978   *De la syntaxe à l'interpretation.* Paris: Editions de Seuil.
Muysken, Pieter
  1981   "Half-way between Quechua and Spanish: The case for relexification" in: Arnold Highfield–Albert Valdman (eds.), 52–78.
Muysken, Pieter–Norval Smith
  1986   *Substrata versus universals in creole genesis.* Amsterdam: Benjamins.
Papen, Robert
  1988   Convergence et divergence linguistique en métif. [Paper presented at the Département de linguistique, Université du Québec à Montréal, May 1988.]
Singler, John
  1989   "Creole genesis and the historical record". [Unpublished MS, New York University, New York.]
Szabolcsi, Anna
  1987   "Functional categories in the noun phrase", in: Kenesei (ed.).
Tremblay, Mireille
  1990   "French possessive adjectives as dative clitics", *Proceedings of the West Coast Conference on Formal Linguistics* 8.